MATERNAL ENCOUNTERS

Many women find mothering a shocking experience in terms of the extremity of feelings it provokes, and the profound changes it seems to prompt in identity, relationship and sense of self. However, although motherhood can catapult us into a state of internal disarray, it can also provide us with a unique chance to make ourselves anew. How then do we understand this radical potential for transformation within maternal experience? In *Maternal Encounters*, Lisa Baraitser takes up this question through the analysis of a series of maternal anecdotes, charting key destabilizing moments in the life of just one mother, and using these to discuss many questions that have remained resistant to theoretical analysis – the possibility for a specific feminine-maternal subjectivity, relationality and reciprocity, ethics and otherness.

Working across contemporary philosophies of feminist ethics, as well as psychoanalysis and social theory, the maternal subject, in Baraitser's account, becomes an emblematic and enigmatic formation of a subjectivity 'called into being' through a relation to another she comes to name and claim as her child. As she navigates through the peculiarity of maternal experience, Baraitser takes us on a journey in which 'the mother' emerges in the most unlikely, precarious and unstable of places as a subject of alterity, transformation, interruption, heightened sentience, viscosity, encumberment and love.

This book presents a major new theory of maternal subjectivity, and an innovative and accessible way into our understanding of contemporary motherhood. As such, it will be of interest to students of family studies, gender studies, psychoanalysis, critical psychology and feminist philosophy as well as counselling and psychotherapy.

Lisa Baraitser is Lecturer in Psychosocial Studies at Birkbeck, University of London, a feminist theorist, writer and theatre director, and a psychotherapist with a particular interest in working with mothers. Her research is currently concerned with articulations of the maternal in the fields of psychoanalysis, social theory, feminism and philosophy.

WOMEN AND PSYCHOLOGY
Series Editor: Jane Ussher
School of Psychology, University of Western Sydney

This series brings together current theory and research on women and psychology. Drawing on scholarship from a number of different areas of psychology, it bridges the gap between abstract research and the reality of women's lives by integrating theory and practice, research and policy.

Each book addresses a 'cutting edge' issue of research, covering such topics as post-natal depression, eating disorders, theories and methodologies.

The series provides accessible and concise accounts of key issues in the study of women and psychology, and clearly demonstrates the centrality of psychology to debates within women's studies or feminism.

The Series Editor would be pleased to discuss proposals for new books in the series.

Other titles in this series:

THE THIN WOMAN
Helen Malson

THE MENSTRUAL CYCLE
Anne E. Walker

POST-NATAL DEPRESSION
Paula Nicolson

RE-THINKING ABORTION
Mary Boyle

WOMEN AND AGING
Linda R. Gannon

BEING MARRIED, DOING GENDER
Caroline Dryden

UNDERSTANDING DEPRESSION
Janet M. Stoppard

FEMININITY AND THE PHYSICALLY ACTIVE WOMAN
Precilla Y.L. Choi

GENDER, LANGUAGE AND DISCOURSE
Anne Weatherall

THE SCIENCE/FICTION OF SEX
Annie Potts

THE PSYCHOLOGICAL DEVELOPMENT OF GIRLS
AND WOMEN
Sheila Greene

JUST SEX?
Nicola Gavey

WOMAN'S RELATIONSHIP WITH HERSELF
Helen O'Grady

GENDER TALK
Susan A. Speer

BEAUTY AND MISOGYNY
Sheila Jeffreys

BODY WORK
Sylvia K. Blood

MANAGING THE MONSTROUS FEMININE
Jane M. Ussher

THE CAPACITY TO CARE
Wendy Hollway

SANCTIONING PREGNANCY
Harriet Gross and Helen Pattison

ACCOUNTING FOR RAPE
Irina Anderson and Kathy Doherty

THE SINGLE WOMAN
Jill Reynolds

UNDERSTANDING THE EFFECTS OF CHILD SEX ABUSE
Sam Warner

MATERNAL ENCOUNTERS

The ethics of interruption

Lisa Baraitser

Routledge
Taylor & Francis Group

LONDON AND NEW YORK

First published 2009
by Routledge
27 Church Road, Hove, East Sussex BN3 2FA

Simultaneously published in the USA and Canada
by Routledge
270 Madison Avenue, New York, NY 10016

Routledge is an imprint of the Taylor & Francis Group, an informa business

© 2009 Psychology Press

Typeset in Times by Garfield Morgan, Swansea, West Glamorgan
Printed and bound in Great Britain by TJ International Ltd, Padstow, Cornwall
Paperback cover design by Anú Design

British Library Cataloguing in Publication Data
A catalogue record for this book is available from the British Library

Library of Congress Cataloging in Publication Data
Baraitser, Lisa, 1967–
Maternal encounters : the ethics of interruption / Lisa Baraitser.
p. cm. – (Women and psychology)
ISBN 978-0-415-45500-8 (hardback) – ISBN 978-0-415-45501-5 (pbk.) 1. Motherhood.
2. Family. 3. Sex role. 4. Feminism. I. Title.
HQ759.B268 2009
306.874'3–dc22
2008022090

ISBN: 978-0-415-45500-8 (hbk)
ISBN: 978-0-415-45501-5 (pbk)

To my mother, Marion Baraitser, with love
and with thanks for so much of hers.
To my dear sons, Joel and Saul,
who bring life itself.

CONTENTS

Acknowledgements   xi

1   Maternal encounters   1
    A maternal anecdote 1
    Maternal ethics 4
    Escaping abjection 7
    Maternal encounters, philosophical perspectives 8
    The feminine and the maternal 10
    Becoming unaccommodated: an anecdotal theory 11
    Protagonists 17
    Terms and conditions: the gendering of the maternal 19

2   Maternal alterity: mum's the word   24
    Jessica Benjamin and the intersubjective turn 29
    Judith Butler and the 'reality' of negation 33
    Levinas 35
    Femininity, maternity and paternity in Levinas 40
    Naming 45

3   Maternal transformations: oi mother, keep ye' hair on!   48
    Maternal transformation: Irigaray and the maternal-feminine 56
    From veil to wig 62

4   Maternal interruptions: I, yi, yi yi, yi, I like you very
    much, Si, si, si, si, si, I think you're grand   66
    Interruption 68
    The cry 69
    Maternal time 74
    Disruption 75

CONTENTS

The tantrum 80
Stammering: the interruption of interruption 84
Coda 88

5   Maternal love: on mother love and unexpected weeping   90
Mother love 92
Love/desire 96
Kristeva's herethics *99*
Motherhood according to Julia Kristeva 101
Maternal tears 107
A tear is an intellectual thing 109
Badiou: one, two, infinity 112
Badiou's love 115
The return of maternal love 120

6   Maternal stuff: maternity and the encumbered body   122
Stuff 122
Maternal embodiment 123
Childhood objects and maternal 'tool-beings' 126
The viscous body 127
Psychoanalytic and philosophical objects 130
Intentional objects 133
Zeug 134
Ethical objects 137
Uncreation and creation 140
Artefacts 143
Motherhood and the ethics of objects 144
The mother in the city: freerunning 146

7   Intentions, inconsistencies, inconclusions   151
The dis-abled mother 153
Inconclusions 157

Notes   160
References   165
Index   179

ACKNOWLEDGEMENTS

My heartfelt thanks to Stephen Frosh and Amal Treacher who, in their subtle ways, facilitated my own peculiarities and particularities to emerge, and in doing so, taught me more than I can say. Rachel Bowlby and Anthony Elliott provided detailed responses to earlier drafts of this manuscript, for which I am grateful, as did Amber Jacobs, Gail Lewis, and Rachel Thomson. Sigal Spigel has been there throughout, so my thanks are for this friendship. Thanks also to Imogen Tyler, Katie Lloyd-Thomas, Caron Evans, Virginia Eatough, Mary Peace, Jane Haugh, and Heather Elliot. Derek Hook and Calum Neill continue to keep me intellectually to task, for which I am truly grateful, and my thanks also go to the Birkbeck Freud Reading Group with similar sentiments. Thanks in particular to Lynne Segal, who continues to be an exemplary colleague and friend.

Special thanks to the many academics, writers, artists, performers, psychoanalysts and students who have been involved in the research network MaMSIE (Mapping Maternal Subjectivities, Identities and Ethics), for so many challenging and stimulating conversations. These maternal encounters have propelled me into unfamiliar and richly rewarding terrains, and I look forward to many more besides.

I am indebted to Jane Ussher for instigating and supporting this project and thereby taking a leap into the unknown, and to staff at Routledge for their editorial assistance. I would like to thank Muriel Dimen at *Studies in Gender and Sexuality* for expert editorial input on earlier versions of two chapters of this work.

And finally, my thanks are with Simon Bayly for the shared project that is our life together, and for, as I always say, keeping his eye on the real subject.

Earlier versions of Chapter 2 and Chapter 3 appeared in the journal *Studies in Gender and Sexuality* (www.informaworld.com) and are reproduced here with kind permission.

1

MATERNAL ENCOUNTERS

A maternal anecdote

In 1980, the performance artist Bobby Baker had the first of her two children. In 1988 she created a performance entitled *Drawing on a Mother's Experience*, telling the story of those eight years. For the show she used cold roast beef, skimmed milk, frozen fish pie, Guinness, sheep's milk yoghurt, tinned blackberries, tomato chutney, sponge fingers, tea, black treacle, eggs, caster sugar, brandy and strong white flour. Her 'canvas' consisted of a large white cotton double sheet, which she spread on the floor. Coming from a background in visual art, Bobby enacted a kind of domestic parody of action painting, only using food instead of paint. The performance took the form of a series of anecdotes about mothering, each featuring one of her chosen food products, punctuated by moments in which she spilt, threw, poured, splashed, squashed and ground her ingredients into the sheet. At the end she poured flour over the whole painting, then wrapped herself in it, took a long look at the audience, and left the stage. Of the original performance, Griselda Pollock wrote:

> Bobby creates delicate and calculated patterns on her canvas and then at key moments rubs our noses in it. She steps on the blackcurrants, grinding them into the sheet; she lies on the canvas, provoking a powerful image of immobilisation in the midst of sanity-threatening chaos . . . . With superb and subtle management of emotions, Baker takes us back through the years she did not make art, calling for recognition of those shared lunacies which only humour can allow us to recall, then momentarily halting the laughter with poignant moments of deep pathos.
>
> (Pollock 1990)

Rather than an exuberant reclamation of feminine experience or a glorification of the joys and pains of motherhood, Bobby's piece was presented as a form of research. She was dressed in a scientist's white coat and her

1

action-painting-in-the-making was performed as a semi-illustrated lecture. She struck a perfunctory tone as she recounted her pregnancy cravings, birth story, post-birth blues, her return to live with her mother, then working full-time while trying to put family meals on the table. The 'subject' of her research however was not motherhood as such, but her own elusive and unstable psychic state during those long years. Literally 'drawing on experience', she attempted to retrace, grasp and illuminate certain subjective moments that baffled her. These moments, though marked by both laughter and poignancy, also appeared to have aimed at capturing a pervasive traumatic quality evading representation. So, both figuratively and metaphorically, her 'drawing on' was a 'drawing over', as she attempted and failed to catch the tail of what really happened. The impossibility of representation, graphically displayed as she poured flour over the entire piece, gestured towards the real of maternal experience. Perhaps we might say that the process of attempting, and perhaps inevitably failing to catch hold of the mercurial mental and emotional currents prompted by maternity is one way to understand what we may call maternal subjectivity.

Of course I missed the original performance. In 1988 I was twenty-one. Passionately interested in the performance-art scene but arrogant to a point of perfection, I could not get excited about a performance about mothering. I have a dim memory of knowing it was on, and posturing about how motherhood was already 'overdone'. After all, I had only just emerged from a childhood peppered with explosions of feminist-inspired maternal rage about just such sanity-threatening chaos. The impossibly paradoxical experience of motherhood and mothering,[1] both liberation and trap, exquisite pleasure and appalling drudgery, were the backdrop to my evolving womanhood. One of the stories that I absorbed from my own experience of being mothered was that mothering was at once deeply fulfilling, and precisely that which drove women away from the domestic scene into an active engagement with the world. I wanted to see performances by brilliant, powerful, sexy, imaginative, worldly women, not half-insane mothers close to the edge of a nervous breakdown.

Bobby Baker went on to perform *Drawing on a Mother's Experience* all over the world. It has been part of her repertoire for two decades, apparently as relevant today as it was then. While writing this book I managed to get hold of a recording of a recent performance of the piece, hoping to find something edgy, risky and raw emerging out of Bobby's continued investigation into the maternal. However, it turned out to be like looking through the wrong end of a telescope. There was Bobby, now middle-aged, with a performance persona that seemed to deliberately court the ordinary, middle England, verging on blue stocking, teetering around in her slightly unsensible shoes, tipping flour, eggs and brandy over her sheet. The performance was tight, but seemed somehow too slick, too sewn up.

2

She already knew in advance the effect she was aiming at, thereby covering *herself* over, leaving nothing at stake. I could only imagine that the original piece held something more enigmatic, disturbing, and exciting. Through the juxtaposition of the mundane tales of mothering and the violent expulsions of food-stuffs, to the white blankness of the flour obliterating her painting, I had imagined that this elusive maternal subject, the 'real subject' of her performance, could have been momentarily glimpsed. In its current incarnation, this was a show I could safely take my mother-in-law to (rather than my still angry feminist mother); one that would make her chortle with gentle recognition at those lost years and the confusion, chaos and mess.

This book is an attempt to glimpse what I long to have been present in Bobby's original performance. The retroactive process of imagining something that perhaps never happened is necessarily performed, and is in fact made possible, through the haze that is my own experience and fantasy of motherhood, mothering and the maternal. It cannot, in other words, be distinguished from my own longing. In my imaginings, Bobby's performance does not just rely on humour and poignancy as a way of marking the maternal. Neither is it pervaded purely by a traumatic quality, though I imagine this to have been present. My hope is that something truly generative, surprising and unexpected may have broken through, furnishing the maternal with another sensibility; precisely a sensibility that I cannot anticipate. I am drawn, in other words, to the notion that motherhood, perhaps through the kinds of particular and peculiar extremities that Bobby charts, opened new possibilities for her; new ways of experiencing herself, new 'raw materials' with which to work, or perhaps, that it even 'made her anew'.

In this book I seek to articulate the potential within maternity for new experiences, sensations, moods, sensibilities, intensities, kinetics, tinglings, janglings, emotions, thoughts, perceptions; new coagulations of embodied and relational modes. I try to pay attention to the ways that motherhood may allow the generation of new 'raw materials' for experiencing ourselves, others and our worlds. In doing so, I hope to map a series of maternal constellations that we may retroactively be able to gather up into something we could name as *having been* a maternal subject, resisting where I can my own impulses to try to build new models for subjectivity that solidify and reify experience, processes to which 'the mother', as metaphor, figure or trope, is particularly vulnerable. I take as my starting point some rather mundane and usually overlooked moments of maternal experience that appear to trip us up, or throw us 'off the subject'. It is to moments of undoing, I argue, that we need to apply ourselves theoretically, if we are to try to glimpse something we may term maternal subjectivity. These moments are presented anecdotally – I describe unexceptional incidents in which a mother crosses a street, bursts into tears without knowing why, goes to a school play, dislikes using her child's name, loses the vital transitional object, watches her child having a tantrum, does not know how to put a nappy on, fumbles with Lego®, waits while her stammering child tries to speak, and navigates the urban cityscape with her buggie and babies and bottles and bags. The overtones of these experiences are those of embarrassment, discomfort, exhaustion, shock, surprise, blankness, uncanniness, bewilderment, oddness, terror, frustration and absurdity. Yet, by thinking through these experiences, something we might call maternal subjectivity may emerge – characterized not by fluidity, hybridity or flow, but by physical viscosity, heightened sentience, a renewed awareness of objects, of one's own emotional range and emotional points of weakness, an engagement with the built environment and street furniture, a renewed temporal awareness where the present is elongated and the past and future no longer felt to be so tangible, and a renewed sense of oneself as a speaking subject. The mother emerges from these investigations not only as a subject of interruption, encumbered, viscous, impeded, but also re-sensitized to sound, smell, emotions, sentient awareness, language, love.

Maternal ethics

What is this longing for motherhood to hold the generative, surprising and unexpected? Why not allow it to be a diverse yet patterned experience, both individually located and yet differing historically, culturally and particularly in relation to class, 'race' and ethnicity, constantly in play with dominant and normative discourses, traditionally those of patriarchy, and more recently those of our post/neo-colonial culture? Why not let motherhood alone as a particular or new experience, and join with those who now speak generically of 'parenting', or even abandon our studies of motherhood in preference for the new turn to fatherhood? Why allude to a potentially transhistorical, transcultural notion like ethics in relation to one of the most locally produced, specifically experienced, and simultaneously heavily regulated practices of all?[2]

In part, my longing for, and wish to articulate the generative, surprising and unexpected in relation to the maternal is a deliberate strategy at both a theoretical and personal level. I understand it as a kind of ethics in itself, an aspirant reaching out towards the good (the difference, that is, between what is and what ought to be). 'The mother' after all, is the impossible subject, par excellence. Caught in an ever widening gap between her idealization and denigration in contemporary culture, and her indeterminate position as part object, part subject within the Western philosophical tradition,[3] the mother has always been left hopelessly uncertain, with all the death-like and dreadful connotations that the abject possesses. In some senses she is everywhere, our culture saturated with her image in its varied guises, and yet theoretically she remains a shadowy figure who seems to disappear from the many discourses that explicitly try to account for her.

4

Perhaps this is unsurprising given that we all, as infants, may have needed to conjure up an ever-present fantasy mother whom we are told must find just the right balance of presence without impingement (Winnicott 1963: 86), and who needs therefore to remain partly in the shadows, and then gradually but appropriately 'fail' (Winnicott 1963: 87), and finally sort of . . . fade away. As the psychoanalyst Erna Furman put it, motherhood is the lifelong process of 'being there to be left' (Furman 1982: 15), one, in her view, that is the hardest and most psychologically threatening to women who mother, one that never ends, that is repeated with each child and constantly stirs up early infantile experiences of separation from our own mothers. While feminist psychoanalytic thinkers have concerned themselves with articulating how the twin poles of idealization and a defensive scorn and denigration of the maternal-feminine covers over a deep-seated fear of a powerful, envied and terrifying mother on whom we were all once dependent, there has been a real struggle to rescue the maternal subject from she who is purely 'there to be left'.[4] However, just as maternal subjectivity is on the cusp of being articulated within the psychoanalytic literature, for instance, the mother appears to slip back into some manifestation of her traditional object-position as container, mirror, receptacle for intolerable feelings, a body with bits attached, or with supposedly vital bits missing, an object to be repudiated, hated or feared, the one who bears destruction and abandonment and still remains intact, more recently an effective and reliable cortisol manager,[5] but ultimately she who must to some degree be left, or more forcefully abjected or killed off, in order that 'the subject' (so often the child in psychoanalysis, gathered up retroactively by the child-now-adult through the process of analysis) can emerge unscathed. Due to her necessary function in the developing world of the infant, and due perhaps to our continued needs for our mothers to remain simultaneously present and yet to disappear, maternal subjectivity persists as ontologically puzzling, both necessary and suspect. Jacqueline Rose (1996: 421), commenting on Kristeva's famous naming of the maternal as 'that ambivalent principle that . . . stems from an identity catastrophe that causes the proper Name to topple over into the unnameable' (Kristeva 1977: 161–162), describes the catastrophe as the simple fact that there is an unconscious, that is, there is a limit to knowledge, and that the name that we give this limit is the mother. The question that then follows is 'what does thinking about mothers do to thinking?' (Rose 1996: 413). To think about mothers is to think about the vanishing point of thinking, to do violence then to what remains resistant to knowledge, to Christopher Bollas' 'unthought known' (Bollas 1987). No wonder we may not really want to know about her, not want to tease out what kind of 'she' is 'there to be left', or who has the capacity to materially produce others, or who somehow continued to love us despite our destructive attacks. My contention is that despite the vast and expanding research field on maternal practice, maternal relations, maternal embodiment and maternal representation, on the new technologies of birth and reproduction and their implications for women, and on the currently rapid rate of change that family structures and parenting patterns are undergoing, the maternal remains haunted by her link with the impossibility of knowing, and hence remains somewhat unspeakable.

In a similar but more forceful vein, Kristeva (1987a) suggests that the simultaneous presence and absence of the mother within the symbolic, thought broadly as the realm of signification, arises from our inabilities to commit a necessary 'matricide'. In *Black Sun*, she writes:

> Melancholy persons are foreigners in their maternal tongue. They have lost meaning – the value – of their mother tongue for want of losing the mother. The dead language they speak . . . conceals a 'Thing' buried alive. The latter will not be translated in order that it not be betrayed.
>
> (Kristeva 1987a: 53)

Instead of being able to accept the loss of the mother which would entail bearing matricidal guilt in order to achieve autonomy, the melancholic negates maternal loss, cannot murder the mother, and instead buries the maternal Thing alive within the symbolic. This unrepresentable Thing is at once lost and present in that the loss is foreclosed but not mourned or worked through in such a way as to render the mother symbolizable. She is therefore preserved in her absence and takes up a position in the symbolic only as an incarnation of the Real in the place of the Other. This gives rise to the classic characterization of the mother as the unthematizable, unrepresentable and unrecoverable presence that haunts each subject. And we can perhaps see some of this simultaneous preservation of the lost maternal thing in the way that those of us who write about maternal subjectivity appear to mourn the disappearance of the mother theoretically without seeming to be able to do anything to recover her. We are perhaps psychologically invested in maintaining her as lost for fear of having to murder her, mourn her, and move on. In addition, Paes de Barros (2004) writes:

> The reality of the maternal body – its biological contingencies, its vast capacity for radical change, its evident sexuality and utility – make it truly Lacan and Zizek's 'Symptom.' That maternal body harbors the inexpressible Real.
>
> (Paes de Barros 2004: 90)

It makes some sense, then, that our dealings with the maternal may attempt to keep her at bay by rendering her as either a function or object in the developing inner world of the child, a metaphorical figure used to signify particular representational modes, or an individual who engages in a set of socially controlled practices and ideologically driven fluxes of power, thereby leaving her struggling to consolidate anything that may be thought of as agency, desire or choice.

Escaping abjection

To escape the tendency for abjection to cling to the maternal we may need to deliberately approach maternal subjectivity from a position that engages with the generative, surprising and unexpected, a strategic valorization of what is excessive (but *not* monstrous) in maternal experience in order to counteract a discourse so mired in loss, murder and melancholia. Kristeva's position seems to destroy the potential for maternal subjectivity at the point that it appears to rescue mothers from their silence. All that may be left to us is a strenuous 'leap' of the imagination. This is akin to the excessive strategy found within Irigaray's project that seeks to run with, flaunt perhaps, feminine alterity as a way to challenge and expand both the masculine symbolic and the masculine imaginary from within. As I argue later, Irigaray's fusion of the feminine and the maternal leads to some difficulties with holding onto the specificity of maternal subjectivity, but the sensibility of this current work is nevertheless indebted to her radical imagination. My longing, then, for Bobby Baker's performance to have marked the maternal with the unexpected, surprising and generative is in part an ethical commitment to rethinking the maternal as a potentially life-changing event brought about by a certain response to an other whom we come to name as our child; a way to counteract the binary options – melancholia or murder.

This deliberate valorization of the generative potential of maternity may appear to be a rather alarming aim; a reactive or cheerful attempt to celebrate motherhood despite the profound psychological, emotional, relational, and financial crises (to name but a few) that it so clearly provokes in so many of our lives, a return perhaps to the rather jubilant maternalist sensibilities of some feminist writers of previous generations.[6] However, my aim is certainly not to write an account of the joys of motherhood. Nor do I advocate elevating the maternal as a specifically feminine bodily or socio-sexual experience, the ultimate sign of sexual difference. Nor am I attempting to chart in any global sense the ways motherhood changes our lives – though I would not deny that it does so. Instead my aims are deliberately more myopic. If we shift from a female subject position to encompass a maternal one when we have a child (be that an adoptive, birth, foster, community or surrogate child, or any other relationship in which one comes to name another as one's child), then we must surely contend with the notion that motherhood produces something new. The questions that concern me are about how we might theorize this newness as a way to claim back something for the maternal that escapes the melancholia-murder binary. Does thinking in terms of changes in internal object-relations, self-image, self-representation, identifications, or social and cultural practices and locations suffice? Or are there other ways in which we could think about these changes, ways that have something more to do with the nature of the encounter between a mother and the one she names and relates to as her child?

Toni Morrison once wrote:

> There was something so valuable about what happened when one became a mother. For me it was the most liberating thing that ever happened. . . . Liberating because the demands that children make are not the demands of a normal 'other'. The children's demands on me were things that nobody else ever asked me to do. To be a good manager. To have a sense of humour. To deliver something that somebody else could use. . . . Somehow all of the baggage that I had accumulated as a person about what was valuable just fell away. I could not only be me – whatever that was – but somebody actually needed me to be that.
>
> (Moyers and Tucher 1990: 60, quoted in Bassin et al. 1994: 2)

Morrison's point is that the 'other' previous to motherhood had interpolated her as a certain kind of person (sensual, attractive, intelligent). The child demands something else, asks different kinds of questions, draws a different kind of 'her' out of her. Though I would want to problematize the notion that motherhood strips us down to 'who we really are', Morrison's reflections are well taken. In part, this book seeks to instigate a dialogue, or at least manage an uneasy tension, between a notion of subjectivity that comes into being through our relation of obligation to an inassimilable otherness in the figure of the child, and a psychoanalytic and feminist tradition that has worked assiduously to flesh out mothers as desiring, fantasizing, remembering, culturally imbued, sexual, agentive subjects in their own right.

Maternal encounters, philosophical perspectives

I begin by drawing on Levinas (1947a, 1961, 1974) in seeking to understand subjectivity as that which emerges out of an encounter with an inassimilable otherness, which I explore in the figure of the child. Here the subject emerges at the point it responds to the Other that it cannot colonize, and ultimately cannot know. To reverse the link between the maternal and the vanishing point of knowledge, I argue that one formulation of the maternal is as an emblematic and enigmatic formation of this subjectivity 'called into being' through the relation to *the child* as 'other'. I contend that this interrupting, tantruming, crying, demanding, questioning, loving, unpredictable and ultimately unknowable other that is a child, can be thought of as a particular other for the mother, the response to whom calls us, as maternal subjects, into being. I end, however, with an almost polar opposite view of subjectivity; one drawn from Alain Badiou's notion that subjectivity happens only to some of us, some of the time, and arises not out of an encounter with alterity, but out of our fidelity to an 'event' that occurs in the realm of the Same through a 'chain of autonomous actions within a changing situation' (Feltham and Clemens 2003: 6). An event can retroactively be named as such only after the event (Badiou 2001, 2003, 2004) and we attain subjectivity by dint of our ability to make a wager that, by acting as if the event has happened, it does turn out to have been one. In other words, by acting as if something has changed our lives, it may just turn out to have been true. Somewhere in between these dichotomous versions of subjectivity, the former premised on ethical relations with the Other, and the latter a rejection of the ethics of Otherness with a focus on the potential for radical innovation in every situation, I believe an articulation of the maternal subject becomes possible. For it is almost impossible to think the maternal without reference to a dependent yet constantly changing other, and yet there is no maternal subject without understanding how this new and transitory subjectivity comes to arise. And just to be clear, like motherhood, this tricky balancing act, this holding in tension, this straddling of philosophical positions, this 'impossibility', *will no doubt end in tears*.

So, despite my attachment to, and gravitation towards, a variety of poststructuralist perspectives, in trying to keep my sights on the radical innovation of maternity and its capacity to produce change other than through repetition or reiteration of the Same, the *sensibility* of the book, its desire and longing, is to work against the grain of repetition compulsion, of my own psychoanalytic attachments. It represents a refusal to deem those years 'lost years' or to fully engage with the poignancy of a subject characterized by emptiness, lack and loss. As Clément writes: 'I do not exclude meeting Freud, even less encountering Lacan, but that is not enough – or rather, it is no longer enough for me' (Clément 1994: 19). This sensibility perhaps theoretically finds itself akin to a philosophical tradition that can be traced from Spinoza through to Deleuze and within this work is evidenced both in Bruno Latour's work on the ethics of objects (Latour 1988, 1992, 1995, 1997) and to some degree in Badiou's work on love. However, emerging out of my own psychodynamic clinical practice with mothers, I do not fully abandon a particular strand within psychoanalysis that continues to hold open the encounter with the 'unknowable' other as formative of the self. Much in keeping with Jessica Benjamin's articulation of holding in tension complementary theoretical views, I aim to try to bear the uncomfortable tension between a view of subjectivity founded on loss, lack and alterity, and one founded on something a little stronger, and which Badiou makes a claim for as 'truth'.

9

The feminine and the maternal

Christine Battersby, in *The Phenomenal Woman*, sets out to think about models for personal and individual identity by taking the embodied female subject as the 'norm':

> Rather than treating women as somehow exceptional, I start from the question of what would have to change were we to take seriously the notion that a 'person' could normally, at least always potentially, become two. What would happen if we thought identity in terms that did not make it always spatially and temporally oppositional to other entities? Could we retain a notion of self-identity if we did not privilege that which is self-contained and self-directed?
>
> (Battersby 1998: 2)

The five features Battersby isolates as marking out the female subject position as both lacking and excessive if the male subject is taken as the norm are: natality (the potentiality to become two); relationships with dependent others in which inequalities and power-dependencies are basic; the emergence of the self from the intersection of self and other; 'fleshy continuity' (premised, in part, on the capability of birthing new selves from within the embodied self); and what she terms 'monstrosity' (a passive thing-like embodiment that is set up in opposition to the rational male subject) (Battersby 1998: 8–14). Her aim is to think about identity if such features are taken as the 'norm'. What strikes me is how fundamental maternity is to her notion of what marks the female subject position as specific. There are instances in what follows where I try to tease out similar conflations of the feminine and the maternal, arguing for the retention of a specifically maternal subjectivity. To fail to do so leaves the mother's particular concerns and paradoxes hopelessly unarticulated. Instead of tying female subjectivity to maternity, and then, as Battersby suggests, investigating identity by taking this female subject position as the norm, my intervention is to adjust Battersby's project by a minute degree, and think about subjectivity by taking maternity as if it were the norm. This would repeat the second-wave move to uncouple maternity and femininity which I believe is vital, not this time for the sake of the feminine, but for the sake of the maternal, and in addition, move us beyond a conception of maternity as the embodied potentiality to become two, towards an account that can include the staggering complexity of what happens for a mother after 'birth'; what arises for mothers during the day-to-day, ongoing and relentless experience of mothering, whether that is with their birth, adopted, fostered, community, surrogate or 'other' children. In other words, what would happen if we took seriously the notion that a 'person' was someone who lived in an ongoing relation to that peculiar species known as a child? Sara Ruddick, one of our exemplary mothers of maternal research, talks of a child as an '"open structure" whose acts are irregular, unpredictable, often mysterious' (Ruddick 1980: 352). What happens to us when, not only do we live in close proximity to this irregular, unpredictable and mysterious other, but also we are somehow responsible for them too? What kind of subjectivity emerges? And what might happen to our understanding of subjectivity if we took this subjectivity as if it were the norm? Although I would want to resist replacing one norm with another, the exercise would be a deliberate imaginative engagement with what it is like to live alongside this other life form, *as if it were normal!*

Becoming unaccommodated: an anecdotal theory

One of the ways I therefore wish to proceed is by asking the question, *'What is it like to stay alongside a child?'* What is it like to be exposed to incessant crying, incessant demands, incessant questioning, incessant inter-ruption? What is it like to love a child? What is it like to bear witness to a child in the grip of a tantrum? What is it like to be physically burdened by a child and their 'stuff', to negotiate the child-plus-buggy-plus-changing mat-plus-nappies-plus-bag-plus-juice bottle around the urban cityscape? What do these experiences feel like and do to us? To ask what experiences are like is to already eschew attempts to build new conceptions of the subject. Instead I try to home in on key moments in which we are disturbed or dislodged by motherhood, but perhaps in very minor, transitory, mundane, silly or occasional ways. I have steered away from big moments, grand realizations or epiphanies. Rather, I have tried to keep my eye on the miniscule and rather overlooked instances in which we are wrong-footed or undone by mothering. Drawn from personal experience, and anecdotally recounted, I argue that these moments have in common a capacity to disrupt, producing a small 'blank' in experience that at once arrests and provides new points of departure. They have the quality of a shudder, or a hiccup in our self-experience, close to what Catherine Clément has called 'syncope'.[7] Although these moments unsettle us, and can be experienced in unusually intense and painful ways, I do not believe they are wholly unpleasant. I think they are experiences of 'becoming unaccommodated', to borrow Steven Connor's phrase (Connor 2008).[8] I argue that, if we are to refer to a specifically maternal subjectivity, then we would have to under-stand it as a transitory state, revealed through numerous 'hiccups', or unaccommodations in the daily lived experience of mothering.

My method for an investigation into the maternal is a little odd, to say the least. I'm not sure I can make a claim for it being a method at all. I could, after all, have interviewed a range of mothers, asked them about their experiences, transcribed their responses, tracked the twists and turns of their stories, and re-presented their storied selves. There are many fine examples of this type of work in the literature (e.g. Bailey 1999, 2000, 2001; Pollock 1999; Miller 2005; Reynolds 2005). However, I was more inclined to heed to John Law's call for 'quieter and more generous methods', for a kind of spreading or diversification of approaches to method, a refusal or desisting of a hierarchy of method, or the adoption of what Law calls 'symmetry'; a way of thinking about all methods in the same terms, whether or not these fit the normative rules of social science or indeed humanities methodologies (Law 2004). He calls for other metaphors for imagining our worlds and our responsibilities to these worlds – for, as he says, that is what methods, or 'method assemblages' do. They call forth worlds, helping us both imagine and take responsibility for them. His metaphors for imagining our worlds and our responsibilities to those worlds are: 'Localities. Specificities. Enactments. Multiplicities. Fractionalities. Goods. Resonances. Gatherings. Forms of crafting. Processes of weaving. Spirals. Vorticies. Indefinitenesses. Condensates. Dances. Imaginaries. Passions. Interferences.' They are metaphors for what he calls 'the stutter and the stop' (Law 2004: 156).

Why begin with an anecdote? Jane Gallop (2002) has evoked the term 'anecdotal theory' to describe a kind of writing that takes the recounting of an anecdote as its starting point. Working from the bottom up, she mines anecdotes for theoretical insights that may be recuperated from them (Gallop 2002). Gallop's anecdotes are themselves about 'theoretical moments' drawn from two decades of working in the academy, making a nice neat link between anecdote and theory. Coming from a perspective that fully embraced the 'theory moment' in the mid-1980s, Gallop continues to blur the distinction between reality and text, approaching her anecdotes as textual fragments that can be unravelled to find within them theoretical insights, while at the same time using them to evoke a relation with what she refers to as 'lived experience' (Gallop 2002: 2). If, according to the *Oxford English Dictionary*, an anecdote is understood as a 'short account of some interesting or humorous incident', then to juxtapose 'anecdote' with 'theory', Gallop (2002: 2) claims, is to cut through the usual connotations whereby 'humorous is pitched against serious, short against grand, trivial against overarching, specific against general'. Anecdotal theory would then 'produce theory with a better sense of humour, theorizing which honours the uncanny detail of lived experience' (Gallop 2002: 2). Anecdote appears to be used by Gallop as a way to dislodge theory from its perch, to try to get it to think about lesser, more mundane matters, and perhaps have a laugh at itself along the way. There is some uneasiness perhaps with the notion that an anecdote somehow brings us closer to 'lived experience' just because it is a recounting of a minor incident that may have actually occurred. In some senses anecdote may take us further away from the original experience. An anecdote, after all, is often recounted orally rather than textually, and usually in expansive circumstances (at weddings, after-dinner speeches, a night in the pub). Told well, it involves embellishment and exaggeration. It may, after all, not even be true. And, while being presented as a fragment, something minor or inconsequential to a main story, it takes on a special significance through being singled out. The anecdote, like its teller, is somewhat pumped up through the process of being told, revealing perhaps the paltriness of the telling experience, which is why it must be told and retold, again and again. To accord anecdote the status of text is perhaps more than it can bear. This may be Gallop's point. Rather than the anecdotal merely performing a 'thumbs up' at theory, Gallop also uses theory to sober up anecdote. Gallop takes herself through a process of systematic reflection on her anecdotes, subjecting them to a level of analysis that they do not, at first glance, appear to warrant. What this renders is a kind of self-analysis, similar to a psychoanalytic procedure that would not wish to censor anything on the grounds of its inconsequentiality, but rather, look in particular detail at that which is relegated to the margins of the main story.

In this book I perform an approximation of an anecdotal theory. As described earlier, I try to isolate key moments of maternal experience that I consider disruptive, but in relatively minor ways. These moments are recounted as short accounts of something that has interested me about motherhood. They are all originally autobiographical, although I no longer really know how true they are, having been embellished, altered, tampered with and edited in the process of recounting. They have been essentially 'overwritten' in the way Bobby Baker's performance drew on her experience of motherhood quite literally, using food. However, rather than subjecting myself to a detailed self-analysis which would seek to uncover unconscious motivations, hidden meanings or agendas, I have used the anecdotes more variously; at times to illustrate, at times to contradict, inform and dislodge the theoretical investigations that form the main body of this work. In doing so, I try to retain something of the indigestibility of maternal experience by leaving these small, unintegrated and perhaps undigestible nuggets of maternal writing within the more formal academic reflections, as well as using them to interrupt myself, or, as much as possible, throw myself off the subject – especially my own tendency to be drawn back towards the relative safety of theory.

I do not mean to make any radical claims for such an approach. Mindful of Blau DuPlessis' dry observation about feminist autobiography, 'but (and) many people have reinvented the essay' (Blau DuPlessis 1990: 175), on the contrary, what I am doing appears to me a throwback to an era in which feminine autobiographical writing, or more experimental writing practices generally, were being explored as ways to escape the closure of subjectivity, with varying degrees of success.[9] In addition, it resonates with many hundreds of years of maternal diary writing, charting women's experiences of attempting to mother alongside writing and the particular tensions, anxieties, joys and despairs that this has produced (Olsen 1978). Though not a justification for such a strategy, I do, however, retain a nostalgia for, and ongoing commitment to the possibility of writing what Blau DuPlessis describes as:

> writing as writing. Writing as praxis. Ongoing. Curious. Situated. Rapid. Rabid. Marked with one's markings. Not uniform. An exposure. Incomplete. Unsafe. Even deplorable.
>
> (Blau DuPlessis 1990: 61)

This notion of a writing 'marked with one's markings', a praxis that does not explore or illustrate the personal, but through which the personal takes place has parallels with the notion that the emergence of maternal subjectivity occurs through the details of maternal praxis. When Kristeva identifies poetic writing, psychoanalysis, and maternity as three types of praxis in which the heterogeneity of the drive breaks through the symbolic, putting the 'subject-in-process/on-trial' (Kristeva 1975: 103), there is a sense in which subjectivity itself arises through negativity, but a negativity that does not entirely destroy the fabric of the symbolic. However, I would see my writing strategy as something much more minor than either the emergence of the maternal subject-in-process/on-trial through poesis, or an attempt at a kind of Deleuzian account of 'becoming mother' through paying attention to the multiplicities and intensities that may pervade the maternal. Instead I simply use small incidents that 'stick out' for me in my experience of mothering as curious, odd, enigmatic or surprising, providing me with starting points for thinking about some of the curious, odd, enigmatic, surprising and therefore *new* experiences that motherhood prompts. Anecdotal writing allows me to begin.

There has been some recent theorizing of what has been termed 'mother-writing'. Juhasz (2003), for example, has posited maternal writing as a site for structuring maternal identity. Juhasz discusses how maternal subjectivity can be achieved through the creation of points of coherence by seeing mother-writing as a creative space that can promote recognition for the mother-author who uses writing to navigate a plurality of self-positions, for the reader who also acts as surrogate mother to the mother-writer, and for the text itself (Juhasz 2003: 395). By bringing together 'multiple maternal identities' within the same textual space, she argues a 'grammar' (Juhasz 2003: 400) can be established, and with it, the possibility of viable relationships among different maternal positions. Though Juhasz emphasizes multiplicity, creativity and recognition, her account rests on a core notion of 'self' onto whom these 'multiple identities' are pinned. She explicitly rejects positions that valorize decentredness. She argues instead that maternal work consists of the twin tasks of caring for the child and simultaneously trying to organize diverse aspects of the self so that they 'seem coherent, viable, or to possess continuity' (Juhasz 2003: 406). Writing, she believes, can create a semblance of coherence out of the self that is fragmented by splitting due to the inherent ambivalence of the maternal. It can help the mother recognize the work she does to hold in tension disparate facets of herself.

In contrast, I do not come to 'mother-writing' to hold in tension disparate facets of myself. Although my anecdotes are autobiographical, I do not wish to use such writing to create the semblance of coherence by patching the self's fissures. Anecdotes are also 'secret, private or hitherto unpublished narratives or details of history' (*Oxford English Dictionary* 1989). We could equally think of secret histories as those imbued with trauma rather than erotic energies, histories that remain private, unpublished and possibly unspeakable because they are resistant to codification in language. Stories about motherhood often have this quality. I suggest, however, that motherhood lends itself to anecdote rather than the grand narrative of 'mother-writing' due to the constant attack on narrative that the child performs: literally breaking into maternal speech, and as well as her own self-narrative which is punctured at the level of constant interruptions to thinking, reflecting, sleeping, moving and completing tasks. What is left is a series of unconnected experiences that remain fundamentally unable to cohere. Secret, private and certainly unpublished, they resurface as anecdote – often in the form of funny stories we tell each other about silly or charming things our children did or said.

Working between the mundane and theory is also in keeping with a broadly phenomenological perspective. If phenomenology seeks to describe conscious experience from a first-person point of view, then human subjectivity is understood as not existing in some space outside of lived experience, but rather, that the space of human subjectivity is produced by embodied or lived experience (Merleau-Ponty 1962). This embodiment occurs at the level of perception, imagination, thought, emotion, desire, volition and action. Though a post-modern feminist perspective would reject a crude notion of a specifically female lived experience (Weedon 1998), there has certainly been a recuperation and engagement with an embodied feminine otherness or difference as a site of both resistance and transformation, particularly in the work of Irigaray, Kristeva, and Clément.[10] Given the almost intractable difficulties with separating the maternal subject from the pregnant body, and then from the maternal body that the child uses in a myriad of actual and fantasized ways, a phenomenological perspective that keeps maternal experience in its sights may help with these delicate processes of separation.

This book is also, then, an attempt to write a necessarily partial phenomenology of motherhood, paying particular attention to some moment-by-moment experiences of being with small children. To ask the question 'What is it like?' rather than 'What does it mean?' in this context is reminiscent of

Steven Connor's notion of 'cultural phenomenology' (Connor 2008) which would 'home in on substances, habits, organs, rituals, obsessions, pathologies, processes and patterns of feeling. Such interests would be at once philosophical and poetic, explanatory and exploratory, analytic and evocative' (unpaginated webpage). Likewise, this work aims to be at once academic and personal, rigorous and oblique, welcoming the delightful in experiences that are also clearly very grim. If my argument is that, out of the kind of Beckettian tragi-comedy that motherhood is ('I must go on, I can't go on, I'll go on', Beckett writes at the end of *The Unnameable*), a new subjectivity is called into being, then to describe this would entail a particular attentiveness to what this experience is like. It recalls Susan Kraemer's words when she writes of the necessity of asking about 'how the mother feels about what she feels and what she does with how she feels' (Kraemer 1996: 768).

As I have noted above, there is something excessive in this approach. Gallop tells us that the notion of excess is related both to the exorbitant, and the real. She notes that the exorbitant is a term Derrida uses in his early text, *Of Grammatology*, as a way to justify his interest in rare and marginal texts (Derrida 1976). The exorbitant is related to exteriority, exits, departures, attempts to get out of ruts. Of Derrida's use of the term, Gallop (2002) writes:

> The rut he wants to get out of is the rut philosophy is in, the metaphysical rut which separates philosophy (or what we could call theory) from empiricism (the link to the real, the here and now). Derrida connects the exorbitant with the attempt to get outside the metaphysical closure that sequesters theory from the real.
>
> (Gallop 2002: 8)

To some degree, this rut is particularly deep when it comes to the maternal; the mother is both the supreme object through which subjectivity is thought, as well as profoundly unable to extricate herself from the empirical. However, I propose that the maternal subject both embodies this rut, this split between philosophy and empiricism and that the lived experience of such a split has a subjective spin-off for the mother, providing both a theoretical and an actual exit from this rut. Both Kristeva (1977) and Battersby (1998) argue that the maternal subject is peculiar in that her subjectivity is premised on being both for herself and for another. Kristeva's notion of *herethics* is that the mother is at once ethical, heretical and feminine (Kristeva 1977: 185), constituting what Kelly Oliver has called an '"outlaw" ethics' (Oliver 1993a: 15) in which the mother sees herself as responsible for the other's life to the point of her own disappearance, which places her outside of the law of the symbolic. My interest is in an account of maternal subjectivity in which something comes back from the encounter with the child. I try to understand the maternal subject as arising out of the

16

paradox of the one who sees the world from the point of view of there being two, which in its turn retroactively produces the one. The experience of loving a child is understood as a momentary flooding of subjectivity arising out of a mother's capacity to attend to the truth of the disjuncture that there are two. Something excessive to the split between philosophy and empiricism breaks out.

In sum, though this work aligns itself with anecdotal theory, feminist autobiographical writing and cultural phenomenology, it does not knit these approaches into a quasi-methodology, but aims at something more tenuous than any of these approaches suggest. It uses whatever it has to hand to ask the question, 'What is it like to encounter a child?', in the hope that the answer to such a question may provide us with an articulation of a specifically maternal subjectivity.

Protagonists

Having homed in on key moments of disruption, I attempt to think about such events through the work of an eclectic group of theorists: Julia Kristeva, Catherine Clément, Luce Irigaray, Jessica Benjamin, Judith Butler, Emmanuel Levinas, Alain Badiou, David Appelbaum, Jean Laplanche, Jerome Neu, Bruno Latour and Elaine Scarry. Taken together, their work does not constitute a coherent research field, and although Kristeva and Benjamin have written on motherhood, it is not a theory of maternal subjectivity that I look to them for. Instead I try to draw out from diverse sources a nexus of ideas about *transformation and change, alterity, interruption, disjunction, love, crying, syncope, objects and ethics*: the particular elements of subjectivity that I believe pertain to the maternal through the everyday experience of mothering, and are shown up in the key moments of disruption that I describe. If there are similarities between these theorists' work, they could perhaps be described as a broad commitment to thinking about ways subjectivity emerges 'otherwise' than the conscious workings of either an autonomous, auto-affective, rational male subject, or his post-modern counter-part; the traumatized, split, mournful, abject (still male) subject. So, for example Kristeva's notion of the heterogeneity of the drive, Clément's exploration of syncope and rapture, and Laplanche's reinstitution of the seduction theory to describe the way the unconscious is formed by an encounter with the 'alien' other of the mother's unconscious, share an interest in articulating disruptive forces that lie at the edge of the symbolic. These forces are usually associated with the feminine, the excessive, the exotic and the unrepresentable, but provide the conditions for the emergence of a subjectivity thought of as 'otherwise' to the traditional male rational subject. We might say that psychoanalysis, certainly from a Freudian or Lacanian perspective, has always kept one eye on the inherent instability of the subject, and the way that the ego is constantly undermined from within. In part, this book represents a wrangle with psychoanalysis about what it does about the subject undermined in a very concrete way from 'without'; how disruption by the other shifts our internal psychic structures, not only during childhood, but also throughout our lives, and therefore how it accounts for the emergence of the new, the unexpected, the surprising or the generative. Motherhood is offered as a model for exploring how the new, at times radically, and painfully, emerges.

This is not to deny the psychoanalytic insight that we come to the encounter with a child from a position of both knowing and unknowing. I would characterize such knowing as what we already carry within us from our own experiences and unconscious fantasies about our mothers and mothering. As well as conscious memory, thoughts, feelings and associations that we have with our own mothering, we carry, following Laplanche, our mother's enigmatic signifiers that give rise to our own unconscious (Laplanche 1999). These we then, in our own turn, unconsciously pass on. This latter unconscious element could be thought about as a kind of 'unknown known' in that the enigmatic signifier is not just 'unthought' in the sense of Bollas' 'unthought known' (Bollas 1987) but coming from the other, it remains totally impossible to decode. This, perhaps, is a way of thinking about the distinction Laplanche makes between the other thing (*das Andere*) that is maintained in its radical alterity only by the actuality of the other person (*der Andere*) (Laplanche 1999: 71) but this time from the perspective of the mother rather than the child. Over and above the child's developing unconscious (*das Andere*) is the radical alterity of the other person (*der Andere*) who, for the mother, is the child. This surely offers the mother something she cannot anticipate, and to which she too responds.

The book does not aim to present a systematic critique of the main protagonists. Nor does it set itself up within either philosophy or psychoanalysis in order to make critical contributions to these fields. Rather, it enacts a heterogeneous foray into unfamiliar terrain, looking for scraps that may help articulate, understand or describe maternal moments of undoing, remaining with the mother in a marginal relation to these main bodies of work. In *The Philosophy of the Limit*, Drucilla Cornell draws on Walter Benjamin's figure of the *chiffonnier*, the nineteenth-century rubbish collector, whom she uses as a model for her ethical subject, picking her way through the refuse of philosophical ideas for bits or scraps that she can recollect, use or recycle (Cornell 1992). Though drawn towards this ideal figure (especially as she merges with a familiar stereotype of the mother, creatively making what she can with what little she has so that her children don't go hungry), it also calls into question my own relation to both philosophy and psychoanalysis. If, as Deleuze suggests, to philosophize is to attempt to write the autobiography of a spiritual automaton, then this work could be thought of as a kind of philosophizing. And in ways that I hope to substantiate as I go along, maternity shows up the limit of psychoanalysis, calling psychoanalysis into question at the point it gives way to ethics. Though I come to philosophy as a willing amateur, I am impelled to look there for different answers than psychoanalysis can provide to the questions I have, and where I find philosophical answers, I am impelled to loop back to psychoanalysis as my own 'first philosophy' to reinterrogate them from a perspective that always reminds us to hold the child in mind. My hope is that in placing itself in proximity to both psychoanalysis and philosophy, this work attempts to overcome the limits of its own specialization, that of maternity, as well as using maternity as a model to ever-so-slightly ruffle the limits of both psychoanalysis and philosophy.

Terms and conditions: the gendering of the maternal

Of whom do we speak when we talk of mothers and what do we denote when we refer to mothering, motherhood, maternal subjectivity, or the maternal more generally? What have the contours of these terms come to signify across different disciplinary domains, what are their genealogies, and where now may 'a mother' begin and end? It is generally accepted that the maternal refers to not only the material and embodied experience of pregnancy, childbirth and lactation, but also to identities and meanings of mothering, the ongoing emotional and relational work of being with children and others, the daily material practices of childrearing, the social locations and structural contexts within which women mother; indeed, to the whole range of embodied, social and cultural meanings, practices and structures associated with reproduction and parenting (Arendell 2000). From an interdisciplinary perspective however, I think it is possible to locate a particular tension between accounts of the maternal that focus on maternal work, thought of as a coherent set of ethical tasks and functions that centre around the preservation of a child's life, the fostering of their growth and the development of a capacity for social acceptability (Ruddick 1989) and accounts that focus on unconscious intersubjective dynamics (Hollway 2001), and the mutual development of 'mother' and 'child' through another kind of maternal work that entails containment and reverie (Bion 1962) (that peculiar psychoanalytic form of thinking), and managing both the child's and one's own ambivalence (Parker 2005). From this latter perspective, maternal subjectivity is a term used to refer to the ways 'fantasy, meaning, biography and relational dynamics' inform how each woman takes up a position in relation to a variety of discourses about mothering (Featherstone 1997: 7), acknowledging not only what we bring to mothering from within and without, but also how the relational dynamics of mothering itself has transformational potential in terms of both the self and the social fabric.

However, although 'parenting' and the 'parental body' is being used more and more to reference childrearing practices that can, and indeed are, performed by both men as well as women, there are difficulties with collapsing the distinction between parenting in the masculine and in the feminine. Sara Ruddick (1997) argues that maternal and paternal practices remain distinct. Although she understands parenting as the 'complex ongoing work of responding to children's needs in particular economic and social circumstances', work that is not prima facie associated with either sex, the younger the children and the more physical their demands, the more likely this work will be assigned to women (Ruddick 1997: 206). To talk only of parenting 'denies the history and current practice of female mothering – including women's disproportionate responsibility for child-care' (Ruddick 1997: 206). And, as Shelley Park has pointed out, it is not only an issue of maternal practice. Paternal bodies are not mediated by the same cultural expectations and norms as maternal bodies (Park 2006: 207). She advocates using the way adoptive maternal bodies are rendered 'queer' by pronatalist perspectives, to critique dominant views of mothering with-out losing sight of the differences between maternal and paternal bodies. Wendy Hollway (2006) makes a different point. Drawing on early debates begun by Nancy Chodorow (1978) in *The Reproduction of Mothering* and extended by Jessica Benjamin (1995), she argues that fathers do not 'mother', but can develop a capacity to care, based, as she sees it on whether fathers, as boys, 'were able to retain their positive identification with maternal capacities to care for them, while at the same time coming to terms with being boys' (Hollway 2006: 99). She argues that maternal subjectivity arises out of a woman's position in relation to 'the absolute, unconditional demands of a dependent infant, especially if that infant has been a part of her' (Hollway 2006: 64). Though she raises the issue of biological mothers having a more immediate experience of embodied subjectivity through the experience of pregnancy, birth and breastfeeding, she is careful to distinguish biological mothers from maternal subjectivity, the latter being open to what she terms 'non-mothers' who remain available for trans-formative experiences through the practices of childcare. The maternal subject is understood, then, as a gendered subject who is structured by a relationship to a child (Hollway 2001). Mothering becomes parenting in the feminine not only due to the particular experiences of pregnancy, birth and breastfeeding, but also because of the uses the child makes of sexual difference.

Susan Kraemer also uses the term maternal subjectivity to include the 'grimmer experiences of "ordinary" maternal hate, aggression, and failure' (Kraemer 1996: 767). Her emphasis, however, is on how the mother comes to own and tolerate the broadest range of subjective responses to her baby or young child that include hate, anger and aggression. It is all very well granting the mother subjectivity, she claims, but it is an examination of what experiencing her subjectivity *means* to her that we need to engage in. In discussing, for example, the maternal analytic metaphor of the container, she proposes that we move beyond caricatured portrayals of the maternal container as either 'empty' (Hirsch 1987; Aron 1991) or 'omnipotent' (Mitchell 1988). Instead, she suggests that:

> these conceptualisations of the maternal container are in them-selves artefacts of fantastic stereotypes about the selfless, self-denying or powerful, dangerous mother. We need, alternatively, to construct maternal containers that are neither devalued nor feared, neither sanctified nor vilified, but are simply subjectively alive and struggling, as ironically, the analytic holding mother is sometimes viewed.
>
> (Kraemer 1996: 769)

Being 'simply subjectively alive and struggling' is the way Kraemer wants to try to hold on to the mother's subjectivity without it being thought about purely in the service of the child. However, one of the tensions in Kraemer's definition of maternal subjectivity is the plea for the mother to have a subjectivity she can call her own, while her subjectivity is thought about as arising through a relationship to a child that is characterized by a one-way, non-negotiable dependency. Maternal subjectivity emerges in her account as a way to describe the experience of managing intense emotional states thrown up by an ongoing relationship to this absolutely dependent other. It suggests that mothering is fundamentally about a particular kind of asym-metrical relationship in which the mother manages the feelings provoked in her by the 'ruthless' infant. Kraemer's work points us towards an under-standing of maternal subjectivity arising directly out of the lived encounter with the child as she actively struggles to manage ambivalence or act as container or mirror. While I think this approach is vital in reminding us that mothers have emotional experiences of mothering that are complex and are inflected by unconscious dynamics including ambivalence, and that it may involve a non-negotiable relationship with a dependent other who is one's child, I think there is a real question about sustaining an account of maternal subjectivity out of the mother's ability to recognize and ultimately hold together feelings of love and hate. The mother is still figured as a container, even if she is now one who has some feelings about what she is being asked to do. My suggestion would be that we need accounts of maternal experiences that move the mother away from containers and receptacles altogether, that have other shapes and contours, and which may allow us to think about other things mothers do for and alongside their children.

At the end of a decennial review of scholarship on mothering; Arendell (2000) highlights some gaps in the literature and asks a series of pertinent questions: How do various women feel about being mothers; what meaning do they ascribe to mothering; how are women's sexual lives, desires and experiences affected by mothering activities and the status of mothering; what is the mothering project, as mothers see it; what is the character of the relationships between particular mothers and their children; what exactly, do mothers do; what is the character of mothers' daily lives; how do mothers negotiate the activities of childrearing; how are women affected by mothering; how do women actively resist the dominant ideologies of mothering a family? These questions have a different kind of slant than the question Ann Snitow (1992) posed, which highlighted the tension between motherhood as institution and identity. They are more concerned with subjective experience, more focused on feelings and meanings thrown up by motherhood, more focused on the detail of lived experience and on agency in relation to maternity. They highlight the direction of current research; a willingness to engage in mother's subjective experiences of mothering while holding in view the context in which such subjectivities emerge, are structured and also impact in their turn on such a context.

Though I want in no way to exclude any of the multiple and complex ways in which people inhabit maternal relations, nor put myself in a position in which what I write would be tantamount to denying anyone a claim on those relations when they feel that claim is their due right, this book explores a very specific area of maternal experience; the experience of rearing young children who are present in a mother's life in a fairly regular way. However, I use the maternal to signify any relation of obligation between an adult who identifies as female, and another person whom that adult elects as their 'child'. It signifies relations between women and their birth children, adoptive children, foster children, community children, family members or children of friendship groups for whom they have informal or formal parental responsibilities, and many other constellations beside; relations in which the adult involved takes on partial responsibility for the preservation of life, growth and the fostering of social responsibility for that other whom they name and claim as their child.

When I talk of 'maternal subjectivity' however, I am attempting to point towards an experience that resides 'otherwise' than, or is excessive to maternal identities, thought of as emerging at the intersections particularly between gender, class and 'race'. Paradoxically arising, I argue, out of the mundane and relentless practices of daily maternal care, maternal subjectivity presents us with particular philosophical and ontological conundrums, not only in terms of the pregnant and lactating body that is both singular and multiple, disturbing notions of unity and the bounded self, but also because maternity is an experience that I maintain is impossible to anticipate in advance, one that unravels as it proceeds, and that one is always chasing the tail of, never become expert at, or even competent, and that always eludes our attempts to fully understand it. It involves relations with a particular and peculiar other whose rate of change is devastatingly rapid, who is always, by definition, 'developing', shifting, changing, and yet it is another to whom one is 'linked' in an equally particular and peculiar way, a way that has something to do with larger issues of responsibility and care but played out in the most seemingly ridiculous forums; those of the daily 'thinking' about feeding, sleeping, dressing, manners, routines, good stuff, bad stuff, schools, friendships, more stuff, influences, environments, time, responsibility, freedom, control and so on. This book attempts to debate the nature of this link, the 'ethics' that is, of motherhood, but for the very specific purposes of understanding what this linking means for women who mother. My concerns are with trying to understand how an encounter with a child, the one we come to name as the child for whom we are responsible, is experienced from the asymmetrical position of being a mother; what this experience may 'offer' a mother that opens her onto the generative, surprising and unexpected; how motherhood indeed makes us anew.

In working from a few isolated personal experiences, I am speaking from the most narrow and particular location one could conceive. I have, for instance, two sons and no daughters. I live in an urban, British city. My partner has played an active role in parenting, and because of the flexibility of my own work arrangements, I have been able to spend considerable periods of time with my children when they were small, despite working full-time, though perhaps at enormous cost to my psychological and physical well-being. I have my own gendered, raced and class relations that are continuously at work in all the choices I make, and fail to make. There is no 'outside' of these experiences, and they deeply affect the ways I read theory, and understand and hear the maternal experiences of others. I do not believe, however, that the specificity of this account invalidates it. In many ways, it functions to keep reminding myself of my specific locations, of the particular ruts I find for myself, and find myself in. And in some ways it is its very specificity that permits the writing of a phenomenology of motherhood at all. I offer it, not as an example of a mothering experience that others may relate to, but its opposite; as what 'sticks out' of just one mothering experience, that may give pause for thought.

2

MATERNAL ALTERITY
Mum's the word

In the attenuated moments after giving birth, while the bloodbath is mopped up around me, in those first blinking, thinned out moments, as I realize the pain has miraculously stopped as inexplicably as it began, and I lie stunned, and somewhat empty, someone asks me if I have decided on a name. What? A name? A name for what? A name for the baby, the same someone says. Now what? I think. Not only must I birth the baby, but I must author it too? My partner and I look at each other. No, we haven't decided, but this seems like an inadequate response to the enormity of the question; a question that begs so many other questions about belonging, memory, culture, taste. So I say, I mean I just slip it out . . . 'Joel'. I just say it, and then it is his name. My partner half shrugs, half nods to me. Like all names, it's the best of a bad bunch. It's not quite right, but it will do. It's at the top of our not-quite-right-names list. Saying it makes it his name, but does not yet make it right. The name is too big for him. Any name would be. I find myself embarrassed saying it. As I say it again and again over the coming weeks, until eventually his name sticks to him, until it becomes, through use, his right name, I retain this discomfort. A whiff of embarrassment lingers in the gap between the child and his name. The child is a stranger to his name. He doesn't respond when I call to him. It hangs around him, as the nappies hang around his tiny bum like ill-fitting sacks. It is inconsequential to him. He didn't choose it. I elected it as his name, so quickly, so arbitrarily. And I am deeply implicated in making what is strange in him familiar, in fixing him in language before he even knows what language is.

What is this discomfort I have with saying his name? Have I still not come to terms with the arbitrary relation between signifier and signified? It comes back to me like a mantra that I realize I have repeated endlessly without understanding at all. I have notebooks full of badly drawn trees and odd-looking toilet doors, but this is nothing compared with the actual responsibility of assigning a name for the first time to the unnamed, and watching it stick. Yes, naming both claims him as my child, and places him elsewhere, given over already to the order of language. Once stuck, he is simultaneously mine and displaced, same and strange. But for a few weeks, he is neither. His otherness appears to be his very own.

24

It is not uncommon for mothers to talk of the first moments after birth as a surprising encounter with otherness. In *Still Life*, A. S. Byatt writes of Stephanie, moments after she has given birth to her son:

> she recognised him, and recognised that she did not know, and had
> never seen him . . . . 'You', she said to him, skin for the first time
> on skin in the outside air, which was warm and shining, 'you'.
>
> (Byatt, 1985: 114)

And yet this 'you' seems so slight in comparison to the weight of the name conferred on him – this scrap of life, in his particularity, his singularity, is almost overwhelmed by the sign of his own interpolation into an already existing network of meanings – cultural, social, familial, personal, this 'being' already so invested with the desire of the other. Even so, there appears to be a time delay, a few uncomfortable, yet intriguing weeks during which the encounter with what is strange, even alien in the child remains tangible through this mother's embarrassment at the name she has conferred. It doesn't fit. Her discomfort temporarily maintains and makes visible the distance between the child and his name. We might say that reciprocally, it holds open the status of she who names. A not-yet-mother in relation to a not-yet-child; between the moment that she names him, and the moment the name sticks and becomes invisible through use, a transitional space appears.

I mentioned earlier Sara Ruddick's evocative description of a child as an '"open structure" whose acts are irregular, unpredictable, often mysterious' (Ruddick 1980: 352). These qualities – irregularity, unpredictability, mystery – perhaps work to maintain the child as an enigma, this originary otherness that is revealed through a mother's discomfort with naming turns out to be constantly transforming itself, defying our initial attempts to 'fix' it through these clumsy processes. Mothers, however, are usually given the unenviable task of being in the position of the one who is supposed to know. From Winnicott and Bion on, mothers have been imbued with capacities for empathic understanding, attunement, reverie, mentalization; capacities that supposedly allow us to make sense on the infant's behalf of their confusing, stricken and contradictory internal world, and so return to them their thoughts and feelings in a more digestible form.[1] As more complex accounts of maternal subjectivity have emerged,[2] the naturalness and ease of these maternal mental processes have been brought under scrutiny. In these accounts the focus shifts from purely how the infant uses the mother, towards how the mother experiences her mothering role, her tasks and her changed identities, as well as her reconfigured internal object relations, and how this may impact, in turn, on a mother's capacity to relate to her child. However, although we may have begun to tentatively ask ourselves that hair-raising question 'What is it like to be alongside a child', an account of maternal subjectivity, as opposed to a description of mothering, would in part entail imagining what it is like to be in close proximity to the 'open structure' that is a child. This would mean thinking more deeply about women's childrearing experiences from the perspective of being responsible for a child who is not just initially experienced as other, but remains irregular, unpredictable and essentially unknowable, and the pressures and strains as well as the generative potential that this may have on the maternal psyche.

The turn to the 'other' ('the ethical question', as Cornell (1992) put it) needs to be understood as a counterpart, in Jessica Benjamin's view, to the question of the subject that was such a prevalent part of social and feminist theory throughout the late 1970s and 1980s (Benjamin 1998). Whether one adheres to the view of the subject as primarily the subject of discourse and power in keeping with Butler's early work (Butler 1990), or the various attempts to recuperate notions of agency, autonomy, desire and the 'self' through resisting the treatment of subjectivity as purely a function of language, from Benjamin's perspective the question of the subject inevitably leads to the question of the other. It seems imperative, then, to try to think about maternal subjectivity and ethics alongside one another, and my suggestion is that one way to begin thinking about maternal subjectivity as an ethical subjectivity is through providing an account of *maternal alterity* – maternal encounters with inassimilable otherness, seen here in the figure of a child.

It is not at all unusual to bring together the terms 'mothering' and 'ethics'. There is a substantial literature on what has come to be termed 'the ethics of care'.[3] Some of the early work in this field theorized mothering as a particular kind of ethical work with specific tasks and functions. This led on to an exploration of an ethics of care that could draw on the mother–child model as a way of describing an ethical sphere that was not purely governed by autonomy, independence and justice (Gilligan 1982; Noddings 1984; Ruddick 1989; Tronto 1993). Mothering was drawn on as a paradigmatic type of caring relation, one that involved empathic understanding, interdependence, flexibility, relatedness, receptivity, responsiveness, attentive and preservative love, nurturance and training. These types of qualities, many of which have 'feminine' overtones, were valorized by early theorists, in part as a way of elevating maternal work to the status of ethical work (this is particularly evident in Ruddick's writing), and in addition, opening up a debate about care and justice in the social and political sphere. Care became a trope used to both soften up moral philosophy with its traditional concerns with justice, and to indicate new modes of social and political transformation (Tronto 1993; Sevenhuijsen 1998; Hollway 2006). Williams (2001) identifies a paradigm shift in work on the ethics of care that has sought to move beyond the binary, care versus justice, with its connotations of public versus private and masculine versus feminine. Here care breaks free from associations with the mother–child model altogether, and can be seen instead to structure all human relationships (Sevenhuijsen 1998). This universalist paradigm (Williams 2001) sees the earlier reliance on the mother–child relation as a model for care as problematic, as it reduces concern with the ethics of justice and of social equality and is also highly normative (Roseneil 2004). It seems then that mothering in the ethics of care literature has been drawn on and then, to some degree jettisoned, as the focus has broadened to include other models of care such as friendship (e.g. Roseneil 2004).

Andrews (2001) argues that much of the underlying concern about the care and justice debate within feminism is the anxiety that care ethics points us back towards Virginia Woolf's famous image of the *Angel in the House* (Woolf 1942). This is an image of the charming, sympathetic, unselfish woman who has neither a mind nor wishes of her own, but feels totally fulfilled by thinking always of other people. Andrews (2001) rightly critiques the Angel fantasy for being a sexist, heterosexist, racist, classist, Christianized ideal of femininity and calls for a different ideal type than the Angel for envisioning the moral woman. This demonstrates the ongoing tension in the care and justice debate between care being understood as a soft 'feminine' trait which then needs to be valorized (i.e. the valuing of relationality, context, emotion, responsiveness, receptiveness and so on), or whether care needs to be reassessed as an activity that encompasses thinking, taking responsibility, skill and competence, with their more traditionally 'masculine' overtones. The question with regards to mothering is whether we want to see mothering as the emblematic instance of the 'feminine' version or try to think about mothering in a way that includes what has been conceived of as these more 'robust' tasks and attributes. Feminists may well want to move women away from the Angel as an ideal image, but, to some degree, mothers are stuck with having to work out their relation to problematic notions (especially for women) of giving, loving, caring, nurturing, being for another and putting the needs of a vulnerable other before ones own. In a highly problematic and controversial statement, Kristeva (2001) writes:

> We still must acknowledge that, no matter how far science may progress, women will continue to be the mothers of humanity. Through their love of men, too, women will continue to give birth to children. That fate, though tempered by various techniques and by a sense of solidarity, will remain an all-consuming and irreplaceable vocation.
>
> (Kristeva 2001: xiv)

My suggestion is that we use a different strand of ethics to propel us away from this debate about femininity, masochism, and the Angel in the House, away from the dualisms of feminine-care, masculine-justice and mother-hood as an all-consuming vocation. What I would like to do is try to move the account of the ethical nature of the mother–child relationship away from its reliance on notions such as flexibility, relatedness, receptivity and responsiveness but without jettisoning the project of mapping out a specifically maternal ethics. My interest, after all, is in motherhood rather than care. Instead of borrowing from the mother metaphorically to help us understand something of our relations to others (as much psychoanalytic literature has done in order to help understand the relationship between analyst and analysand), I want to return to the mother–child relationship itself to probe the complexity of a specifically maternal ethics. To do so requires understanding maternal ethics as less to do with an unstinting commitment or caring attentiveness towards an other, and more to do with the way otherness is always at work, structuring, infecting and prompting human subjectivity. This implies understanding not only the ways that otherness figures in the developmental trajectory of the child, but also crucially in a mother's own developmental process too. This would go some way towards recuperating something for a mother out of her often bewildering encounter with a child, which could then be used to shore up the notion of a specifically maternal subjectivity.

To do this, I am going to draw on the work of Emmanuel Levinas (1961, 1974, 1985). Levinas' philosophy proceeds from a refusal of the traditional primacy of the subject. There is no clearly defined individual human subject describable as an ontological entity prior to our responsibility for others. First and foremost there is the Other. Subjectivity is seen to emerge through a relation to this radical alterity, this irreducible otherness. However, setting up the question of the other as a counterpart to the question of the subject is precisely one of the difficulties with the so-called 'ethical turn'. In figuring the other as counterpart to the subject, the other remains within the realm of a signifying system that Levinas would call the Same, thus calling into question the possibility of distance and therefore difference. Before turning to Levinas, it makes some sense, then, to begin with a discussion between psychoanalysis and philosophy, one staged between Jessica Benjamin and Judith Butler around different readings of intersubjectivity, drawing, as they both do, on the work of Hegel to try to understand how we come to have relations with others at all. Part of this discussion involves the status of the Other as radically other, as opposed to another subjectivity or ego.[4] As I understand it, at the core of this debate is whether *difference* can be thought of in the same terms as *alterity* – whether being other to me, beyond my control, and thereby recognizable as another, like me, can be thought of in the same terms as radical alterity, an Otherness that is, by definition, beyond notions of 'me-ness'. This is perhaps already a dialogue in different registers, psychoanalytic and philosophical. If Levinas' position is useful, it is perhaps because of his assertion that there is no me before or beyond the Other. Subjectivity is understood as emerging through particular relations with alterity – the Other shown up as 'face' in the child, persecutor, stranger, brother, lover, neighbour.[5] The child in Benjamin's account of intersubjectivity emerges through relations to the other, but, as we shall see, the account remains reliant on the mother as the ultimate site of otherness that structures notions of both self and other, but without articulating maternal experiences of alterity. Without figuring the child as essentially an enigma, a stranger who calls the mother to ethical responsibility, it is difficult to see a way of theoretically sustaining maternal alterity, and without a relation to alterity, I believe the mother will always be in danger of being co-opted to serve the child in all her classic manifestations: object, abject, container, receptacle, mirror, or absent 'Thing'.

Jessica Benjamin and the intersubjective turn

Intersubjectivity has become a major theoretical addition to psychoanalysis, emerging largely within the relational tradition through the work of Benjamin (2004), Mitchell (1988, 2000), Aron (1996) and others. In Benjamin's work it is through her account of reciprocity, recognition and intersubjectivity that she arrives at how we experience otherness (Benjamin 1990, 1995, 1998, 2004). Benjamin moves away from psychoanalytic formulations that seek to understand how the infant internalizes real and fantasized interactions in the interpersonal domain, and which, through the dynamics of projection and introjection, come to shape in their turn, that domain. Instead, she holds out for an understanding of intersubjectivity that is more than merely internal object relations, and that exists in tandem with the interpersonal. In this sense Benjamin keeps in sight a distinction between the interpersonal and the intersubjective, or the object and the other. She writes:

> If we take the tension between recognition and omnipotence to be the inner conflict that shapes the interpersonal world, then I think we are taking the intersubjective to be an axis that cuts across intrapsychic and interpersonal.
>
> (Benjamin 2000: 297)

Benjamin's notion of the intersubjective rests on an otherness that remains beyond one's control, resistant to the pressures of an internal split complementarity governed by omnipotence. If omnipotence is the condition in which the subject attempts to control the other by forcing the self and other into complementary polarized positions, then the other is reduced to the status of internal object and the distinction between other and object is destroyed:

The tension between recognizing the other and wanting the self to be absolute (omnipotence) is, to my mind, an internal conflict inherent in the psyche; it exists independent of any given interaction – even in the most favourable conditions. It is not interpersonally generated but is, rather, a psychic structure that conditions the interpersonal. The problem of whether or not we are able to recognize the other person as outside, not the sum of, our projections or the mere object of need, and still feel recognized by her or him, is defining for intersubjectivity.

(Benjamin 2000: 294)

One inherent aspect of our psychic world, Benjamin argues, is the defensive structure that involves splitting and is governed by the need for omnipotent control or independence, the philosophical roots of which can be seen in her use of both Hegel's master–slave model and Freud's notion of narcissism (Benjamin 1995: 36). Another aspect of our psychic functioning, however, is what Benjamin calls 'intersubjective space' in which it is possible to identify with the other's position without losing one's own. This space is characterized by mutual recognition, in which the self can recognize the other as a like subject, and in turn be recognized by such a subject. Mutual recognition is achieved through a process in which the other survives destruction, albeit in fantasy, and is thereby established in the subject's mind as beyond omnipotent control. Benjamin here draws heavily on Winnicott's ideas about the 'use of an object' (Winnicott 1968) where he marks out a developmental phase that comes after object relating and involves object use, which is made possible through seeing that the object survives unconscious destruction. The object in question is the mother, and 'survival', in Winnicott's terms, describes the mother's ability to respond in a non-retaliatory manner to the infant's unconscious attacks. In intersubjective space both reflection and also analysis become possible on the mother/analyst's side because the infant/patient experiences the other as truly external through survival of its own destructive impulses. And it is through this process that the mother/analyst attains subjectivity in the mind of the infant/patient. When intersubjective space breaks down (when destruction is truly destructive, if you like, when the other does not 'survive' but instead retaliates, or abandons), there is a return to the complementary positioning of internal objects. In Benjamin's view there is an ongoing and endless cycle of the establishment of mutual recognition followed by its negation, constituting a never-ending tension between complementarity and mutuality, between relating to the other as object or like subject.

Benjamin's position clearly has implications and consequences for the mother and her own relation to otherness. There are some important points in Benjamin's theorizing when she specifically addresses the issue of the mother's subjectivity in relation to the child (Benjamin 1995). Given that she is concerned with tracing the development of our capacity to experience otherness, as well as wanting to accord the mother a subjectivity of her own, Benjamin maintains that the mother's subjectivity is necessary for the development of the child's separate experience of self. She asks some crucial questions pertaining to the development of maternal subjectivity starting back in childhood:

> How does a child develop into a person who, as a parent, is able to recognize her or his own child? What are the internal processes, the psychic landmarks, of such development? Where is the theory that tracks the development of the child's responsiveness, empathy and concern and not just the parent's sufficiency or failure?
>
> (Benjamin 1995: 32)

In many ways this looks promising. Here the capacity for recognition is seen as a developmental achievement in childhood, and is later extended to the new child of the child-now-parent. Recognition is not something the mother just does naturally or altruistically for the child. However, what Benjamin does with the mother in this early work is complex.

First, as we can see from the quote above, what interests her in terms of the mother's subjectivity is the mother's capacity to recognize the child. Second, although she argues passionately for the importance of mutual recognition of maternal subjectivity, she relies on the maternal subject's ability to respond benignly to the child's attacks as the cornerstone for the child's development of the capacity for recognition. However, mothers are not always able to do this. More often than not, they find themselves in a losing battle to maintain any sense of separate or autonomous 'self' in the face of the dramatic and relentless onslaught of the child's needs and demands, especially their needs to destroy their mother's separateness (Kraemer 1996). In addition, they must then contend with the sense of failure, hopelessness and despair that arises from their awareness that they have not 'survived'. Although it could be argued that this is a form of survival in its own right – the capacity to contend with these feelings and to evolve in the face of regularly 'losing it' – Kraemer argues that this amounts to a re-idealization of motherhood, just at the point that it appears that we have become able to think about maternal ambivalence. Mothers live with strong, normative social and cultural messages that constantly remind us that, although we all have a range of powerful and conflicting feelings about our children, we still need to act responsibly in the face of infantile ruthlessness, for the sake of the developing child.

One of the examples Benjamin gives of the mother's survival is her ability to set firm, but not too rigid boundaries during the child's second year of life, as the child becomes consciously aware of the mother's separateness and stages a battle against it. The battle is one in which the child attempts

31

to destroy the mother by attacking her difference; when the child cries 'want what I want', it is the mother's otherness that is under attack. If the mother, attempting to leave the protesting child to go to work, for instance, still leaves, but communicates to the child that she misses him or her, the child comes to realize that the mother is outside of the self, an other who cannot be coerced, and paradoxically, as Benjamin claims, through omnipotence the child comes to experience otherness. The child can later identify with the mother who misses the child and repair the breakdown in recognition (Benjamin 1995: 92).

I think, however, that although it appears that we have kept our eye on the maternal subject throughout, she has, in fact, slipped out of the frame. Benjamin's account relies on a reworked version of a 'good-enough' mother who will bear the destruction and deal with it creatively in order for this to happen. She writes:

> Let us imagine a mother who gives in to the child and never leaves. The child feels she or he has succeeded in controlling Mother, and this means 'Now Mommy is still my fantasy, Mommy is also afraid, and I can never leave Mommy without great anxiety either.' Thus, even as the child loses contact with the real independent mother, the omnipotent fantasy mother fills the space . . . . If alternately, the mother leaves and returns, followed by a happy reunion, the child feels that the danger – the projection of his own anger onto Mother – was not real.
>
> (Benjamin 1995: 91)

The mother must, in other words, have the capacity for what Kleinians would describe as depressive position functioning. However, in Benjamin's account, the mother who is able to do this must be drawing on her own childhood experience of intersubjective space in order that she now has the capacity to relate to her child as other rather than purely as object. The mother's abilities to set boundaries, to experience her child as separate, to know not to cave in, and to manage to do this consistently without burdening the child with her own distress or despair, is presumably *a mother who had a mother who managed the crisis brought on by separation*. Now a mother in her own right, she is the one who can maintain herself in the face of the child's demands because she can experience her child as another locus of subjectivity rather than purely an internal object. This, in its turn, allows her child an experience of her as a subject, and therefore an experience of intersubjective space.

One of the questions this circularity begs is how we account for those who have not had such 'good-enough parenting' but who go on to parent as adults effectively and with imagination and skill. The notion that good-enough parenting begets good-enough parenting presents a highly deterministic view of human development. Moreover, it has implications for a mother who is struggling to, and at times managing to overcome inadequate parenting, perhaps through the very task of parenting a child herself (Raphael-Leff 2003). In addition, how do we account for those who have had good-enough parenting but when faced with their child's omnipotence, still cave in? And who is to really say that caving in is wrong? As Frosh (1997) writes movingly of fathering in a clinical vignette:

> Sam's father has stayed at home with Sam since his mother died, not sending the boy to school. 'I want to be everything to him now,' he says, 'but people tell me he will cope with the separation; they say I should send him to school.' I think, I wish nobody had to go to school. Perhaps people's criticism of Sam's father reflects their discomfort with – and their envy of – his decision not to act in accordance with what Sam might 'cope' with, but with what he and Sam want.
>
> (Frosh 1997: 47)

It is interesting, perhaps, that Sam's father holds out against the criticism that he should be sending the boy to school. Frosh, as the therapist here, supports the father's resistance to external pressures, supports him 'caving in' to the demands of the child. One wonders if such support would have been maintained had it been the father who had died, and the mother who decided to keep the child home with her.

Finally, though Benjamin does talk about how the mother may experience the demanding omnipotent child as a disillusionment (Benjamin 1995: 89), causing her to relinquish the fantasy of both the perfect child, and herself as the perfect mother, her subjectivity is not seen to stem from the negotiation of the feeling states that this provokes. The mother is expected not to throw a tantrum, after all. In order to assign the mother her own subjectivity, Benjamin then looks to the mother's engagement with what is not her child: her work, lover, political activity and interests outside of the child's sphere. As de Marneffe (2004) has powerfully argued, Benjamin is not concerned with how caring for children might itself express autonomous desires rather than impede them (de Marneffe 2004: 75). Equally, at a theoretical level, the mother is required to shore up the development of intersubjective space, without much regard for how this positioning affects her capacities to sustain both subjectivity and alterity in relation to the child.

Judith Butler and the 'reality' of negation

One of the questions Judith Butler (2000) raises in relation to Benjamin's work is to do with the way recognition, in facilitating the transformation of object into other, itself becomes valorized, figuring as both a norm and an ideal form of communication. Against the ideal of recognition, destruction becomes an 'occasional and lamentable occurrence' (Butler 2000: 273) and one that can be reversed and overcome through therapeutic dialogue. According to Butler, although recognition and destruction coexist in tension in Benjamin's schema, it is only by overcoming destruction, by moving through it and realizing that the destroyed object is still there, that recognition, and thereby an experience of otherness, is made possible.

But what is destruction, Butler asks, if the whole point is that it does not destroy? Benjamin works with a notion of unconscious destruction *in fantasy* drawn from Winnicott, but at the same time bringing it alongside Hegel's account which is closer to a murderous impulse towards the other. Hegel (1807) imagines a fight to the death between two subjects struggling for a self-consciousness which requires recognition from the other. Butler argues that Benjamin wants to make a distinction between destruction and negation, where destruction must be continually survived as negation, so that eventually destruction is overcome. But what Butler goes on to argue is that in Hegel's famous 'master–slave' model in *The Phenomenology of Spirit* (Hegel 1807), the encounter with the Other is seen as encompassing self-loss as well as the possibility for recognition. Butler's reading is that in Hegel:

> whatever consciousness is, whatever the self is, it will find itself only through a reflection of itself in another. To be itself, it must pass through self-loss, but when it passes through, it will never be 'returned' to what it was.
>
> (Butler 2000: 286)

This leads to an inherent ambivalence in our relation to the Other. As well as self-knowledge through recognition, there is also self-loss to contend with. Self-loss is not the same as surviving the other's fantasy of destroying you. The encounter with the other fundamentally marks you, changes you. With self-loss, the self 'never returns to itself free from the Other' (Butler 2000: 286):

> Its ontology is precisely to be divided and spanned in irrecoverable ways . . . . It is transformed through its encounter with alterity, not in order to return to itself, but to become a self it never was.
>
> (Butler 2000: 286)

To become a self, in Butler's account, is to be outside oneself, or 'other' than oneself, and to have always already lost oneself through a relation to the Other that returns one to oneself as different – as other. What Butler identifies is that this is only really possible in Hegel when the two self-consciousnesses recognize each other at a point of extreme vulnerability – precisely a life-and-death struggle. When true destruction is imminent, when the self truly stands to lose itself, then recognition can emerge to keep destruction in check. As a result, the self is 'not its own' (Butler 2000: 287). The relationship with the Other is aligned as ethical – we are reciprocally 'given over' to each other.

What is most useful here is Butler's reinstalment of destruction as destruction, the fundamental risk the self takes in its encounter with the Other in order to become a self. From the mother's perspective, we could say that as the infant destroys her, she is marked by the other, contending with self-loss, through which, according to Butler, an altered self may also emerge. From the infant's perspective, omnipotence functions to protect the child from the fantasy of maternal aggression – the baby is fearful that the devouring or powerful mother will really harm it, and must protect itself. For the child to move beyond this, the child must experience the mother as having survived destruction, rather than be marked by destruction itself. The mother and analyst, on the other hand, are relied on to risk being psychically destroyed and to retain the capacity to think; that is, to bear and contain the awareness that they have not survived. The mother may destroy the infant in fantasy (the destruction may be notionally reciprocal in this sense), but her primary task is to survive the destructive attacks that the infant makes in a non-retaliatory manner. The continual and relentless attacks on the mother's psyche that the infant and toddler perform are described by Kraemer as putting the mother 'in a losing battle to retain her center of gravity and solid sense of subjective choice or desire' (Kraemer 1996: 771). In her view the mother struggles with feelings of 'enormous shame, confusion, self-reproach and anger' (Kraemer 1996: 771), as, with difficulty, she struggles to maintain herself in the face of such attacks. In other words, she may well not bear it. The mother truly risks something in the encounter with this other, but, following Butler's argument, she also stands to gain something through 'giving herself over' to the other. It is in this sense that I understand Butler's notion of the self that 'never returns to itself free of the Other' (Butler 2000: 286). It is 'transformed through its encounter with alterity, not in order to return to itself, but to become a self it never was' (Butler 2000: 286). This, then, goes some way towards an account of maternal subjectivity in which subjectivity is understood as the remainder, or what is returned to the self through the encounter with the Other, a self necessarily different than before.

Levinas

At some point in his fifth year, Joel, the named one, starts to call me by my first name. Initially I thought he had learnt a clever way to get my attention. Realizing that I no longer responded to 'Mum', I would at least lift my head if

I heard 'Lisa'. But later, I thought that perhaps he was retaliating, or just playing with that same making-strange experience that I had had with him. As far as he was concerned, my name was 'Mum'. That was the name that stuck to me. By renaming me 'Lisa' he renews my strangeness, opening a gap between myself and who he elects me to be. Again, for a few weeks I experience an uncanny sensation, only this time myself made-strange, until, eventually, his election of me as 'Lisa' re-sticks itself to me and the gap closes.

The notion of maternal subjectivity as the remainder that is returned to the self through the encounter with the Other leads us directly into a discussion of Levinas' work. Since the late 1970s, Levinas has been taken up widely in diverse disciplines, drawn, it seems, towards his careful and highly original account of ethics. C. Fred Alford rather damningly talks of how Levinas has become everything to everyone. 'We pretend we get it, writing in much the same style, so as to say whatever we wanted to say in the first place' (Alford 2002: 1). Given the difficulty and complexity of his work for those of us outside of academic philosophy, it is perhaps worth asking what it is about his work that might be so compelling. At the centre of his thinking is the notion that we are for the Other before we are even a self who can be for ourselves. Ethics is 'first philosophy', both prior to and beyond ontology. Before we are selves who can respond to the other, there is the Other, the radically other Other who cannot be co-opted into the realm Levinas terms the 'Same'. To be for the other first and foremost seems a grand thing indeed, and perhaps Levinas appeals to a need in all of us to show ourselves in our best altruistic light. But how on earth are we to achieve this? We read on, in the hope of finding out, but reading Levinas is like trying to read water. In Tina Chanter's words:

> There is a drive to continue reading despite the diminishing returns
> it seems to yield: the more one reads, the less one understands . . . .
> The effect is to induce more reading.
>
> (Chanter 2001: 1)

She goes on to link this with the very structure of Levinas' ethics:

> The more I do, the more responsible I become. This infinite call,
> which deepens as I try to fulfil it, draws me in, captivating me.
> There is no escape. I am responsible despite myself and prior to
> any debt I incur.
>
> (Chanter 2001: 1)

Through the dynamics, then, of diminishing returns, Levinas draws us into his account of infinite responsibility for the Other. Bordering on the mystical, prophetic even, he returns us to the meaning of Dostoyevsky's words: 'we are all responsible for all for all men before all, and I more than all the others' (Levinas 1974: 146).

In understanding ethical relations with the Other as both prior to and beyond ontology, what Levinas alludes to is a sphere that is not that of being, nor of nonbeing, but what he describes as 'otherwise than Being' (Levinas 1974). Before and beyond meaning, consciousness or any notion we could term 'I', there is simply the response to the call and the demand of the Other:

> I speak of responsibility as the essential, primary and fundamental structure of subjectivity. For I describe subjectivity in ethical terms. Ethics, here, does not supplement a preceding existential base; the very node of the subjective is knotted in ethics understood as responsibility. . . . Responsibility in fact is not a simple attribute of subjectivity, as if the latter already existed in itself, before the ethical relationship. Subjectivity is not for itself; it is, once again, initially for another.
>
> (Levinas 1985: 95–97)

It appears that Levinas is attempting to exit from the inevitability of colonizing the Other through knowing. As soon as we know the Other, the Other is returned the Same and remains within what Levinas terms 'totality'. In contrast, if the Other is 'infinity' to the extent that it exceeds or overflows the idea or representation we have of the Other (it goes beyond what we know of it), then the distance between the Same and the Other, between totality and infinity is itself infinite. Radical alterity can be maintained, preventing the collapse of otherness back into the realm of the Same.

Levinas' argument is in a different register from that of sameness and difference, recognition and reciprocity. Recognition, as discussed above, is not identical with responsibility. Self-recognition that relies on recognition by another subject will perhaps always run into difficulties with how to prevent an infolding of alterity due to the colonizing impulse that is inherent, not only in 'knowing' another but in recognizing too. In contrast, describing the relationship with the Other as an ethical relationship prior to self, a relationship that establishes the subject as a responsible subject prior to 'being' a subject at all, Levinas redefines both the notion of the subject and the Other, as well as the nature of their relationship and that of recognition itself:

> [if] responsibility is a form of recognition, it is not recognition as cognitive act, that is an identifying, re-presenting, re-cognising act.

It is effected in expressive acts by which one expresses oneself,
expresses one's own being, exposes oneself, to the other.

(Lingis 1978: xix)

Responsibility redefines recognition as an exposure of the self to the Other
for whom one is responsible.

Levinas' first mature work, *Totality and Infinity* (Levinas 1961) is perhaps
less insistent and extreme than his later *Otherwise than Being, or, Beyond
Essence* (Levinas 1974). In *Totality and Infinity* Levinas is concerned with
initially establishing a sphere which he names 'interiority', characterized by
sensibility, enjoyment, dwelling and being at home with oneself. These are
elements of egoism, but do not, as such, constitute subjectivity. Levinas
then goes on to describe the sphere of 'exteriority', that of infinity. Infinity
(as described above) is that which overflows its own idea, escaping compre-
hension and containment, and thus breaking with the mode of totality
which is the mode of content, theme, unity, knowledge, reason. The relationship with this radical alterity of infinity arises in the face-to-face
position in which language takes place. The 'face' here is another word for
infinity in that it refuses to be contained. It is the place of the 'exposure' to
the other that Lingis refers to above. It cannot be comprehended, which
means it also cannot be encompassed:

It is neither seen nor touched – for in visual or tactile sensation the
identity of the I envelops the alterity of the object, which becomes
precisely a content.

(Levinas 1961: 194)

The thrust of *Totality and Infinity* is to describe the relationship between
interiority and exteriority in such a way as it does not fall back into the
terms of totality. Interiority and exteriority are not complementary, dialectic or unified. Exteriority by definition exceeds totality, cannot be contained within it. The relationship with alterity is therefore asymmetrical,
paradoxically both 'height' and 'destitution' (Levinas 1961: 215). Levinas
uses the figure of the 'master' or 'teacher' (1961: 72) to indicate this
asymmetry, which again could be read as a move away from reciprocity or
mutuality as we would normally understand it. In this sense, Levinas does
not figure the Other as another person in a straightforward sense at all.
The Other cannot be thought of as another locus of meaning, subjectivity
or me-ness. This would again locate the Other within totality, and imply
that there is an objective position from which the two relating others could
be viewed. Although Levinas insists that the Other is neither 'religion'
nor 'mystification', he often refers to the Other as God, or like God
(Levinas 1961: 79). One could argue it is ultimately a transcendent Other,

whose proximity to the Same demands a response through which subjective responsibility figures.

Otherwise than Being, or, Beyond Essence (Levinas 1974) pushes the relationship with alterity further, and perhaps to more extreme ends, concentrating on ethical subjectivity and language, as opposed to the more schematic exploration of ethical alterity in *Totality and Infinity*. Here Levinas drops his notion of interiority, and the focus of his argument is on the moral sensibility of the subject awakened by the Other. This is a traumatized, decentred self, a self-held hostage by the Other. As Cohen (1998) puts it:

> The moral subject arises in subjection, 'despite itself,' introjected deeper than its own synthetic activities, suffering an 'immemorial past' never contracted to the present, the trace of a diachrony, to the point of obsession, substitution for the other, turning the self inside out, hostage to and for the other, for the other's needs, for the other's life, to be sure, but also for the other's responsibility, even for the other's evil, in an an-archic moral inspiration expiating even for the other's persecution. I am my brother's keeper, all the way.
>
> (Cohen 1998: xii)

The psychoanalytic understanding of recognition that I explored above through Benjamin's work relied on the presence of a non-retaliatory maternal figure who bears destruction so that the infant can develop the capacity for intersubjective space. This is a long way from the notion of the mother who recognizes her infant through her exposure to her infant's otherness. The latter is closer to Butler's critique, that gave us the notion of the self marked by the other, the self returning from an encounter with the other, changed, thereby opening the possibility of a maternal subjectivity arising out of an encounter with alterity, rather than through the processes of surviving destruction. Here, in Levinas, we find responsibility redefining recognition. The issue becomes one of ethics – *how do we take responsibility for the other through exposure to the other prior to the possibility of recognition by that other?* This shift into an ethical domain has particular implications for the mother, given her skewed relations with her child; that is, the ways that the maternal subject tends to collapse in the face of the needs of the fragile and developing child. Here I am suggesting we rethink the maternal position from the perspective of the mother's exposure to the other who is her child, an exposure that entails beginning with responsibility for that other, but one that gives rise to maternal subjectivity in the process. In order to pursue this further, we need to look at what Levinas does with femininity, maternity and paternity – three key tropes in his work.

Femininity, maternity and paternity in Levinas

Peppered throughout Levinas' work we find references to maternity, paternity and the feminine to figure various privileged aspects of alterity. In *Time and the Other* Levinas writes:

> I think the absolutely contrary contrary [*le contraire absolutement contraire*], whose contrariety is in no way affected by the relationship that can be established between it and its correlative, the contrariety that permits its terms to remain absolutely other, is the *feminine*.
>
> (Levinas 1947a: 85, original emphases)

The feminine here is elevated to an almost ultimate form of alterity, a name for the transcendent Other that cannot be confined within the realms of the Same. In that alterity is alterity by dint of remaining unknowable, Levinas' characterization of the feminine in *Totality and Infinity* as 'modesty', 'hiding' and 'slipping away from the light' (Levinas 1961: 256–266) lends her an extra-special otherness, while constraining her within the most traditional figurations. In addition, Levinas writes:

> And the other whose presence is discreetly an absence, with which is accomplished the primary hospitable welcome which describes the field of intimacy, is the Woman. The woman is the condition for recollection, the interiority of the Home, and inhabitation.
>
> (Levinas 1961: 155)

In linking the feminine with dwelling, with inhabitation (Levinas 1961: 156), the one who is 'silent and 'welcoming', or in the realm of eros as the 'weight of non-signifyingness', coquettish and 'a bit silly' (Levinas 1961: 155, 257, 263), the feminine therefore hovers between an ultimate signifier of alterity and being 'otherwise' to any possibilities for transcendence herself.

The feminist response to Levinas begins with a much-quoted footnote in Simone de Beauvoir's *The Second Sex* in which she criticizes Levinas as he 'deliberately takes a man's point of view, disregarding the reciprocity of subject and object' (de Beauvoir 1949: xxii, quoted in Chanter 2001: 2). Since then, the feminist critique seems to have centred on two sides of a debate: those who read Levinas as de Beauvoir suggests, as writing blindly within a patriarchal system that assigns women to their traditional position as other, denying the potential for reciprocity between the sexes and subjectivity for women, or those, including Derrida, who read Levinas as a 'sort of feminist manifesto' since it defines the 'welcome *par excellence* . . ., the pre-ethical origin of ethics, on the basis of femininity' (Derrida 1999: 44, quoted in Chanter 2001). Bracha Ettinger (2006) helpfully works a pathway between the two. In her view, the feminine becomes self-sacrificial only if the woman-as-feminine stands for absolute Otherness and 'infinite disappearance from light'. Instead she proposes a model for femininity as 'almost-Other and partial-subject in-between appearance and disappearance by way of jouissance and trauma in real and phantasmatic psychic and mental transconnectedness of I and non-I' (Ettinger 2006: 101). Ettinger's notion of the 'matrixial' (Lichtenberg-Ettinger 1995) works with a Levinasian ethics, but proposes a way of imagining feminine specificity through no longer needing to think only in terms of I or non-I, but in terms of 'feminine almost-Otherness and side-by-side-ness: a besideness that permits to think coemergence of I and non-I' (Ettinger 2006: 101–102).

In *Otherwise than Being, or, Beyond Essence*, we find the most extreme formulation of subjectivity, in which the subject gives herself over entirely to the other in an act of *substitution*. Levinas uses maternity to figure this ultimate substitution, with the pregnant body being drawn on to describe responsibility as the point at which one gives one's own substance or flesh over for the other:

> Maternity in the complete being 'for the other' which characterizes it, which is the very signifyingness of signification, is the ultimate sense of this vulnerability.
>
> (Levinas 1974: 108)

Levinas' language becomes seeped in bodily sensation at this moment in the text (Brody 2001), and it is through this invocation that Levinas wants to describe responsibility as 'contact' or exposure to the Other, an order of experience in which the Other is now thought of as 'the-other-in-the-same' (Levinas 1974: 55), or the other within. It is the maternal body that is used to invoke this 'within-ness'. Sikka (2001) notes that Levinas invokes the maternal body as:

> a condition in which one is responsible for the Other with the very substance of her being, prior to any acquaintance with him or her, prior to any knowledge of his or her characteristics, and prior to any choice, but a subjection that is election rather than enslavement.
>
> (Sikka 2001: 106)

Even more than the feminine, the maternal body appears to be both elevated to the site of an ultimate ethical gesture while simultaneously disappearing as it is given over completely to the Other. Maternity is this principle of absolute substitution that underpins Levinas' notion of the feminine. What is at stake in both the maternal and the feminine is the capacity to believe that there is the possibility of reality and meaning without me (Levinas and Lichtenberg-Ettinger 2006).

> Woman is the category of future, the ecstasy of future. It is that human possibility which consists in saying that the life of another human being is more important than my own, that the death of the other is more important to me than my own death, that the Other comes before me, that the Other counts before I do, that the value of the Other is imposed before mine is.
>
> (Levinas and Lichtenberg-Ettinger 2006)

While all human beings have the capacity to affirm that without me, the world has meaning, and the name that Levinas gives this capacity is the feminine, it is the maternal body that is used to figure this absolute substitution of Other for self.

Along with femininity and maternity, Levinas also brings a notion of paternity into play. Paternity has a very different function from the maternal-feminine. The terms paternity and fecundity are used interchangeably and the adult-child relationship is exclusively discussed in terms of fathers and sons. These discussions take place in a section of *Totality and Infinity*, entitled 'Beyond the Face' (Levinas 1961: 254), which is concerned with love, eros, paternity and filiality, all of which are somehow conceived of as outside the realms of the face-to-face, and in this sense beyond infinity. However, it is through paternity that the 'father' is returned to ethical subjectivity through an encounter with infinity that in addition engenders time.

First, paternity is closely tied to eros. It is through eros that one goes:

> towards a future which *is not yet*, and which I will not merely grasp, but *I will be* . . . this unparalleled relation between two substances, where a beyond substances is exhibited, is resolved in paternity.
>
> (Levinas 1961: 271, original emphases)

However, Levinas does not tie paternity to the biological fact of having a child:

> Biological filiality is only the first shape filiality takes; but one can very well conceive filiality as a relationship between human beings without the tie of biological kinship. One can have a paternal attitude with regard to the Other. To consider the Other as a son is precisely to establish with him those relations I call 'beyond the possible'.
>
> (Levinas 1985: 70–71)

What does Levinas mean when he talks of paternity as a set of relations 'beyond the possible'? In paternity we relate to what is both same and other, ours and not ours. Unlike maternity, the relation is not one of substitution. Paternity establishes a particular ontological category in that the I is both singular and multiple simultaneously. The I transcends itself in paternity, but is also returned to itself, as the son both is and is not the father.

> Neither the categories of power nor those of knowledge describe my relation with the child. The fecundity of the I is neither a cause nor a domination. I do not have my child; I am my child. Paternity is a relation with a stranger who while being Other ('And you shall say to yourself, "who can have borne me these? I was bereaved and barren . . ."' *Isaiah, 49*) *is* me, a relation of the I with a self which yet is not me.
>
> (Levinas 1961: 277, original emphases)

So, multiplicity here is not to do with multiplying oneself in the sense of having many children. It is to do with facing what is beyond one's own possibilities, but recognizing this beyondness (described as the son's possibilities) as also part of one's own possibilities. This can be done with anyone whom one elects as a 'son'. In this sense the paternal relationship is the relation with what is beyond the possible taken into the self.

> The fact of seeing the possibilities of the other as your own possibilities, of being able to escape the closure of your identity and what is bestowed on you, toward something which is not bestowed on you and which nevertheless is yours – this is paternity. This future beyond my own being, this dimension constitutive of time, takes on a concrete content in paternity.
>
> (Levinas 1985: 70)

Second, out of the situation that can be described as paternal, a special kind of identity of the I arises, one that is also 'constitutive of time'. Only in paternity can the self go beyond itself in 'trans-substantiation' (Levinas 1961: 266) without losing itself – otherwise logically the I dissolves as it transcends itself. Paternity is unique in that the 'I breaks free of itself' (Levinas 1961: 278) without ceasing to be I. 'Fecundity evinces a unity that is not opposed to multiplicity, but, in the precise sense of the term, engenders it' (Levinas 1961: 273). As Kelly Oliver puts it, it is 'the only relation in which the self becomes other and survives' (Oliver 2001: 229). In Levinas' words: 'The I is, in the child, an other' (Levinas 1961: 267).

So, as well as engendering multiplicity, paternity engenders time, and in re-establishing a relation to infinity, paternity re-establishes ethics. Paternity is a promise (Oliver 2001: 226), but not one premised on a promise of authority or position within the symbolic as in Freud, but 'a promise of nonrecognition, of strangeness, of an open future, of what he calls infinity' (Oliver 2001: 226). Time is the infinite engendered through finite beings coming together, and it puts the ethical back into the relation between finite beings that otherwise folds back into the realm of the Same. In a way, the engendering of a child saves eros from becoming pure pleasure, and the trap of a kind of sterile virility. It is the possibilities of the child that allows desire to renew itself (the child now desires, so in this sense desire is engendered).

Importantly then, in Levinas it is not that the father recognizes himself in the son, but he *discovers* himself there for the first time. Paternity engenders the father as much as it does the son. In relation to his son, who is both himself and not himself, the father discovers his own subjectivity. As he discovers that his son is distinct, a stranger, he discovers that he too is distinct, even a stranger to himself. Paternity challenges what Levinas calls the 'virile' subject (Levinas 1961: 270) that always returns to itself, the subject of the 'I-can' of traditional phenomenology. Again, you return different.

Oliver asks how Levinas' 'father' may relate to a daughter who represents a more radical 'otherness' than a son. But perhaps another question we might ask is what happens if we think through Levinas' paternal figure from the perspective of the mother. After all, Levinas has already told us that a biological relation is not necessary for constituting filial relations. All human beings are open to electing anyone as a 'child'. A mother too, discovering her child as a stranger, may discover her own distinctness, her own subjectivity, herself as ethical, not in the sense of her ability to give herself up for the child, but in the sense that the relationship to her own infinity gives rise to an ethical subjectivity. This would be a very different ethical mother than the mother of Ruddick's 'Maternal Thinking' for instance (Ruddick 1989). In Ruddick, maternal practice, understood as a discipline in which the one who mothers develops intellectual capacities, judgements, attitudes and values, becomes a moral choice. The mother, in her view, attains an ethical subjectivity through her ability to deal with the uncertainty and conflict inherent in child-rearing with grace, humour and good will.

Of course there are real difficulties with simply co-opting Levinas' notion of the paternal in order to think through maternity, of performing a simple gender flip-flop. Ettinger (2006) makes a more complex suggestion. Rather than having to choose between femininity as Otherness on the one hand, and masculinity as eros and subjectivity on the other (with all the connotations of activity and libido, virility and paternity), we could understand femininity as both transcendent alterity and the alterity of 'transitivity and jointness', in keeping with her model of the matrixial. The matrix is the symbol Ettinger uses to propose another mode of human subjectivity linked

44

to archaic traces of inter-uterine life in which the maternal and the unknown other within the mother coexist. The matrix, she writes, is 'a sex-difference that "remembers" the female body but is based on "webbing" links and not on essence, identity or negation' (Lichtenberg-Ettinger 1997: 367). Where these two 'femininities' meet is through an understanding of transcendent alterity as 'a quality – and not a logic distinction – of difference' (Ettinger 2006: 112). Femininity is neither constituted in relation to masculinity nor derived from it, but is that which 'qualifies' difference itself. If this is the case, then perhaps the task is not so much to swap the paternal for the maternal, but to keep trying to understand relations from the perspective of the matrixial. As Ettinger says, 'I interpret even the relation of filiation as feminine-matrixial: the father/son relation of filiation is "a woman"' (Levinas and Lichtenberg-Ettinger 2006: 139). Although the matrixial is not identical with the maternal, it allows a broadening of perspectives on Levinas' filial relation that can then include the maternal subject in a capacity otherwise than substitution. And given, as Lisa Walsh (2001) puts it, that Levinas, in proposing paternity as the ethical transcendence of sexual materiality, thereby 'somehow manages to wipe away every last trace of the engendering force of the feminine-maternal' (Walsh 2001: 83), there might even be something ethical in reworking Levinas' paternal from the perspective of the feminine-maternal. In the same way as he reminds us that paternity is not about the biological condition of having children, he also reminds us, despite naming it in the feminine, that the capacity to affirm that without me the world still has meaning, is open to all human beings. I believe that paternity and fecundity are used much more clearly as tropes than the way maternity functions in Levinas' work, perhaps due to the difficulty of reading gestation unhooked from the female body. In this sense I think it is possible, even desirable, to construct a reading of the paternal in Levinas as a figure for motherhood, and hence to reclaim this notion to think about aspects of maternal subjectivity.

Naming

Let us then briefly look again at fecundity from the perspective of the maternal. What we have established is that the maternal could be thought of as a new subjective category, the condition of being both singular and multiple simultaneously, while still being figured in the feminine. However, I want to argue that unlike Ettinger's matrixial, which uses the image of female bodily space in pregnant subjectivity to describe a mode of human subjectivity that could be thought of as feminine, I want to try to stay close to the specificity of the maternal, not understood as a pregnant subjectivity, but as a set of ethical relations with the post-birth child as radically Other (an otherness made temporarily tangible by that whiff of embarrassment as the mother confers a name on this stranger with no name, in the gap before the name 'sticks'), an encounter with what is fundamentally strange, as well as being the same, that establishes this relationship as ethical, and hence as one in which we can begin to talk of the emergence of subjectivity. In recognizing the child as a stranger, as distinct, the mother also recognizes what is distinct about herself. Motherhood can then be thought of as a particular form of female subjectivity, one in which we transcend our own possibilities while recognizing this beyondness as also our own. Something comes back from the experience which is the self taken as other, similar, perhaps, to Butler's notion that the subject's encounter with the other is always transformative. It is this excess, an excess which is nevertheless returned to the subject in our reworked notion of maternity that Levinas evinces, and that distinguishes his notion of ethics from that of reciprocity or recognition. I suggest that this ethical turn may go some way towards deepening our understanding of the developmental trajectory of motherhood.

Something of this movement in which what is traditionally thought of as a paternal function is widened to encompass the maternal seems to also show up in the anecdotes about naming. In Lacan's early reworking of Freud's Oedipal complex, naming is the paternal function par excellence. Lacan's 'Nom-du-Père' (Lacan 1956) is perhaps the prime example of the link between the paternal name and the conferring of identity. It is the father's name that positions the child in the symbolic, as well as signifying the Oedipal 'no'. The Nom-du-Père enacts a crucial separation between the child and its mother. Foreclosing the Nom-du-Père leads to psychosis. And yet, later in Lacan's work we see the Nom-du-Père subtly shifting to 'Les noms du père' in an almost mythical seminar that was never given (Verhaeghe 2000: 143). The number of names of the father turns out to be infinite, and the focus shifts to their function – that of keeping the real, the symbolic and the imaginary distinct and separate from one another. This 'paternal' function is performed through the act of naming (Verhaeghe 2000: 143), taken up by me, the mother, and accepted by my partner's nod. Did my discomfort around using Joel's name stem, in addition, from my unfamiliarity with this 'paternal' function, with the responsibility for processes of distinction and separation that are supposed to allow the child to separate from me, his mother?

But then, how often do any of us get a chance to name the unnamed? Naming the unnamed is in fact a thing of childhood. We name our dolls or stuffed animals, our transitional objects, our imaginary friends. We name places and things that do not exist, or whose existence we can manipulate and change. It is only perhaps our pets whom we name in such a way as the name sticks. Some animals come to recognize their names in the way a stuffed toy cannot, and then it feels unfair to keep changing it. To give something a proper name is precisely to confer a fixed point within the symbolic. Proper names are for keeps. And yet, as Deleuze (1977) puts it:

To say something in one's own name is very strange, for it is not at all when we consider ourselves as selves, persons or subjects that we speak in our own name. On the contrary, an individual acquires a true proper name as the result of the most severe operations of depersonalisation, when he opens himself to the multiplicities that pervade him and the intensities which run through his whole being.

(Deleuze 1977: 114)

It was not just me who named, but I was also renamed by my child. When the child (the one named Joel) calls his mother 'Lisa', she is called into a peculiar awareness of herself. Mum, after all, is a command to silence. 'To mum' is to mime, to act without words. The actors in such silent plays were called mummers. This is why to 'keep mum' means to keep silent, usually about a secret. Mum is then a sounded word that signifies a command to silence. When my child renamed me 'Lisa' he performed, for a second time, my original positioning in the symbolic by calling me out of my silence; he performed, that is, an act of separation. For a few weeks I notice that I am no longer mum (silent) but Lisa (worded). I sense other people's discomfort – why does your son call you by your name? Did you ask him to, did you teach him that? I am truly as bewildered as they are, but I am also made aware of myself made-strange, with my distinctness that is a particular kind of indeterminacy; with, might we say, my maternal subjectivity?

3

MATERNAL
TRANSFORMATIONS

Oi mother, keep ye' hair on!

Motherhood is the pitilessness of the present tense. Reflective space is obliterated. This relentless and infinite present destroys all that is subtle, indeterminate, unknowing in one's thinking. It's not that mothers stop being able to think. It's that we think in another order – the order of immediacy. Ha! Is this what is meant by maternal instinct? That we are forced into a kind of survival mode, a chronic crisis, the endless horror of Groundhog Day? In this immediacy, I am brought face-to-face with the patched-over, broken bits of myself, the cracks in relations with mother, lover, siblings, friends. Everything is challenged, like in analysis, painfully peeled back.

During the days and weeks after the birth of my first son, in the grip of a mute and helpless grief, I feel chained to this tiny creature, chained by an invisible thread, a shadow of the umbilicus, in oh so many subtle ways restricting the movement of my very being. Movement, as Irigaray would have it, is the being of woman. Is this why so many women feel such terrible loss after the birth of their first child?

It is the first day I leave the house alone after giving birth. My son is perhaps two or three days old. He is sleeping, his face set like a tiny Celtic high priest, sleep draining the colour from his cheeks, in a deep, lost place. And I am in search of a maternity bra, so unprepared am I for the trappings and para-phernalia of new motherhood. As luck would have it, there is a famous bra shop on the Whitechapel Road. Its name is Carol's. Carol says her family have run a lingerie shop there for generations. Plump and matronly, she swishes around, breathing womanly secrets, as she measures and hoists, clasps and tugs. She is aghast, horrified that I am out of bed, that I show no visible signs of having given birth three days ago other than my tender leaking breasts. She views me with a faint edge of irritation. I catch a glimpse of myself in Carol's mirror. I notice that despite my body's refusal to let on, something very odd has happened to my hair. My hair, usually so unruly, so rude, has straightened all by itself. It has assimilated. It lies in a neat bob, pretending to have always been so well behaved.

And I know now that everything has changed. I am unsteady, dizzy, like I'm relearning to walk after a long illness. I imagine a war has taken place while I've been away. I look for the signs. I can't understand that no one else has noticed. I want to rush up to the thin stream of Bangladeshi men, moving up and down Brick Lane, and confer with them, join them in their huddled groups to discuss in hushed voices the catastrophic shift that has taken place. I stand on the kerb waiting to cross the road, fearful should anything happen, conscious of needing to protect myself in a way that has never occurred to me before. Not trusting that I know what to do, I waver, looking left, then right, twenty, then thirty times, still unable to propel myself off the kerb. I have to stay alive. I am two. Maybe more. I don't know myself. Severed from myself, like the cut end of a worm, I am disorganized, stunned.

In *Misconceptions*, Naomi Wolf's disturbing account of giving birth in North America, she writes with some surprise at the profound changes that occur for women when they become mothers. Her focus by the end of the book sits squarely within a discourse that understands these changes in terms of the social, political and economic realities that structure motherhood. However, she seems elsewhere to be genuinely surprised by the extent and sheer arduousness of the psychological work that accompanies this shift from womanhood to motherhood; the quiet mourning, for example, that she detects in so many mothers' accounts of this oddly painful transition:

> When I spoke to new mothers, it seemed to me that although a child and new love has been born, something else within them had passed away, and the experience was made harder because, at some level, underneath their joy in their babies, these women were quietly in mourning for this part of their earlier selves.
>
> (Wolf 2001: 6)

Although her 'Mother's Manifesto' (Wolf 2001: 243) is full of the usual call for changes in working patterns and child-friendly facilities, things that *are* vital in returning to women the hard-won independence they achieved before having children, a kind of despair infusing the personal stories seems to undercut the possibility of such a return. There is a quiet acknowledgement that perhaps things will not be the same again. Though one gains a child, one loses, I think she suggests, the irreplaceable clarity of the borders of the self. From now on one's 'self' is crucially changed by the presence of this particular 'other' who is one's child. Wolf writes that it is a 'messier, more inter-dependent new maternal self that emerges' (Wolf 2001: 6). This discourse turns on the supposition of an earlier independent, solitary, unitary self that must yield to a more fluid self capable of bearing a much more porous relation to another. Motherhood, it appears, is a condition in which the self budges up to make room for another, and is radically changed in the process. The self undergoes a fundamental transformation of state; from something solid, unified, singular, to something messy, interdependent, and altogether more blurred.

This unity/fluidity dialectic that provides a starting point for tracking the psychological work entailed in transforming woman to mother, belongs to the highly contested notion of feminine identity that informs any discussion, whether feminist or psychoanalytic, of the maternal subject. Psychoanalysis has long troubled the notion of a clearly bounded self, working instead at the very border of self-knowledge that would ground such a concept. We are constantly undone from within, carrying with us, under the sign of the unconscious, our own self-dissolution. From a Lacanian perspective the unitary 'I' was always a fiction anyway, one we glimpsed in a jubilant moment of misrecognition, and which we absurdly mourn as if we once had. The psychoanalytic subject is understood to be under constant maintenance because of these inherent threats to its real or imagined stability, a shifting process of negotiation between material conditions and unconscious desire. And the feminist analysis of such a position has assiduously uncovered the gendered split in this dialectic, pointing out how the masculine usurps the position of unified subject, and relegates the feminine as the necessarily unthematizable excess which serves to give the masculine its consistency, form and visibility.

My concern, however, is this: if the old independent self/new messy maternal self are refigured as two poles of the same unity/fluidity dialectic, it is the maternal, instead of the feminine, that is now relegated beyond unity. Maternity, containing the messy and unthematizable excess signified by femininity, produces retroactively the old (feminine) self as a fictional unitary subject that must be mourned and then given up. Contemporary accounts of motherhood that articulate the confused and painful movement from one state to the other, do so by (perhaps necessarily) misrecognizing the feminine as a lost unitary fiction. Rachel Cusk (2001), for instance, in her popular account of the transition to motherhood writes:

> The vision of myself that I . . . glimpsed in the park – unified, capable, experiencing 'the solidarity of life' – is one that I will continue to pursue over the coming months. It proves elusive . . . . To be a mother I must leave the telephone unanswered, work undone, arrangements unmet. To be myself I must let the baby cry, . . . forestall her hunger or leave her for evenings out, . . . forget her in order to think about other things. To succeed in being one means to fail at being the other. The break between mother and self was less clean than I had imagined . . . . For later, even in my best moments, I never feel myself to have progressed beyond this division. I merely learn to legislate for two states, and to secure the border between them.
>
> (Cusk 2001: 57)

The 'unified capable' self is retroactively glimpsed, only to be lost again under the weight of the child's demands.[1] Ah, we seem to be saying, only now can I see, too late, what I was, now that I must give up this version of myself for a more interdependent version, one that is premised on being able to make room for another. Ironically, here the feminine takes up a position under the unified sign of the masculine, at the point that the mother gives way to the true demands of the other – her child. Imbued with both loss and shock, the maternal emerges in these popular accounts as the most confusing of subjective positions, full of fissures and splits, illusions and hopes, broken apart by violent emotions.

The cost of the psychological work involved in moving from womanhood to motherhood has certainly been recognized in the psychoanalytic literature too. With it is an acknowledgement of the debt psychoanalysis owes to the mother as a key model who has been plundered for metaphorical significance and then abandoned when it comes to applying psychoanalytical insights to helping mothers understand their complex reactions to mothering. As Nancy Chodorow writes in her 'Reflections on *The Reproduction of Mothering* – twenty years later':

> *The Reproduction of Mothering* is written from the daughter's point of view more than that of the mother, even as the kernel of the mother's viewpoint, in the psychological capacities, desires, and identities whose development it describes, can be elicited from within it.
>
> (Chodorow 2000: 348)

It is exactly this kind of looping of the mother back to her daughter position that enacts the disappearance of the maternal. It is only through having children herself that Chodorow thinks she has begun to understand 'the powerful, transformative claims that motherhood would make on our identities and senses of self' (Chodorow 2000: 348). As Jacqueline Rose (1996) asks in her exploration of the relationship between the mother and knowledge in Christopher Bollas' work, 'when does a mother get to speak, where are the case studies of women as mothers in the work?' (Rose 1996: 419). Susan Kraemer (1996) has argued persuasively that, as psychoanalytic constructions of the mother have shifted from Winnicott's rather idealized good-enough mother to a more subjectively complex one, she now risks being valorized both 'for her resilience and for her ability to play easily with her feelings of hate and aggression towards her baby' (Kraemer 1996: 765). The mother, in other words, is now seen to be able to move fluidly in and out of intense emotional states, with no apparent consequences to her mental health. Kraemer claims that re-idealizing the mother in such a way misapprehends what experiencing intense hate, aggression, envy and sadism towards children feels like, and does to mothers. Yet again, the complex

51

and at times treacherous process of 'claiming oneself' as a subject (Kraemer 1996: 775) is replaced with a fantasy mother who can simultaneously claim herself and navigate her baby's needs with grace and charm. Kraemer contends that 'inter-dependence' is not some easily attained fluidity. She refocuses us on the important question of what a mother feels about her own destructiveness in relation to her baby. The mother in her view has to *bear* her subjectivity, not by gracefully juggling with constant tensions, but by tolerating very difficult and largely unconscious feelings – those of hatred, ambivalence, failure, shame and remorse. This juggling exacts a price, and at times causes us to go under.

There appears, then, to be a need to understand maternal subjectivity as a fundamentally changed or transformed state, a state at or beyond the border that we once would have recognized as a self-boundary, and from which we may glimpse ourselves anew. On the one hand, transformation, with its magical overtones, tends to gloss over the profound struggle with overwhelming experiences that motherhood prompts. On the other, like all experiences that put the subject 'on-trial', it alludes to the way motherhood can create substantial shifts in both material and semiotic conditions, prompting a renewed configuration of self. Bracha Lichtenberg-Ettinger (1997), for instance, describes how both mother and the 'post-mature' prenatal infant (that is, the infant during the last part of prenatal life) are each other's 'part*objects*':

> To the idea that the mother transforms the infant by transforming the infant's surrounding (Aulagnier, 1975; Bollas, 1987) I would like to add that the 'transformed' prenatal infant *transforms* the mother-to-be's trauma, phantasy, and desire. Transmissibility of phantasy, joint trauma, and shareability of affects is bi-directional though not symmetrical. While the mother participates in the shaping of the infant's phantasy *via* her alpha-function, she herself changes.
>
> (Lichtenberg-Ettinger 1997: 381, original emphases)

Speaking of the relationship between the post-birth infant and the mother, Kraemer also reminds us that these changes that women undergo can exhilarate as well as daunt, that mothers can find satisfaction in anger and aggression as well as feel crushed by them, and that part of a complex notion of maternal subjectivity must also include a relation to creativity and hope.

Both early and later psychoanalytic work suggests that motherhood's transformative potential resides in its ability to cause a kind of *psychic crisis* in the lives of women. If crises can prompt breakdown, they can also allow a reconfiguration of our relation to new and necessary fictions of who we once were, are, and would like to be. Benedek (1970) takes up classical psychoanalytic concepts in the 1960s and applies them particularly to the psychology of parenthood. She notes that the psychoanalytic literature is slanted towards an understanding of the child's development. She focuses instead on:

> the proposition that the parents' drive-motivated, emotional investment in the child brings about reciprocal intrapsychic processes in the parents, which normally account for developmental changes in their personalities.
>
> (Benedek 1970: 124)

Motherhood, according to Benedek, changes you at an intrapsychic level. She talks of the way parents take children as 'total objects', not as 'part objects' in the way children respond to adults.

> The parents . . . live with the real child at the same time that they are fostering the intrapsychic child as a hope of their self-realization.
>
> (Benedek 1970: 125)

Parents are narcissistically invested in their children and through this investment, they come to *receive* something from the child. Negative behaviour in children, for example, forces the parent to see what he or she does not like within themselves causing a regression to infantile positions. With any luck, the idea is that this gives the parent a chance to rework infantile issues, and for the child to play a reciprocal role in fostering the intrapsychic development of the parent. Benedek asks:

> Is there, however, any psychoanalytic evidence which would support the thesis that the child, being the object of the parents' drive, has, psychologically speaking, a similar function in the psychic structure of the parent? Does the child, evoking and maintaining reciprocal intrapsychic processes in the parent, become instrumental in the further developmental integration of the parent?
>
> (Benedek 1970: 127)

She comes to an affirmative answer to these questions. Although the parent's development occurs through the repetition of childhood conflicts, this, she claims, does not lead necessarily to a pathological condition. It is more likely that this process leads to a resolution of such conflicts.

Joan Raphael-Leff's (2003) work takes up this theme again, and asserts that infants force into awareness split-off aspects of the parent's self, causing a re-experiencing of helplessness, neediness, frustration, abandonment and so on. She claims that:

the motivation to become a parent is often accompanied by an unconscious wish to release archaic raptures, to retrieve and rework undigested experiences and heal early scars.

(Raphael-Leff 2003: 57)

While she warns that where the full force of the baby's impact can be too much for a parent's fragile defences, the parent's unresolved issues can 'distort the child's being' (Raphael-Leff 2003: 57), she also stresses the creative potential that parenting can release. Given that the very wish to parent may be bound up with a desire to rework infantile issues, parenting can be viewed as an unconscious encounter with ourselves through an encounter with a child. While this is in keeping with Freud's assertion about the narcissism of parenting and the investment of unfulfilled longings in the child's development, it also opens a space for thinking about the creative potential of parenting as a spin-off from this process.

Raphael-Leff's work is related to a wealth of writing that acknowledges the way a girl's identification with her maternal object comes to the fore as she becomes a mother in her own right. For example Chernin's *The Woman Who Gave Birth to her Mother: Tales of change in women's lives* (1999) and Stern and Bruschweiler-Stern's *The Birth of a Mother: How the motherhood experience changes you forever* (1998) explore the notion that girls' internal maternal objects are drawn on in a new way when she becomes a mother. Balsam (2000: 483) states that in every analysis 'the patient discovers either overt or hidden beliefs that the parent's way of doing things is still the gold standard'. Major events such as pregnancy, childbirth and aspects of child care 'heavily bear the imprint of the mother' (Balsam 2000: 483). Through this re-connection with an internal maternal object, the new mother's relation to the maternal object is revisited and reworked. Stern (1998) states that what he terms the 'motherhood constellation' is a 'new' and 'unique' psychic state because it brings into operation 'the mother's discourse with her own mother, especially with her own mother-as-other-to-her-as-a-child; her discourse with herself, especially with herself-as-a-mother; and her discourse with her baby' (Stern 1998: 172). Kristeva also maintains that it is first and foremost the mother's mother who is encountered in the mother's relationship with the child (Kristeva 1975: 303).

It is only really when we go to Rozsika Parker's work on maternal ambivalence, that we see some prising open of the relentlessly backwards movement of psychoanalytic theorizing of the development of maternity. Parker (1997) states:

The traditional focus of analytic understanding has meant that maternal ambivalence, and the associated desire to make repara-tion to the baby, have been considered primarily as an action replay in the mother of her infantile experiences of ambivalence towards her own mother. How she became (or failed to become) an ambivalent baby delimits how she becomes (or fails to become) a mother who can manage the vicissitudes of her adult experience of maternal ambivalence. In my view, this overlooks the specificity of maternal ambivalence and the ways it may be different from infantile ambivalence. The particular fears, desires and passions of motherhood – for example, the intense adult wish to protect a powerless baby – inflect a woman's experience of ambivalence in particular ways.

(Parker 1997: 19)

I have quoted this in full, as it seems to be one of the few instances I have found in the psychoanalytic literature that opens up a space to think about the particularity of maternal experience uncoupled from the mother's infantile experience, while still working within an analytic framework.

Cusk's (2001) quote voices the commonly felt experience of having to choose between one's own and a child's needs. This new, interdependent, porous relation between self and other suggests a particular openness and responsiveness to the other in which this choice is no longer simple, opening us, once again, onto the ethical. The dilemma of choosing between one's own and the child's needs has been voiced within feminist psychoanalysis as a tension between the psychical and social mother, the maternal imago whom psychoanalysis repeatedly tells us plays such a vital role in the child's developing internal world, and the mother as a desiring subject in her own right. If the mother is maintained as *the* unconscious object, and the unconscious can only figure as the 'unthought known', then this appears to be the point that the mother is both found, and simultaneously knowledge qua knowledge 'unravels from its own self-possession' (Rose 1996: 413). An emphasis on reciprocity and recognition, particularly in Jessica Benjamin's work, has gone some way towards softening this polarity between the mother as almost hyper-real and simultaneously the vanishing point of self-knowledge. Benjamin (1995), for instance, argues persuasively for the need to recognize the mother's subjectivity as a locus of self-experiencing beyond that of the child. If the child does not have a mother whose subjectivity is recognizable, then the child cannot hope for recognition herself. In its crudest form, the mother can finally be thought of as having a life of her own, beyond her function as a mother to the developing child. The choice is no longer cast as either/or, but the holding in tension of both mother and child's needs, uses and desires.

However appealing at an egalitarian level, as I have noted previously, there is a danger that reciprocity glosses over the skewed nature of the relationship between mother and child, and gives way to the characteristic collapse of the maternal subject in the face of the needs of the fragile and developing child. It is still the child here who is seen to benefit from a mother who has a life outside of the child's sphere. In the process, I believe we lose sight of the way maternal subjectivity is structured through the very relation to the child. I would argue instead that one's subjectivity as a mother is precisely what emerges through this real and imagined relation. The positioning of maternal desire as that which goes beyond the child may be necessary to protect the child from what Kristeva terms 'the caring and clinging mother' (Kristeva 1987b: 34). It does not, however, necessarily help us understand maternal desire itself.

A return to the binary mother–infant relationship is clearly problematic and prompts a reconsideration of the role of the third, though this time from the mother's perspective. It is possible that the child's *otherness* can function as a third term for the mother, and therefore prevent the regressive pull of the mother–infant dyad while allowing us to understand her desire as the desire for the child. When Kristeva poses the question 'what does a mother want?' (1987b: 41), the answer she provides is that she wants her own mother, even in the figure of the child. All desire, in other words, is understood as desire for the lost mother, including our desire for our children. But surely the mother also has a relation to the child that at times escapes this repetition?

Psychoanalysis variously configures maternal desire as the desire for the missing penis, the longed for union with the imaginary mother, or the desire for the 'father' (or lover, work, politics – whatever takes the mother away from the child) which plays a vital function in breaking up the dyad with the child. If the focus shifts from the child's psychic health, however, to the mother's, it may be possible to consider how maternal desire, proceeding from the direct encounter with the child, fundamentally changes the way we mothers feel and think about our partners and lovers, work and politics, our own mothers and ourselves. In other words, although we constantly allude to the felt experience that we are 'transformed' through our relations with our children, we are perhaps fearful of dwelling on how or why, because in doing so, we may jettison the precious connection we have with the world beyond our babies. We fear we will fall into a regressive symbiotic relationship with our children, to their and our own detriment.

Maternal transformation: Irigaray and the maternal-feminine

Transformation: an induced or spontaneous change from one element into another. In common usage it describes what happens when something is changed utterly, like the miraculous metamorphosis of runny egg whites into those elusive 'stiff white peaks' of children's recipe books. Perhaps transformation's fascination lies in our difficulty in deciding when the egg whites really are standing up on their own, knowing that, if you beat for a moment too long, they disastrously dissolve back into their runny form. In Eric Carle's children's book, *The Very Hungry Caterpillar* (Carle 1969), transformation itself is not depicted. The caterpillar disappears into the brown cocoon, and magically emerges as something completely different. The children squeal in disbelief. In this sense, transformation mines our never-fully-relinquished belief in magic. We know the change has taken place but missed the point, the exact moment when one state slipped into the other. Inherent then in the notion of transformation is a blurred boundary and a questioning of limits or edges.

Transformation has least two other intriguing etymological meanings. First, it has roots in the theatre, describing 'a sudden and dramatic change of scene on stage' (*Oxford English Dictionary* 1989). Whether via the sudden dropping of a backdrop from the fly bar or a piece of scenery flown in from the wings or the visible molting of characters into the pantomime figures of Harlequin and Columbine, the scene supposedly transforms before our very eyes. With a dull thud of hessian, we move from inside the witch's hovel to the lakeside at twilight. We will ourselves to believe what we see, despite the noisy clunk as the backdrop hits the floor.

Second, and wonderfully, transformation is an archaic term for 'a woman's wig' (*Oxford English Dictionary* 1989). Conjuring dilemmas of mind and matter, this odd definition contains a constellation of interrelated meanings about performance and mimicry, and by association, female sexuality and madness. It also holds a double allegiance to materiality: when the caterpillar becomes a butterfly, or the runny whites turn stiff, is that a change of state or stuff? While transformation wants to pass itself off as the magical movement between one state and another, it finds itself caught by the coarseness of its own material effects. Just as the backdrop's clunk can never be completely edited out, so the wig's synthetic nylon never fully convinces. Even a 'real' human hair wig does not pass itself off as anything other than a wig. In fact, the closer the wig gets to looking 'real', the more we seek to examine it, to touch it, to ascertain its credentials, and inevitably the more drawn we are towards its ultimate artificiality.

Perhaps we can conclude that transformation contains its own impossibility. A paradox, transformation simultaneously signals a movement towards change and exposes its own mimetic strategy, showing itself up as a fake.

Irigaray (1985a) claims that indeterminate being, being as a state of transformation itself, is the very scene of 'woman'. For Irigaray (1985a), woman is neither closed nor open. In a much quoted passage in *Speculum of the Other Woman* she writes:

> She is indefinite, in-finite, *form is never complete in her.* . . . This incompleteness in her . . . morphology, allows her continually to become something else, though this is not to say that she is ever univocally nothing. . . . But she is becoming that expansion that she neither is nor will be at any moment as definable universe.
>
> (Irigaray 1985a: 229, original emphases)

Unlike the more popular notions of selves and identities, fixed entities in and out of which we move, losing one, gaining another, Irigaray posits the notion of woman as never complete, exploding the conceptualization of woman as possessing one or in fact multiple selves: 'One woman + one woman + one woman never will have added up to some generic: woman' (Irigaray 1985a: 230). Woman is not multiple, but fluid, an endless 'expansion' that escapes its own definition.

In Irigaray's terms, woman (in a notion that appears close to Levinas' concept of infinity) is that which overflows its own idea; it is what goes beyond its own conceptual frame for understanding itself. In other words, Irigaray takes the notion of the feminine as unthematizable excess and jubilantly pushes it to its limit. In direct response to Lacan's situating of the feminine as the other of the Other, Irigaray's 'other woman' of the title of *Speculum of the Other Woman* is a woman 'without common measure' (Whitford 1991: 28). Margaret Whitford writes: 'an "other woman" whose volume is "incontournable", whose lips touch without distinction of one and two' (Whitford 1991: 28). This is the image of contiguity, of two lips touching, which runs through much of Irigaray's work.

> This (self-)touching giving woman a form which is in(de)finitely transformed without closing up on her appropriation. Metamorphoses where no whole ever consists, where the systematicity of the One never insists. Transformations, always unpredictable because they do not work towards the accomplishment of a telos. Which would imply one figure taking over – from – the previous figure and prescribing the next: *one* form arrested, therefore, and becoming *another*. Which happens only in the imaginary of the (male) subject who projects on to all others the reason of the capture of his desire: his language, which claims to name him adequately.
>
> (Irigaray 1985a: 233, original emphases)

Cutting across notions of one self giving way to another self, the self that is woman *is* unpredictable transformation. And yet, when Irigaray extends this metaphor to motherhood she writes:

> And for her, the danger of motherhood is that of it/her being arrested in the world of *one* child. If she closes up around the unit(y) of that conception, enfolds herself around that one, her desire will harden. *Will become phallic because of this relation to the one?*
>
> (Irigaray 1985a: 229, original emphases)

Her expression of the tension between woman and mother is precisely in the danger that this overflowing will harden around the singularity of the child.

The maternal represents a threat to the very being of femininity, in terms of the hardening of desire and the freezing of fluidity.

Likewise, Judith Butler (1994) shows us that Irigaray's version of the feminine-as-other exceeds those binary pairings within which it is usually located – male self/female other, matter/form, body/rationality. Both displaced by and produced by them, the feminine as excessive otherness – a name, that is, for radical alterity – is itself necessary for these dichotomies' ontological status and internal coherence. The feminine does not, however, possess an autonomous ontological existence of its own. Produced at the point it is also excluded, the feminine becomes the necessary outside which is always already inside, showing up 'within the system as incoherence, disruption, a threat to its own systematicity' (Butler 1994: 152).

In her critique of Irigaray, Butler seeks to problematize the way 'matter' is figured as irreducible, prior to discourse, and used to ground claims about sexual difference. Matter itself is, she argues, already imbued with discourses on sexuality, reproduction and signification that prefigure and constrain its nomination. In addition, matter as category is founded on a set of violations or exclusions that shadow its use. She argues that although feminist scholars have worked to reveal the link between women and materiality, especially the body as matter, Irigaray's strategy is more subtle, showing how matter within philosophical discourse is both a substitution for and also a displacement of the feminine. The displaced feminine is positioned beyond or excessive to matter. It is the feminine that therefore cannot be figured within the terms of philosophy proper, because it is the necessary exclusion of the feminine from philosophy that enables philosophy to speak itself.

Irigaray's critique of the origin of matter in philosophy and its consequences for the feminine occurs in *Speculum of the Other Woman*, in her discussion of the receptacle, or *chora*, in Plato's *Timaeus* (Irigaray 1985a: 168–179). What I want to do here is tease out the troubled relation between femininity, maternity, matter and transformation in order to show how Irigaray reinstitutes femininity at the expense of maternity.

Briefly, Plato's *chora* or 'receptacle' is the site of transformation, where matter, through its resemblance to a Form, comes to be recognizable as a material object. Referring to this place as the 'receiving principle', Plato uses the analogy 'nurse' or 'mother'. Because it is the place in which shapes take on their Form, this receptacle cannot itself have shape. Because its function is only to receive and effect transformation, it cannot transform itself. The *chora,* figured as the mother/nurse, is entered, but cannot enter: she conceives form but lacks form herself. In this sense the receptacle escapes definition and can only be known by the analogy mother/nurse.

Interpreting Irigaray, Butler usefully distinguishes between the 'specular figures' of mother/nurse and the 'excessive feminine', which is what is displaced by such figures. The mother/nurse represents the feminine within the binary pair form/matter, both of which are subsumed under the masculine and work to displace the feminine at the moment they purport to represent it. In this sense, Butler (1994) argues:

> This receptacle/nurse is not a metaphor based on likeness to a human form, but a disfiguration that emerges at the boundaries of the human both as its very condition and as the insistent threat of its deformation; it cannot take a form, a morphe, and in that sense, cannot be a body.
>
> (Butler 1994: 154)

In this reading of Irigaray, the maternal becomes the lesser feminine. Just as the receptacle exceeds its metaphorical figures (mother/nurse), so femininity exceeds the receptacle as the 'impossible yet necessary foundation of what can be thematized and figured' (Butler 1994: 154). If the maternal is a specular figure for the feminine, one that, when (mis)taken for the feminine, exacts its erasure, then the maternal always threatens the feminine, and in particular, the feminine's fluidity. The maternal becomes one of Irigaray's names for the fixing of femininity. Butler writes: 'taken as a figure, the nurse-receptacle *freezes* the feminine as that which is necessary for the reproduction of the human but is itself not human (Butler 1994: 155, emphasis added).

If the feminine is thus understood as that which exceeds the maternal and at the same time makes the maternal possible, the maternal subject is left in a difficult position. Irigaray's claim stands as an interesting theoretical counterpart to the more personal articulations of the difficult move from femininity to maternity, as recounted by Wolf (2001). The maternal, made possible by this 'other' site of the feminine, is left by Irigaray as a 'disfiguration', the poor imitation of the excessive feminine, the other to the male same. The maternal is like a poor relation, suspect, and threatening to constrain the feminine. Under the very sign of transformation, the maternal restricts movement, oddly coming to be appropriated, this time, by the masculine. This demotion then reverses the assumptions made, as we have seen, about maternal transformation as a process of moving from independence to interdependence, unity to fluidity.

Irigaray might be read to mimic the exclusion of the feminine in order to point towards the exclusion already evident in Plato, and hence within phallogocentric discourse as a whole. However, I think Irigaray reinstalls the feminine at the expense of yet another shadow – that of the maternal. Elsewhere, seeking to reverse the unacknowledged matricide on which Western culture is based, she deliberately collapses the distinction between woman and mother. For example, her positing of woman as never complete can be read as a mimetic response to the mother's body, which she describes as having been 'torn to pieces' between fathers and sons, leaving her fragmented and unable to speak her difference (Irigaray 1991: 38). 'Every utterance, every statement', writes Irigaray, is 'developed and affirmed by covering over the fact that being's unseverable relation to the mother-matter has been buried' (Irigaray 1985a: 162). Her mimetic strategy is then a jubilant articulation of fluidity in order to both reveal and reverse this fragmentation. The 'maternal-feminine' (Irigaray 1993a) becomes its own kind of fluid entity, irresolvable into one or the other, at all times both.

But this account erases the specificity of the maternal as a subject position. This is evident again when we look at Irigaray's important treatment of the under-representation of the umbilical cord, the placenta and the moment of severance between mother and child. Because the cut from the umbilicus marks her entry into motherhood, obscuring it leaves a specific void for the mother herself. The cut may, of course, restimulate infantile fantasies of guilt and abandonment, as well as prompt intense identification with the mutilated body of her own mother. But it also represents a specific loss for the mother: of an intimate connection with the fantasy-other within her. The child, Irigaray reminds us, is left with a kind of scar, an irreducible mark of birth in the form of the navel (Irigaray 1991: 38). But the mother is left with no mark of the cut at all, nothing to represent her entry into this new intimacy. Perhaps her stretch marks and scars hint at this loss, but these marks of absence seem only to reinforce the cut's lack of representation. Irigaray reminds us not to collude in matricide. But remembering our mothers comes too late if the mother's 'birth' has already been forgotten. Perhaps this erasure is part of the vague unspeakable loss she experiences immediately after birth, and that haunts the early weeks and months of motherhood?

Moments after the birth I feel a huge sense of elation. I want to run around the corridors telling people what I've done. I want someone to congratulate me, to be as astounded as I am at what I have achieved. I need to eat and then sleep. My labouring work is done. So preoccupied am I with the event of the birth itself that I struggle to remember that something was produced with all that labouring. I am shocked when the nurse wakes me up to inform me that the crying baby lying in the plastic tub by my bed is my baby, that this is disturbing the whole ward, and would I mind, by any chance, feeding it. I think why is she waking me? What I need most in the world now is to sleep. This is not my responsibility. Isn't someone supposed to take the baby away? As far as I am concerned, the baby has passed through me. I housed him, accommodated him, made space for him as an act of hospitality, a profound gesture of generosity. And then I birthed him. The cord was cut. My work was done. What more did he want of me?

Let us imagine the mother's 'birth' from a kind of originary state of transformation by tracing the umbilical cord back to the placenta, described by
Irigaray (1993b) as 'the first veil'. Schwab (1994) explicates the connection
of this metaphor with the early work of the feminist biologist, Hélène
Rouch. Upturning our simplistic notions of the placenta as the organ that
nourishes only the foetus, Rouch (1987) describes how the placenta benefits
mother too, regulating her immune system so that the embryo is not
rejected, while providing high enough levels of immunity to protect her
from disease. In doing so, the placenta mediates, establishing a unique
relationship between mother and foetus by maintaining a connection that is
characterized by neither separation nor fusion.

From this view, the placenta holds both mother and foetus in tension,
unresolved in terms of their boundaries, their beginnings and ends. What is
more, the placenta is made of the genetic and cellular material of the
embryo itself. In fact most of the so-called 'pre-embryo's' cells go toward
creating the placenta and the membranes that surround the foetus, with the
embryo itself forming from a tiny mass of cells known as the primitive
streak. When the umbilical cord is cut, the baby is, strictly speaking, cut not
from the mother's body, but from the placenta, something that was already
part of itself. So the foetus was always already other within the mother.
Passing through. Cutting the umbilical cord for the mother terminates an
intimate dialogue, one she will have to painstakingly rebuild with her child.

*My ten-day-old child talks to me. Really he does. Back and forth, back and
forth, ahhhghoo, ahhhghoo, ahhhghoo. It's a secret. No one believes us, so we
keep it that way. No, we are not 'dancing'. We are speaking. Nor is this a
manifestation of our sticky bond of love. He speaks to me. He pushes a sound
out into the space between us and I receive it, and send it back. We're both
delighted. It's so clear and simple. Sound moving across a space. That vital
ten inches that we need to focus. He's ten days old. Really he is.*

From veil to wig

Writing about the transition from woman to mother, then, seems to draw
on metaphors about excess and otherness that have been previously used in
discussing femininity and its relation to masculine unity. On the one hand
the current popular literature unwittingly figures the feminine as the lost
unified subject, and maternity as the messy interdependent excess, with
transformation producing both a 'new self' as well as prompting a kind of
mourning for the 'lost self'. Here the lost feminine comes to be figured as a
unified subject, traditionally associated with the masculine, while maternity
is understood as excessive, messy and interdependent, covering over the loss
of what we think we once had. But to call this process 'transformative' is
something of a misnomer. Transformation suggests a magical movement

from one state to another. But the transition to motherhood entails a certain horror; disintegration, the birth of a state of being excessive to unity. Being a 'subject-in-process/on trial', to borrow Kristeva's term, is not exactly pleasant. Yet this unpleasant state also has creative potential. In some senses it is logical to turn to Irigaray. For one thing, she uses the notion of transformation to figure the feminine itself. For another, her whole strategy is to try to release the creative potential of restrictive practices and discourses through engagement rather than critique (you could say this is what mothers do on a daily basis!). At the same time, however, Irigaray runs this argument the other way, which I believe does not necessarily help. Though she works hard to rescue mothers from their silenced and unrepresented position, I think she ends up associating motherhood with the unified (which in her terms means ossified and also masculine) figure, against femininity which is seen as a kind of jubilant excess. Of course, through her mimetic strategies, Irigaray's celebration of excess is not entirely a simple valuing of one thing over the other. It is her way of doing something creative with what little we've got, in order to reveal the paucity of a space and language left for women to operate in. But when the maternal is associated with ossification, lack of fluidity or movement, it is left even more unrepresented than before. Although Irigaray does not address the process of becoming a mother from the perspective of the mother (hers is mostly a daughter's perspective), or moving from singularity to a relation with the child, she uses notions of transformation as a way of articulating the maternal-feminine – a kind of composite woman-mother who must resist the pitfalls of motherhood in order to retain a relation with fluidity (i.e. femininity). So something is left unspoken in her work about maternal subjectivity, about the transition to motherhood and about loss.

We need, I am suggesting, to move away from a simple reliance on the notion of transformation as a way of dealing with the transition to motherhood. Keeping in mind that, as I said earlier, 'a transformation' is an archaic term for a woman's wig, I want to use wigs as a metaphor to address the problematic of holding onto the intransigent or resistant aspects of transformation – the way it contains the paradox that we both can and can't change, and also, much in keeping with Irigaray, of motherhood as a version of going over the same ground as a way of bringing something new into being. To do so, I want to return to Irigaray's reading of the placenta as a veil, and then move from veil to wigs.

Some years of my childhood appear dominated by my sister's hair. It is matted, unruly, knotted, wiry, rude. My mother runs after her with a comb in her hand. Her Jewish hair must be brought under control: it is the site of the family's shame. How beautiful it is now. Soft, silky, naturally streaked blond. Her hair assimilated all by itself! Mine, like Christopher Robin's, so straight and compliant, has grown a little ruder over the years. I have allowed it to

*recently, since having children, and as they say, 'letting myself go'. It no
longer needs to be cropped, cancelling out a passing comment that still festers;
that I don't look like anything in particular, just the Jewish girl next door.*

Irigaray's use of the term 'veil' is, of course, a reappropriation of that which
has for centuries been a site for the control of women's sexual desire. As a
covering for women's hair in both Judaism and Islam, the veil has traditionally signalled modesty, sexual maturity, and consent to the patriarchal
order which makes woman man's possession (Koppelman 1996). In her
analysis of veils and wigs in Jewish history, for instance, Leila Bronner
(1993) locates the moment in the sixteenth century when Jewish women
stopped veiling their hair and donned wigs instead. The challenge to veiling
came from women themselves. Wanting to emulate French fashion, they
convinced the upholders of rabbinical law that wearing a wig was tantamount to wearing the veil. After the resulting controversy, some of the most
orthodox women took to wearing wigs, which they then covered with a veil
– just to make sure! In some ways, this push towards the acceptance of wig-
wearing within Jewish law could be seen as assimilation to the dominant
cultural practices at the time. But there is something equally delightful
about the notion that Jewish women, whose hair was seen within their own
cultural context as dangerously sexual, found a way around this suppression
by covering their hair with someone else's hair, 'fake' hair to mimic their
own. So long as their own hair was discreetly hidden, they could flaunt
someone else's, as it wasn't technically their hair.

Unlike the veil, the wig, thus historically situated, then allows us to play
with the notion of transformation itself and to return to that difficult
binary, femininity/maternity. Like masks, wigs are odd cultural objects,
working their effects not through a suspension of disbelief, but through an
engagement with their artificiality. We are not asked to believe that the wig
is 'real hair', but we engage with it as if it were real all the same. The 'me/
not me' quality of this play is again reminiscent of the function of
Winnicott's transitional object. The wig does its work through the ability to
get close to real hair, and the simultaneous exposure of its own fakeness.
Wigs therefore allow a process of mimesis to occur.

'One must', writes Irigaray (1985b: 76), 'assume the feminine role
deliberately.' Mimesis defines her strategy of reappropriation, as opposed
to 'just playing the game',

> which means already to convert a form of subordination into an
> affirmation, and thus to begin to thwart it. . . . To play with
> mimesis is thus, for a woman, to try to recover the place of her
> exploitation by discourse, without allowing herself to be simply
> reduced to it.
>
> (Irigaray 1985b: 76)

Mimesis is close to parody, in which parroting becomes a commentary on what is being parroted, not merely a misguided reappropriation. At another level, however, mimesis can also be understood as allowing a new way of being to emerge, through the parodic imitation of a tired discourse, just as both actors and children can 'go through the motions' in order to bring on an 'authentic' emotion. Mimesis, exceeding that which is being parodied, could be understood as a more anarchic reappropriation, a subversion that allows something altogether different to emerge.

In its mimesis, can motherhood also subvert? Among the various discourses on maternity, there is, I have been saying, a dialectic that understands motherhood as either a movement from unity towards fluidity, or the opposite, the moment that fixes fluidity in relation to the unity of the child. Wanting to move beyond matter, while being caught by this impossibility, I have tried to show that transformation itself contains this double allegiance to materiality. Like the transformation from veil to wig, the shift to motherhood may fix or free, trap or liberate. In all likelihood, it does both. If mimesis produces a kind of creative excess, as it seems to in wig-wearing, then transformation points towards something which is excessive to this dialectic: the woman becoming mother. In liberating as it binds, motherhood is perhaps closer to the repetitive, but also creative motion of mimesis than to the magical transformation of caterpillar into butterfly.

Transformation, when applied to motherhood, appears caught in a dialectic about the promise and failure of movement. Does motherhood really change us? In which direction? From what state to what state? Can I tell any more which is my 'real hair'? My changing hair may seem a very odd place to start and finish this chapter, but I think it performs the myopic task that a partial phenomenology requires, bringing us back to the concrete, mundane, overlooked, everyday places where changes occur and are experienced. It asks us to look askance, 'otherwise' than this rather entrenched argument about fluidity and unity, towards the materiality of motherhood, its textures and tinglings. I had a baby and my identity changed, as did my socio-economic status, my work–life balance, my relationships, my internal object relations, my aspirations, my bank balance, my shopping habits. But, perhaps, as we continue through this exploration, something more interesting emerges if we try to keep our eye on the fact that, among other things, my hair changed too!

4

MATERNAL INTERRUPTIONS

I, yi, yi, yi, yi, I like you very much, Si, si, si, si, si,
I think you're grand[1]

Aren't mothers supposed to be attuned to the particular cry of their infant? The nurse has to shake me awake to tell me my baby is crying. I am in a sleep so profound it is akin to a coma. Now it dawns on me that the cry is for my ears. I am the chosen audience for that cry. I must elect this child as my child by dint of my response to that cry. The cry comes to me from the outside, from a creature I have not yet claimed as my own. Now, in this first moment of surprise, it dawns on me that I must rouse myself to action, and try to do something to stop its whole tiny frame shaking with uncontrollable spasms of pain.

The cry induces a sweaty panic as I look for a place to stop at the roadside to breastfeed, trying to get the baby latched on, fill its mouth with something sweet and warm and wet. It generates an intense frustration and desperation bordering on despair, as I try to continue a conversation over the top of it, pacing up and down, holding the baby, swimming upstream to 'get back to what I was trying to say'. Worse still it generates a terrifying level of rage when I'm continually shaken out of a deep sleep, sometimes for hours at a time; tiptoeing out of the room like a guilty lover, only to be called back to the bedside just as I am about to sidle out.

Yes, motherhood is the pitilessness of the present tense. The cry pulls me out of whatever I was embedded in, and before I have a chance to re-equilibrate, it pulls me out again. There are days that follow nights that follow days in which I am punch-drunk from interruption. These periods of time, no longer governed by circadian rhythms, like one long cinematic take act to obliterate the passing of time from what is to come, to what is, to what has been. The interruption constantly re-establishes the present by demanding a response now. The interruption is such that it cannot wait, or it struggles to wait, or teaching it to wait is in itself another interruption, a doubling of the interruption. No one seems to want to let on. In conversations I have with other mothers we all nimbly dance around, pretending that our speech is not slurred, that we are not falling over, staggering to right ourselves as we cheerfully pronounce: 'It's really hard work', the sentiment of which is immediately negated with what usually follows: 'But it's really worth it'.

In this chapter I want to explore the notion of the maternal subject as a subject of interruption; both she who is subjected to relentless interruption, and she whom interruption enunciates; a subject, that is, who emerges from the experience of interruption itself. In some senses it is barely possible to conceive of maternal subjectivity outside of interruption. The daily breaches in maternal thinking, maternal activity and maternal repose conducted by the infant, toddler and young child add up to an onslaught on a mother's mental, emotional and social functioning that can be experienced with nightmarish intensity. Though the relation between maternity and interruption has been commented on at a more global level in terms of the ways having children can interrupt a woman's career or life-plan (Orenstein 2000: 33), there has been little attention paid to the psychological effects of being constantly interrupted on a moment-by-moment basis by small children.[2] As a mother turns herself towards a child mid-sentence, mid-mouthful, mid-thought, or in the middle of the night, she often makes herself available without finishing the things that replenish her. In the face of the infant's needs, a mother may struggle with feelings of shame, confusion, self-reproach and anger when she feels anything other than being nourished and sustained by her maternal work. This struggle to own and embrace the full range of maternal reactions is always present. Although it may be tempting to think of the mother as she who has a tendency to persevere in the face of interruption,[3] it seems important to resist this romanticization. We need to confront the possibility of the mother's right of refusal, of her retaliation or even her breakdown. Kraemer calls on us to think deeply about what it is like for us to sit, again and again, with our children's feelings of need, desire, hate, destructiveness and greed; think, that is, about what it feels like, what emotional intensity it provokes in us, and what we do with this in relation to the infant and ourselves.

My interest here is to draw the focus towards the 'again and again' of this description, and to notice how the expression of these infantile and childish feelings punctures a mother's self-experience through the minute and daily processes of interruption. Psychoanalysis, and in particular object relations, is rich in descriptions of infantile emotion and utilizes the mechanisms of projection, projective identification, and introjection to understand how these emotional states are communicated from infant to mother, and to some extent back again (Klein 1935; Frosh 2002). Psychoanalysis has also long drawn on maternal experience to illuminate the analyst's position, both to help the analyst understand something of what she should be doing, and why she may be feeling how she is feeling. However, perhaps because the therapeutic encounter is temporally boundaried (with the exception of the Lacanian variety), and is predictably and regularly closed down after the standard fifty minutes, there is a tendency to discuss these processes in a temporal vacuum. Infantile emotional events are discussed in a suspended space-time, decontextualized and uncoupled from what precedes and proceeds from them.

These emotional events however, in their multiplicity, their relentlessness and their ability to dis-organize experience form the very ground of mothering. The lived experience of mothering is closer to a seemingly endless series of 'micro-blows'; what I am referring to as breaches, tears or puncturings to the mother's durational experiences bringing her back 'again and again' into the realm of the immediate, the present, the here-and-now of the child or infant's demand. In a myriad of ways the child's 'command' (whether that of early infantile needs, the toddler's demand that cannot be gratified or the child's eventual desire, structured through gradual entry into language) is 'respond to me', 'deal with me'; not later, and not because you've already dealt with me before, but now, and again now, and again now.

> '*Mum.*' '*Yes?*' '*Mum.*' '*Yes?*' '*Mum.*' '*Yes, what is it, Saul?*' *He looks*
> *at me mischievously.* '*Mum.*'

Though the child may be in a process of learning slowly and painfully to delay gratification, psychoanalysis would maintain that the mother is needed as a sustained presence in the face of such demands. In fact the mother must be prepared to come back for more. Whether she decides to gratify the need or respond to the demand, or instead takes on the struggle to hold a firm boundary in the face of fierce opposition while also dealing with what this provokes in her (for example, it may provoke uncomfortable feelings about how similar she finds she is to her own mother, or she may feel manipulated in such a way as to cause her to spiral into a rage from which she emerges shaken and full of self-hatred and despair), she is required to somehow 'right herself' again and again. My point is that this process calls on the mother to confront her own worst nightmares – her rage, aggression, hopelessness and despair, and mothers who spend long periods of the day and night with their young children can find themselves feeling mentally, emotionally and at times physically bruised.[4]

Interruption

What is an interruption? *Inter* means between or among, and *rupt* is from *rumpere*, to break. An interruption is an insertion of a break between or among something that is otherwise continuous, which has ongoing movement or flow. To interrupt is to perform a stop in this flow, to punctuate the flow thereby creating a 'between' or 'among' in an otherwise undifferentiated continuum. And of course, paradoxically the break gives rise to something. It creates a segment, a discrete object where before there was just flow. In doing so, this intervention into flow shows up flow as flow. The so-called 'arrow of time' becomes a dotted line, a series of segments with breaks between. Like its close allies, disruption and eruption, interruption reveals the taken-for-granted background of experience through its power to chop it up and to intervene. Interruption segments, divides, dislodges, unbalances and disturbs the continuum. But in doing so, it creates a form in what is otherwise formless; what Steven Connor, in his discussion of the difference between music and undifferentiated noise calls the 'structured community of sensation' (Connor 2000a: 28). Similarly, if the continuum is figured as the Same (that which is undifferentiated) then interruption is the appearance of difference that dislodges the Same from itself; difference understood as a breach in the fabric of the Same. This can also be voiced in Lacanian terms as the 'punctuation', which momentarily produces the illusion of a fixed meaning in a signifying chain that endlessly defers meaning. So interruptions appear to have a productive force as well as a destabilizing one.

In order to produce an interruption, there has to be the insertion of a gap, however narrow its dimensions, however sharp the cut. Gaps, breaks, intervals and the like, are notoriously hard to get close to. By definition they elude scrutiny, showing themselves in their non-being. Perhaps the frustration caused by constant interruption is in part about having to face these elusive blanks. The moment is covered over quickly as we pass from self-absorption into the sphere of the other. But I want to suggest that in this elusive moment, the moment in which we are interrupted by the other, something happens to unbalance us and open up a new set of possibilities. In Lacanian terms, what is produced by punctuation is more speech; for Connor, the structuring of sensation produces music as opposed to noise. This raises the question of what might be produced for a mother by the endless interruptions by her child. What might her 'structured community of sensation' be like, if we understand relentless interruption as not just depleting but generative?

> *We got cake in ina ina in in in ina ina in in in ina tube station.*
> *R R R R R R R R R R R R R R R Ruth, can I pick those up for you?*
> *W W W W W W Where is Mahmuda going?*
> *I knew that.*
> *Ruth, I say silly words sometimes.*[5]

The cry

The first interruption is the infant's cry. The cry used to be deemed the vital sign that the baby was breathing, so newborn infants were held upside down and smacked on their bottoms to bring crying on. Now that this practice has fallen into disrepute, many mothers note that their babies seem remarkably calm after birth, reporting that they appear to see them, some say they even smile.[6] There are stories from 1970s natural birth manuals of babies crawling up their mother's stomach to latch onto the breast instinctively (Balaskas 1983). The cry comes some time later, after an interval. It appears, reveals itself as a surprise emanation from another being. Naomi Wolf, lying on the operating table after a Caesarean section, writes: 'There is a cry. I do not recognize it. "That's your baby! Do you hear that?" Dr. Yemeni says heartily' (Wolf 2001: 118).

Pain, hunger and the cry, inextricably bound up in the early moments of being human. René Spitz has called the mouth a 'primal cavity' (Spitz 1955), a strange inside/outside space through which, and out of which, emanates the most terrifying, and perhaps also exhilarating sound. Terrifying, not just to the listener, but seemingly to the infant itself. In Connor's analysis of the voice, he posits a Kleinian reworking of the good and bad object in terms of the infant's relationship with its own cry – one that experiences the cry itself as a part-object, splitting it into a 'good' and 'bad' voice.

> If the cry is the form of the infantile hallucination of the breast, it is a disappointment. The child attempts to feed itself with its voice, but its voice simply crams starvation back down its throat.
>
> (Connor 2000a: 31)

He imagines that the bad voice is the voice of the self become other (the cry) and the good voice is the voice of the other (mother) become self, in that the infant takes in the good voice that the mother surrounds it with, and eventually comes to recognize its own voice as good. But he also notes that 'excessive sound is associated, not only with unpleasant or terrifying subjection, but also with experiences of intense rapture' (Connor 2000a: 26). Drawing on the work of Guy Rosolato (1974), he shifts the emphasis seen in Didier Anzieu's classic work on the sonorous envelope, where the baby has a largely passive or reactive experience of sound, towards something more active:

> Right from the beginning, the cry is the manifestation of the excitation of living matter in pain or pleasure, at once autonomous and reacting to stimulation – an excitation which is life itself.
>
> (Rosolato 1974: 76, quoted in Connor 2000a: 29)

And, after all, a mother may respond to this cry with equal excitement:

> The mother gains an enormous sense of relief, satisfaction, and even pride when she sees her baby's vitality confirmed through his or her angry protests, even when they are expressions of the baby's feelings about her and how she makes him or her feel. When the mother can recognize her contribution to her baby's freedom of

expression, she may feel a flush of pleasure (although she may also need to contend with some envy as well).

(Kraemer 1996: 788)

In one sense, we could say that it is the voice or cry of the infant that exists, and 'the infant' comes to be understood as merely the mode of the cry's existence. As a mother, one arrives 'in the middle' of this force. The cry reveals itself as a mode of excitation, the full force of which is received by the mother in its insistence and intensity. The crying infant forces the mother, in other words, to confront the infant's subjectivity as a site of extreme affective states. This may vicariously excite the mother, and through the child's vitality she may allow herself to recognize her own split-off aggression. I can recognize a subtle mixture of pride and shame when my children shout in restaurants, when they are too full of themselves, even when they throw a tantrum in the street. They do things that I would not dare to do, and there is part of me that is secretly glad that they transgress the usual confines of social etiquette on my behalf.

However, rather than understanding a mother's relation to the child's vitality as a vicarious one, we could say that the child proposes, through demonstration, a kind of subjectivity that is bound up in extreme affective states. In doing so, the child calls on the mother to question her own subjectivity. The child's question to the mother is: 'What kind of person would you be, if you allowed the intensity of emotion to course through you in the way it courses through me?'

K K K Katy, K K K Katy, you're the only one that I adore.[7]

Spitz figures the mouth as the primary means for the infant to explore the world because of its unique assemblage of sensory receptors; those of touch, taste, temperature, smell, pain, and also 'the deep sensibility involved in the act of deglutition' (Spitz 1955: 221). He understands the mouth as a unique primary area for the development of all human perception, as it bridges the gap between internal and external organs. This cavity, then, is a place of transition where intentional activity develops, the initial locus of the infant's move from passivity to volition. It is the perceptual modality of the oral cavity which forms the basis for later developmental stages which use as their precursor the 'inside-outside mode established by the intra-oral experience, as for instance in the distinction between the 'I' and the 'non-I', the 'self' and the 'non-self' (Spitz 1955: 228). So the cry, the voice, and later speech, emanate from an organ where the senses coagulate, where perceptions are formed which go on to structure the very basis of the infant ego. And, in keeping with Anzieu (1989), the baby's cry goes out from the infant into the 'sound bath' provided by the mother, supported by her caresses, and physical holding, as she feeds warm, sweet milk to the baby's stomach.

The cry calls forth a response that not only fills the infant's mouth, digestive tract and stomach, but also bathes the infant's ears and nose, and the actual skin-surface of her body (Anzieu 1989).

Wait. Something inevitably has been skimmed over and lost in this account. It is the moment that the cry reaches the mother. It is the minute blank created in stopping her flow, the punctuation mark, the grammatical syncope. What state is she in? Is she sleeping or exhaustedly awake? Perhaps she is already immersed in something she hates to be wrenched from. How does the cry enter her, how does her initial somatic response get converted to a pattern of thinking, as she begins to juggle with what to do, whether to feed on demand, whether to try another form of soothing as she knows she has just fed the baby and he cannot be hungry, whether she can leave it a moment longer to finish her mouthful, what to do with the voice in her head, which is her mother's voice, saying, 'You fuss the baby too much. In my day we just left them to cry'? The cry, initially plaintive, ramps up into the rhythmic blare of an air raid siren, blotting out all thinking, and stimulating a more compulsive need to shut it out or shut it up. A spark leaps from one side of the blank to the other, reconnecting the circuit, as the mother turns towards the baby.

The so-called 'human infant cry literature' seems fraught with controversy, not only as to the nature and functions of this primordial cry, but also to the behaviour it elicits in the adults around it. An evolutionary approach posits that the essential role of infant crying is to maintain the proximity of the caregivers and to elicit care from them. The acoustic properties of the cry itself appear to function as a graded signal with regard to levels of pain (Craig et al. 2000). Soltis (2003) tells us that during pain-induced autonomic nervous system arousal, neural input to the vocal cords increases the pitch of the cry. Caregivers then seem to use this acoustic information, along with other visual clues, to guide their caregiving behaviour. What we 'hear' in the cry is the primordial expression of pain.

Many studies on mothers' responses to their infant's crying involve getting mothers to rate their own reactions to tape recordings of infant cries. Generally, high and variable pitched cries are rated as aversive, urgent, arousing, grating, piercing, distressing, saddening or sickening, compared to lower and less variable pitched crying (Craig et al. 2000). High and variable pitched crying raises the autonomic arousal levels in the listener, increasing the heart rate and skin conductance. What is far less clear from the research, however, is what this may cause us to do. It appears that consistent levels of arousal of this type can lead to some adults abusing or killing their infants, while in others it leads to appropriate soothing strategies (Soltis 2003).

From a psychoanalytic perspective, we could surmise that how a mother experiences and interprets the cry may be intimately bound up with her own history; with issues of control and omnipotence, dependency and impingement, on how successfully she developed a capacity to be alone, or developed a relationship with her own good and bad voice. But these relations are never simple or directly correlative. We hear an infant cry: our heart rate goes up, and we get sweaty. That much at least is official.

It is a universal human feature that the infant cry increases over the first three months of a baby's life. Excessive crying, or colic, is now thought of as the upper end of this normal increase. So the interruptions come thick and fast. The more the mother appears to know about or understand her baby's crying in those first three months, the more the baby actually cries. The 'knowing' is really a kind of imagining, a guessing in order to make some kind of coherent narrative in the face of the absolute impossibility of really knowing; she's hungry, wet, cold, hot, over-stimulated, bored, tired, teething, windy, has growing pains. . . . They are all stabs in the dark. Like the operation of punctuation in Lacanian psychoanalysis, the mother interprets the cry in one way or another, establishing meaning retroactively, fixing meaning momentarily, allowing the illusion that we know what is going on.

> *Joel stammers with his words, but he always finishes what he is saying.*
> *'W W W W W W W W What is this for?*
> *My car's got a puncture, m m m m m mum's car's got a puncture and I think we'll have to get a new one.*
> *L L L L L L L L L Look out L L L Linda! There's a rabbit behind you.*

The cry interrupts all durational activities. Nothing is sacred unless you physically remove yourself from the baby, which is the one consistent piece of advice given to mothers who feel they are not coping and think they may hurt their babies. When you're finally at the end of your tether, when you've tried everything and the baby is still screaming, put the baby in a cot and leave the room for twenty minutes. Beyond the bodily functions, beyond the interruptions of activity and speech, perhaps most disturbing is the interruption in one's capacity to think; to follow through a thought, reflect or dwell in thought, or gather one's thoughts. What kind of thinking is possible in these situations? For, although there have been far-reaching discussions in the literature about the necessity for the mother to 'reverie' about her child (Bion 1962), is it not this very capacity that is so consistently under attack?

Perhaps what is required is a shift of perspective. Interruption is usually figured as the exception, a break in continuity that must be overcome, patched over, worked around, neutralized, or denied. Interruption must be ironed out as it is what impedes us achieving our goals, stops us from getting wherever we are trying to get to, what keeps interfering with the forward thrust of our lives. But what emerges from the discussion so far is

73

that interruption forms the ground of maternal experience against which all other maternal experiences are understood. If interruption is the given of maternal experience, then what this fundamentally changes is a mother's experience of her temporal being. To the extent that we are partly constructed as temporal entities, this also changes the nature of maternal subjectivity. Perhaps maternal subjectivity is a kind of subjective state in which it has become impossible to operate in the realm of reflective thought, and forces into awareness another form of subjective experience and thinking. Though it feels very hard to give up the psychoanalytic insight that maternal containment is largely about the kind of active thinking about the child that Bion describes (Bion 1962: 110), perhaps this is just not possible if you are thrown into the realm of the immediate all the time. We have to allow for another description of the kind of 'thinking' that is possible for a mother to do in these situations.

Wass zzis? Brick. Wass zzis? Brick. Wass zzis? Brick, it's a brick, a blue brick. Wass zzis? Saul, it's a brick. A blue brick. Can you say brick? Wass zzis? Would you like some juice now? Iiick. Yes! A brick. Jus. Yes! Have some flipping jus.

Maternal time

In *Women, Time and the Weaving of the Strands of Everyday Life*, Karen Davies (1990) looks at how women's identities are moulded by their access to different social spheres, particularly for women who are both carers and wage earners and therefore move between different spheres, and the role of contemporary temporal consciousness in structuring these identities. Charting the coincidence of modernity and the development of the clock measuring linear time, she describes the emergence of both cyclical and linear time as the two prevalent ways of conceiving time in Western Europe. How we conceive ourselves as structured by time changes dramatically according to gender, and historical and cultural context. In Western Europe in the modern period, we have come to broadly delineate linear clock time as male time, and process or cyclical time as female time, in keeping with the traditional linking of female subjectivity with the natural cycles, gestation and biological rhythms, and male subjectivity with the relentless movement forward, the thrust of 'project, teleology, departure, progression and arrival' (Kristeva 1981: 13). Male time, though currently the dominant temporal consciousness in the West, has, according to Davies (1990), become distinctly dysfunctional for the majority of men *and* women in the current economic structure.

Davies (1990) argues that women tend to experience time itself as relational, in that women's time is more readily seen in relation to the time of significant others, due, in part to their caring responsibilities. Male interests have played an important part in establishing linear time as the dominant temporal consciousness by exerting power and control over women's time. In looking at the ways women often take on both caring responsibilities and paid employment, Davies argues that women's time can be better understood as continuous and men's time as discontinuous, rather than the traditional linear/cyclical dichotomy, as men's timetable tends to be chopped up into work time, and then the time after work which is figured as a 'break' from work. Women's time, on the other hand, is more like a cat's cradle with multiple points of intersection, and few lacunae, in that there are rarely allotted moments in which women can be idle, and taking 'time out' becomes impossible, as it leads to a breakdown of the cradle's structure. So, regardless of the dominant temporal consciousness of contemporary society (whether linear or cyclical) it is the dimension of continuity and discontinuity that differentiates women and men's actual relation to time. Lacunae have always existed in men's lives, while in women's they have not, due to their responsibilities for children, the sick and elderly people, none of whom, Davies asserts, can *wait*. Care has been seen as 'need-orientated communication' based on the task at hand rather than the clock. The temporal nature of care means that women cannot stop, and the caring supposedly goes on and on. Davies wants to represent women's time as a spiral which none the less moves forwards, and men's time as a dotted arrow, always moving forward but broken by 'time out', which really means their 'own time', a commodity which becomes a resource controlled by men at the expense of women.

However, though the need for care may go on and on, care is not a continuous flow that moves from women out towards children, the sick and elderly people. As I have described, maternal care is elicited by a 'command' made by the other which constantly interrupts the mother, bringing her to a myriad of points of disjuncture in which she is surprised, dislodged or shaken from whatever she is embedded in. She does not just wait, making herself endlessly available for caring for the one who cannot wait. She finds herself embedded in certain durational experiences from which she is disturbed. This disturbance, which I am arguing structures maternal subjectivity, can be experienced as depleting, exhausting, disabling and controlling, but also seems to have the potential to be an enlivening and productive encounter, one that forces a mother to access a kind of thinking and feeling outside of her usual repertoire, pushes her to a state of being 'beside herself' with all the overtones this brings of intensity, exhilaration and excitation as well as anxiety and despair.

Disruption

But what is this other way of thinking and feeling? To understand this may require looking more closely, not at the segments of time created by breaks in continuity, but at the nature and experience of the break itself. This is the focus of the philosopher David Appelbaum's three-volume work, *The Intervening Subject*. In *The Stop* (Appelbaum 1995), *Disruption* (Appelbaum 1996) and *Delay of the Heart* (Appelbaum 2001), the encounter with 'the stop' and with what Appelbaum calls 'its sibs, the blank, the gap, the gape, the lacuna, the caesura, the hiatus, the chasm, the hole, the canyon, the gulf, the abyss' (Appelbaum 1996: 19) is understood to be intimately related to the emergence of both subjectivity and, interestingly, *conscience*.

In a detailed and rigorous reappraisal of the work of the Enlightenment philosophers, Locke and Hume, Appelbaum shows how the stop gives rise to a turn of awareness by which we pass from ignorance to knowledge. For Appelbaum this is specifically a somatic or sensory knowledge, a knowledge uncoupled from the intellect, and which brings forth consciousness (the I) and turns us towards conscience (ethical awareness of the other). Although there may be some discomfort, disruption even, in turning to such an esoteric and abstruse philosophy to try to think about the very concrete, lived experiences of motherhood, it is this very disjuncture that I am hoping may prove productive. In what follows, I try to give an account of Appelbaum's line of thought, as his work engages directly with the notion of an ethical subjectivity emerging out of an engagement with interruption as a productive force. Given I am arguing that interruption constitutes the ground of maternal experience, this may allow an articulation of maternal subjectivity that does not necessarily devalue or seek to eliminate such experiences, but seeks to foreground them as providing access to new subjective experiences.

Appelbaum critiques the tendency for philosophy, specifically a philosophy of being, to devalue disruption, equating it with notions of disintegration, and leading to a desire to eliminate disruption and rid ontology of this unruly force. In formulating the question 'what is the signification of that which disrupts the human act, particularly the act of signification?' (Appelbaum 1996: vii), he reintroduces this unruly force as a positive force for change; what he terms 'movement' and 'alteration' (Appelbaum 1996: 58). In keeping with Levinas, he understands that to pose this question requires the bracketing of ontology, due to the way 'being draws consciousness to it' (Appelbaum 1996: vii). His interest is in what breaks into and breaks up conscious thought, the very point that consciousness and hence being (as characterized in the analytical tradition) encounters a blank.

It is these events, the ones that break into consciousness with a signification *other than being*, that promise movement and alteration. But again, in a line of argument that closely resembles Levinas, an event that breaks into consciousness gives rise to an ethical imperative. A disruption in consciousness engenders a kind of self-remembering (as I understand it, a re-collection of the self), which in turn leads to the development of an 'organ' that is the conscience.

Appelbaum's work traces both internal and external interruptions; both breaks in 'inner speaking' performed by what happens when memory fails (the blank or amnesia when memory encounters the forgotten, like when we forget a person's name even when their face is clear in the mind), and the exigency of the other in front of me – the plight of the neighbour, friend, enemy, stranger, or child whose presence disrupts us. Being disrupted by the other brings us face-to-face with both our own blanks, which memory is constantly seeking to patch over, and the paucity of our own response. And in doing so, it calls us to remember 'the forgotten' – an originary forgotten, without origin or principle (Appelbaum 1996: 52). This is the fundamental gap out of which all thought is born – a kind of archaic blank that the mind constantly seeks to patch over. Remembering the archaic blank, returning to and re-encountering this blank in thought is essentially what he calls conscience.

Remembering the immemorial through an encounter with a blank in consciousness is, by definition, a meeting which cannot take place *in* thought, in consciousness, and so Appelbaum develops the notion of the *soma* as the first place we notice a shift or alteration of consciousness. Appelbaum's point is that the 'retentive mind' (thought which tries to retain itself and holds onto itself), comes into being simultaneously with loss; the loss of that which is vital and somatic:

> A blessing that belongs by right to the red twin is stolen away. The white twin, its thief, retains it. Jacob rather than Esau succeeds Isaac, Esau who by right of birth should. The rightful bloodline, vital, somatic, and silent, is cut short by deceit. Only the sickly pallor of thought, the cunning, contriving, manipulating line is victor. Thus is retentivity forever scarred, forever bent over to protect itself against a loss that, being coeval – *being twinned* – with itself, is irradicable in time.
>
> (Appelbaum 1996: 17, original emphases)

In the same way, memory is always twinned with the forgotten, that blank that memory is always trying to cover over. 'Awareness' then faces a choice in this encounter – either a kind of 'death of intellect' or its regeneration through noticing and being 'touched' by a somatic response:

> To lessen the weight of intellect is to permit an equilibration with the weight of the soma, hitherto unsensed. The deeper action of an anarchaic function is to turn awareness beyond the arche of thought, its raw substance, its unprocessed *hyle*, its state of nature, its stuff.
>
> (Appelbaum 1996: 21, original emphasis)

Shadowing an object of perception, sensation is figured as 'an unframed, nonfocal accompliment to a cognitively endowed impression' (Appelbaum 1996: 24), a kind of 'thereness' without 'thatness', what Appelbaum calls 'the unparticularisable universal' (Appelbaum 1996: 24). This is the 'other than being'. Though sensation shadows the perceived object, doubles it, sits that is, in the background, it is 'a dimension higher than depth that at each point defines depth. It is the hidden body' (Appelbaum 1996: 24).

Drawing on Kant, the uniqueness of sensation is that it cannot be anticipated:

> Unanticipated shadowing, 'sensation occupies only an instant [Augenblick]' – or less. Opaque, untranslatable, irreducible, fluid, and unframed, sensation blurs intellectual focus – a catcall just when the mind is taking aim.
>
> (Appelbaum 1996: 25)

The mention of a catcall may well draw our attention to the way an unacknowledged discourse of gender is at work here. A feminist critique of such a statement may take issue with the division between the rational (male) intellect which draws consciousness to it, and its shadow, the irreducible, fluid and unframed 'body' of sensation, marked in the feminine by that catcall. However, as in Levinas' work, the feminine yet again gets elevated as the dimension that brings us into contact with the ethical, and with our obligation to respond to the other which renders us human. Though it may be problematic to think about Appelbaum's elevation of the somatic, of sensation and percipience in relation to the maternal, I think, on the contrary, it may be very useful. Instead of separating off the masculine and feminine, assigning them different realms and spheres of influence, he shows how the somatic and vital force in the human economy is always being denied as disruptive and dangerous, and needs to be brought into awareness (through the process of remembering the immemorial) in order to establish both subjectivity and conscience. We come into both subjectivity and ethical awareness when we can notice the somatic shadow of conscious thought, and when we can, in addition, notice difference within somatic percipience:

> Existence arrives, if it arrives at all, as a disruption to a global sensation . . . . The specificity of its resonance – I – breaks up the monotony of intellectual production and recalls me to the difference I make . . . . From within the sameness of intellect, the soma appears. From within the sameness of soma, I appears. These are separate disruptions, different steps. They are ascendent. Vitality, quality, and inclusiveness increase, not by degrees, but by quanta.

A human being opens to an actuality of impermanence, movement, and disruption.

(Appelbaum 1996: 29–30)

I am wary of suggesting a crude overlaying of Appelbaum's ideas with the realities of a mother's daily life, as she is constantly interrupted by her child. I am not suggesting that at the moment the mother is interrupted, she suddenly becomes aware of sensations in her body! Appelbaum's soma is only metaphorically to do with the body. He is really trying to describe consciousness in movement, consciousness aware of what consciousness is constantly trying to cover over, and in its awareness, how both subjectivity and conscience arise. However, given the thrust of my work is to think together the mundane and the theoretical, looking for something productive that may emerge out of the gap between them, then perhaps what is useful in Appelbaum's account is a notion that the kind of 'thinking' that psychoanalysis requires of a mother, the kind of thinking that perhaps Bion alludes to in his description of 'reverie', becomes possible if we no longer expect the mother to think in a 'retentive' or static sense, but rather, to become aware of the shadow of thinking itself. At a theoretical level this leads us towards a different articulation of the mother as ethical subject; the blanks created by interruption may offer the mother something that is not 'content or intention but an eruption of being' (Appelbaum 1996: 30). At the level of lived experience, it allows a mother to stop 'trying to get back' to what she was saying, thinking, remembering, doing, and to recuperate some of this experience as a new way of thinking.

In his discussion of the blank and its siblings, Appelbaum inevitably draws us into a complex discussion about time. In a fascinating passage in *The Stop*, Appelbaum seems to describe exactly what happens in moments when time itself is arrested, moments I have tried to describe as at the core of the maternal:

When the stop arrests the intellectualising tendencies of the mind, the concept of time is also affected. Time is ordinarily understood through succession (one event follows another), direction (movement from past to future), insufficiency ('Never enough time'), and extraneousness (Being outside of and containing events.) When time comes to a stop, one experiences, not timelessness, but time unqualified by intellect. In the new order, the a priori form of intuition (Kant) or internal time sense (Husserl) gives way to an organic apprehension of the present moment. A reversal of ordinary assumptions takes place. Events are linked by nonlinear relations rather than by succession. Time ceases to be past, present, and future, and instead either moves or is frozen. Time becomes

79

ample enough to allow an event to occur without crimping it. Time ceases to exist apart from what takes place; instead, it becomes a quality specific to that event.

(Appelbaum 1995: 85)

This seems to me a good description of the way interruption transforms maternal time. Though thought is arrested by the constant interruptions that a child performs on the maternal psyche, a more 'organic apprehension of the present moment' is made available – those intense moments of pleasure or connectedness that mothers report, moments that may para- doxically allow access to a somatic or sensory mode of experiencing which may have been unavailable previously, and may constitute a new mode of self-experiencing.

The tantrum

Soneeta was showing us her arm (eczema patch on it). She said it was sore. 'I I I I I will heheheh heheheh help you' said Joel, and he put his hand on her arm and gently rubbed her arm for a few moments.

After the first month of life the cry gives way to babble. Only later does it re-emerge, transmuted into that peculiar Western childhood ailment known as the tantrum, that 'outburst of bad temper or petulance' (*Oxford English Dictionary* 1989). In Europe and the United States there is a fast developing psychological literature on the tantrum. One study has analysed hundreds of parental narratives of tantrums, building a model of the tantrum as an expression of two overlapping but interrelated emotional and behavioural processes: those of anger and distress (Potegal et al. 2003). Manifestations of anger are described as dropping down, kicking, throwing, stamping, stiffening and attempting to escape, and those of distress as whining, affiliating and crying. The researchers mapped the course of these behaviours to form a 'tantrogram'. Anger rises quickly at the onset of the tantrum, peaking soon after onset, and giving way to symptoms of distress. They note how the full range of tantrum behaviour can stretch to head-banging and deliberate holding of the breath. Parents report how their children scream so violently and so long that the capillaries in their cheeks burst and the eyes become bloodshot, or they vomit or become so rigid with tension they topple over if left unsupported. Cries emanate from their children, which are described as the cries of a 'prehistoric bird'. The 'dropping down', though sounding more like a swoon or faint, is in fact more like a dramatic throwing of the self to the floor, abandoning oneself to these raw and consuming emotions. The cry is closer to a shriek, a wail and a shout all in one. Notice me, notice me, notice me.

Catherine Clément's work on syncope is situated in a similar realm (Clément 1994). Clément describes syncope as a 'faltering' in time (1994: 1) or a 'miraculous' or 'abrupt suspension' of time (1994: 5). In its most colloquial sense it means radical surprise, but the French word contains both the notion of 'loss of consciousness' or 'fainting' as well as 'musical syncopation'. Syncope can also stretch to describe other forms of momentary loss, such as an irregularity in the heartbeat, or a grammatical elision (O'Driscoll and Mahoney 1994).

Clément focuses on those peculiarly intense experiences that are at once sensory, somatic, extreme, intense, and put oneself 'beside oneself'. She fleshes out an area of experience that provokes a 'little suspension of being', or what she calls an 'apparent death', an 'absence of the self' (Clément 1994: 1). In a beautiful taxonomy of syncopic experiences, her examples begin with those things that suspend breathing, which in their extreme state can give rise to real fainting fits, such as tremors, coughing, sneezing, hiccupping, laughter, asthma, screaming, wheezing, sobbing, and when included with uncontrolled excretion, and foaming at the mouth, can be brought under the mantle of epilepsy. Next is the fainting fit itself, the trance, attacks of sleep, repetition of physical activity such as the spinning of the dervishes. Then comes ecstasy; experiences that take one outside oneself such as the delirium of mystics and tantrics. Here she draws on Bataille's list of processes through which one can come to ecstasy; 'laughter, drunkenness, eroticism, meditation, sacrifice, poetry' (Clément 1994: 13). Then come experiences that bring us closest to death; experiences of orgasm or jouissance. Beyond this is love at first sight, and beyond this there are more and more (Clément 1994: 1–21).

All are experiences of momentary disappearance in which the subject comes back *fundamentally changed*. They are therefore generative experiences, out of which newness can emerge. Syncope is a lapse and then a new departure. Clément is at pains to flesh out an experience that is not linked with death itself, but with a simulated death. She describes syncope as 'this eclipse of thought, this game of following death' (1994: 20). In syncope, one always comes back. The point is to 'play-act death, but in order not to die' (1994: 15), passing beyond consciousness and returning changed. 'It would be too easy', she writes, 'to interpret syncope as a lapse, a failed act; in short, it would be premature to put it in the huge cupboard of products of the unconscious' (1994: 19). This would be to write it off as either a psychosomatic phenomenon with hysterical origins, or a series of signifiers covering up 'emptiness, lack, internal twisting' (1994: 19). Though these interpretations would not be wrong, she is looking for something else.

This desire to look beyond a discourse of lack and emptiness and interminable mourning for the unrecoverable, echoes Appelbaum's desire to re-establish a place for the somatic and vital in the philosophy of the subject, and my own desire to look beyond the conflicting emotions of maternal containment to something altogether more generative and enlivening – the 'something' that may happen in the gap itself. Reminding us of the musical meaning of syncope, Clément describes how the first part of the syncope (the weak beat) prepares for the dissonance struck by the second part (where the emphasis falls) but also resolves the dissonance that precedes it. She therefore picks up on the momentary disappearance of the beat in order to draw our attention to how rhythm is born out of this missing moment (Clément 1994: 4–5). By asking the question 'where do we go to when we faint?' she aims to notice the productive and harmonious discord that is produced from this momentary loss of consciousness. Her focus, in other words, is on what we come back with. In an important sense, she minutely shifts us away from 'gap' or 'lack', to this tiny interval, this lost beat that then re-appears; 'from delay to anticipation, *dissonance* and then its *resolution*' (Clément 1994: 120, original emphases).

Where are the mother and child situated in all this? Can a tantrum be thought about in terms of syncope? It has all the characteristics of one. The child falls to the ground, overcome with emotion, and disappears somewhere unfathomable in those moments, not far removed from an epileptic fit, sometimes literally foaming at the mouth. The child reappears changed, shaken by the experience but holding on to something within, something that will have to be revisited again and again in order to ascertain that it is really internalized, that these feelings are tolerable, that they do not kill you off even though they appear to.

And the mother? I would like to suggest that bearing witness to a tantrum is a form of syncope too. After all, what is it really like, not only to constantly bear witness to the child's syncopic experience, but also to be the object of a syncope, and, moreover, to be responsible for the one caught in the 'disappearance' of the syncopic moment? Is the expressive interruption that a tantrum performs akin to a syncope itself, where the mother also momentarily disappears to re-emerge changed, shaken but holding on to something too, something about the survivability of her brush with a 'little death'? These are not issues Clément concerns herself with, but the interruption performed by being with the other who has disappeared may prompt a complementary, or perhaps identificatory experience. The infant cry of need escalates to the intensity of the toddler's display of anger and distress. At least with needs, whose source the mother cannot precisely divine, she nevertheless has some strategies to meet. The tantrum is the extreme expression of the unreasonable, irrational demand whose object cannot exist. In fact she, the object, must be obliterated. The excessiveness of the emotional display is deeply disturbing; when infants have tantrums, especially in public, it can induce in mothers a sense of shame, humiliation, rage, despair, hatred, anxiety, compassion, helplessness, disbelief, a dispassionate separateness, aggression, sadism, concern, boredom and distress. I suggest that the expressive force emanating from the toddler shakes us to our core and brings us back changed.

This also brings to mind the force of both interpretation and punctuation more generally in psychoanalysis, in the way it aims to shock the analysand into a less defensive structuring of self, bringing a moment of connection with what is dis-organized within us. The Lacanian psychoanalyst, according to Clément, approaches treatment practices precisely as an exercise in punctuation. By punctuating the analysand's discourse in unexpected ways, the analyst aims to retroactively change the intended meaning of the analysand's speech (Evans 1996: 157). Changing the punctuation 'renews or upsets' the fixed meaning that the analysand had understood his own speech to mean, showing the analysand that he is 'saying more than he thinks he is' (Lacan 1953–1954: 54, quoted in Evans 1996). Punctuation can take the form of repeating back part of the analysand's speech to him with a different intonation, thereby showing up a different meaning, it can take the form of a silence, or an interruption that is an interpretation, or finally by stopping the session at an opportune moment – what Bruce Fink calls 'scansion' (Fink 1997). The purpose is to interrupt the session at the exact moment when the break would be most effective, thus bringing about both shock and illumination. In this sense, Clément claims that the Lacanian psychoanalyst's job is to 'look for an effect of syncope during every session' (Clément 1994: 125), where syncope is understood in the sense of 'radical surprise'. Scansion is the 'protecting of the element of surprise in the subject's recourse to the subject' (Clément 1994: 125).

Similarly, interpretation itself, instead of seeking to uncover the true meaning of a symptom, slip of the tongue, association or dream, should instead be aimed at disrupting meaning. In *Seminar II* Lacan states:

> Interpretation is directed not so much at 'making sense' as towards reducing the signifiers to their 'non-sense' in order thereby to find the determinants of all the subject's conduct.
>
> (Lacan 1953–1954: 212)

In this formulation, the analyst plays on the ambiguity already present in the analysand's speech, bringing out its inherent multiplicity of meaning. The effect of a Lacanian interpretation is to produce more speaking by allowing the analysand to continue when his flow of associations has become blocked by closure around one particular meaning, as meaning is always produced in the gaps between irreducible signifiers. The way the analyst must proceed is not to listen for underlying meaning, but to stay operating at the level of the signifier; that is, by taking what the analysand says literally – a kind of deliberate staying in the present. Lacanian punctuation, then, is yet another description of this elusive generative power of interruption, in its ability to both render a moment of surprise which is a moment of self-knowing, without self-knowing closing in around fixed meaning.

Stammering: the interruption of interruption

At some point, Appelbaum tells us, during the second month of life, babble evolves from crying. Before the infant can babble, lallate or coo, it cries. However, after this point, crying and babble diverge. Crying takes its own independent course onto which language is grafted, leaving babble 'to be buried alive as desire replaces need' (Appelbaum 1990). What Appelbaum appears to mean by this is that crying and speaking are both born out of absence (the cry gives voice to the absence of food, warmth and love, while language is structured by the desire of/for the other) whereas the babbling period, which reaches its peak between three and ten months, is an unfettered experience of pleasure, where the infant produces sound purely for its own interest and excitement. Babbling is pure autoerotic play, process rather than production. In babbling, sound is continually in the process of being made and yet left unfinished with respect to a closure of meaning. Slowly, as the infant replaces pulmonic-lingual consonants, plosives and dentals and a variety of vowel-like sounds, with stable phonemes, babbling disappears, getting buried beneath desire-as-language.

This may not strictly be the case. Lois Bloom (1993) concedes that for a long while it was thought that infant babbling was unrelated to the sounds of speech. However, research on the nature of infant expression since the 1980s has revealed that babbling contains the same preferences for certain kinds of phonetic elements and sequences found in later meaningful speech (Bloom 1993: 68). The consensus now is that early words which develop towards the end of the first year of life grow out of a small number of core sounds that the infant has favoured in babble, and that the particular sounds that infants babble before speech, determine which words are subsequently acquired and which are not (Bloom 1993: 68). Babble therefore is more directly related to language acquisition than Appelbaum would suggest.

In addition, by 'playing' with language through repetition (ba ba ba ba ba, da da da da da da, aaachoo, aaachoo, aaachoo), the infant calls forth a similar response in the mother who responds with her own set of repetitions and variations on repetitions, enabling the infant to regulate his engagement with her, and revealing the innate communicative function of babbling, already then a precursor to language. Stern (1985) makes this argument, describing how infants seek invariants so as to order the world, while needing a certain degree of familiarity so that the invariants can show up as invariant (Stern 1985). This allows the infant to reach an optimal level of excitement without tipping over into uncomfortable intensity. What the infant is doing when she babbles is regulating her own affect and excitation in her contact with another. Winnicott also notes the role of babble in establishing an 'unchallenged' space to explore me/not me phenomena in conjunction with transitional objects. In the transitional space, along with the sheet, or blanket, thumb or chewed ear of a cuddly rabbit, the infant mumbles, '"mum-mum," babbling, anal noises, the first musical notes and so on' (Winnicott 1951: 235).

> *I, yi, yi, yi, yi, I like you very much. Si, si, si, si, si, I think you're grand*

Stammering retains something of the buried babble; at once, a regression to a state of free-play, the beginnings of affective regulation of communication, and the crucially unchallenged transitional space in which me and not-me is still undifferentiated. The stammering child particularly struggles with I I I I I. The adult stammerer stammers with his own name (Gggggggggraham), and then when he changes his name to something simpler, he can now miraculously say Graham, and stammers instead on Bob. The non-stammering child says Mum, Mum, Mum, Mum, Mum. You, you, you, you. Does the stammerer, already rattled by something, need to revisit this transitional space? Both a block and a repetition, a repeated interruption into the flow of speech, staging again and again a breach in the signifying chain. Begin again, begin again.

My child is devouring language. The sophistication of his two-year-old turn of phrase is charming, compelling and disturbing all at once. What do I do? Respond, feed him more of what he demands, more words, more descriptions, more explanations, more and more access into a complex world where things are not what they seem, where language does not say what it means, where mechanisms are not simple chains of events? The other route: 'Joel, it's a dinosaur. Even the spiky ones. Just dinosaur. I don't know its other name. They are all called dinosaur'. Caught, language delights me too. It is hard to hold back, when he's going so fast. I'm proud of him, secretly pleased that he's so 'grown up', though I catch the way others recoil slightly from him. His propensity for language is almost unsightly, smells a little of hot housing, of parentification, of someone too old for his years. But he lures me in, with his language, he wants to play with me, with language. I am swayed.

A bang on the head. Another child is wheeling him in a trolley at ferocious speed towards a wall. The child lets go. He doesn't know what else to do – he 'loses his head', so to speak, though perhaps not, perhaps he just needs to see what happens. Perhaps the implacable wall is too much for him, too much to negotiate, too much temptation. So I watch him, as he lets go. Two frozen moments, joined together by the horror of the impact. The unreal time as I watch my son hurtling towards the wall. Then the silence between the impact and the cry. My mind cannot contain the moment itself, his head smashing against the cold wall. Time skips a beat, skirts around the obstacle, the indigestible, unrecordable event that dislodges a much more archaic memory, that of repeatedly falling. Then, with his scream, the beat resurfaces. He's alright, look he's screaming, no concussion, alive, in pain.

I I I I. I I I I. I cccan't talk mum! I am overwhelmed with a slow, sick despair. He is so innocently mystified, baffled, as if someone had jolted him in a crowded place and stolen something that meant nothing to them, but is the very fabric of his being. For days now, since the accident, I have been noticing a kind of stuckness, as he tries to propel himself into the sentence. Like a diver wavering on a high board, now not so sure if he wants to plunge, now feeling something like fear, something that he has never felt before, that he knew nothing of until this moment. Now the most ordinary things are called into question. Yes, you want to say something, and it cannot come out. Something, that was once fluent, generative, easy, is tripping you up. I have a confused conversation with a doctor friend about delayed concussion.

Bizarrely, at nursery they insist on writing down his actual words. We receive strings of consonants, lists of ornate vowels, fragments of language strung out across the page like an ee cummings poem. Joel, the rap artist of Columbia Market Nursery.

I grope my way towards some kind of understanding, trying to make a story for myself, as I did in the days when I didn't know if his cry was an expression of cold, hunger, tiredness or some other unfathomable pain. Now the interruption of his interruption has the odd effect of slowing us all down. It opens up a space for thinking.

My story goes like this: language was the way he could mime being an adult, his way of collapsing the space between him and us. Because of his innate proficiency and my enthusiastic delight, he rapidly closed this gap, his language overleaping his emotional pace. The blow to his head was like a warning sign, shaming us both into an appreciation of his own fragility, and my difficulties with protecting him. Now he produces his stammer to hold him back, like a second perforated skin, only allowing a trickle of exchange, where the first skin, my containment, was an inadequate boundary. Now he has some protection from what he doesn't want to know; from knowing he is not the only one, that there is an inevitable delay before he can fully take up his position within the symbolic, that language, however sophisticatedly he tries to use it, cannot catapult him into an adult relation with his parents, cannot make him one of us. As Kristeva writes:

> In being able to receive the other's words, to assimilate, repeat, and reproduce them, I become like him: One. A subject of enunciation. Through psychic osmosis/identification. Through love.
>
> (Kristeva 1987a: 26)

86

Freud's story about stammering is full of anal-sadistic impulses, writing to Ferenczi that 'stutterers . . . have projected shitting onto speaking' (Freud 1915: 91–92), rendering their speech dominated by anal-sadistic conflicts. Fenichel also understood stuttering as an expression of intense ambivalence; simultaneously wanting to speak and not speak, reflecting an unconscious conflict over expelling or retaining faeces (Fenichel 1931: 170, quoted in Plänkers 1999). Glauber, who has written extensively on stammering, homes in on the symbiosis with the mother, seeing stammering as an expression of a traumatic experience of separation conflict (Glauber 1968: 97). He surmises a highly ambivalent mother, who stutters in her attentiveness, giving rise to a traumatic infantile experience of object loss.

Plänkers (1999) draws together the psychoanalytic literature on 'psychic withdrawal' and its link with the fantasy of the mother's anal claustrum because of the common association between stammering and intense withdrawal from object relationships. He arrives where we were previously, at the work of Spitz and Anzieu on the role of very early acoustic and olfactory experiences at the origins of our intellectual capacities. Anzieu, in describing words as a symbolic skin, establishes a new conception of speech disorders as disorders of this fundamental symbolic envelope, the sound envelope, which is the first psychic space, corresponding to the form of the mouth in which 'rustles, echoes and resonances orbit' (Anzieu 1989: 224). Not only would shitting be projected onto speaking, but also

in the stutterer the mouth as the space of the sound envelope is projectively identified with an anal claustrum in which there is both a violent attack on the musical sound envelope and also, on the other hand, a phobic fear that every object caught in the analized envelope will disintegrate.

(Plänkers 1999: 243)

The speech therapist makes a series of videos of myself and my husband playing with Joel. His speech is not mentioned. We are the focus of the therapy. We watch, frame by frame, stopping to speak about what we see: the micro-dynamics of playtime. Like Douglas Gordon's breakdown of a Hitchcock movie, what we see, frozen and captured in each frame, is horrifying. There we are, always a step ahead, there, interrupting him. In the minutest of ways; a gesture, a small movement of the hand towards the puzzle piece that he hasn't yet noticed, our fingers dextrously slotting the Lego® together while he fumbles next to us, giving up, waiting instead to play with the tower we have made. A drama of interruption. Joel is stammer-free within a few months of therapy.

I want to return to the suspended moment produced by the stammering child, the suspended present tense created by his endless beginnings. What does this prompt in the one who listens? Frosh has suggested a kind of compassionate waiting, as well as a powerful aggression which can be evidenced, not only in deliberate teasing, but the accidental mimicking that can leak out from even the most sensitive listener (Stephen Frosh, personal communication, 2003). I suggest that in this compassionate waiting, a stop is created in the interruption that the child is for the mother; that the stammer itself stages for the mother something that allows her to grasp hold of the tail of her own experience of interruption. The stammer, produced out of interruption, and given back as an elongated interruption, paradoxically creates reflective space. In being with my stammering child, I am compelled to stop, wait, anticipate but not foreclose the child's meaning-making. The demand that the stammer makes to stay in the present tense, in the suspended non-time of interruption, allows the child to momentarily return to a state of primary narcissism and the mother to pause for thought.

As Clément (1994) says of Lacan's re-punctuation of Descartes' '"I think, therefore I am", forming "I think: 'therefore I am'"' (I am the one who thinks: "therefore I am")': 'From that moment on, "I" am nothing but a syncope, a fault line between thinking and being, a subject that is suspended, "shifted," fainting' (Clement 1994: 126). Perhaps, in the moment the mother waits for her stammering child to speak, this is what she experiences, with shock and surprise.

Coda

In her bitter poem 'Thoughts about the person from Porlock' (Smith 1975: 385), Stevie Smith chides Coleridge for blaming the Person from Porlock for interrupting him, and so stopping him from finishing *Kubla Khan*. Coleridge's story is that he fell asleep while he was staying at a farmhouse near Porlock in 1797. He had taken opium as he was reading about Kubla Khan's palace, and in his opium dream imagined an epic poem of perhaps 200 or 300 lines. When he woke, he began writing, seeing the whole piece in his mind, but he was 'called out by a person on business from Porlock, and detained by him above an hour' (Coleridge 1816). That, he claims, made him forget the rest of the dream, which is why *Kubla Khan* remains unfinished. Hearing in Coleridge's story a lame protestation, Stevie Smith sardonically surmises that Coleridge was already stuck, in fact longing for interruption, the blame for which he conveniently dumps on this unsuspecting stranger. This person, like the paternal function or third term, steps in, interrupts the enmeshed relationship between Coleridge and his text, breaks up the suffocating dyad and offers Coleridge a way out. Named only by reference to the place he is from, the Person from Porlock is also the classic figure of the stranger. Smith, always with an eye for the ordinariness of existence, domesticates him, gives him a history ('His grandmother was a Warlock'), as well as a cat named Flo. But she too longs for her own Person from Porlock.

In Smith's rendition, Porlock comes to signify death, an end to interminable thinking, a benevolent other who will come to put one out of one's misery, so that there will be nothing left to stay for, no reason to keep dwelling in one's own thoughts. The death drive is projected onto this unsuspecting Person, expelled from the self, so as to turn back on the self to relieve it of its burdensome consciousness. If only the Person from Porlock would come, one could be relieved of one's being. Porlock, as a literary term, has come to signify not only an interruption, but also an evasion, an excuse not to engage in creative work, and more particularly, not to live.

But a longing for interruption is also a longing for love. To long to be interrupted by the other is to be open to an encounter that goes beyond the borders of one's ego in the hope that the loved one will break up this narcissistic relation to the self. The romantic tradition figures love as a disease, a cantankerous tumour, making us sick, disturbing our thoughts from within, driving us crazy. The loved object gets into us, causing us to faint and swoon. But the other great strand of Western love is courtly love, born out of that unbridgeable gap between an inaccessible lady and a troubadour, a passionate encounter paradoxically created by the injunction on touch or sexual union. What the lady and her lover exchange are words. Lacan, Clément notes, picked up on this when he said that 'to speak of love is in itself a jouissance' (Lacan 1972–1973, quoted in Clément 1994: 188). The chatter is the essential component of courtly love. As Kristeva puts it simply, 'love is something spoken, and it is only that' (Kristeva 1987a: 277).

Not everyone longs for a child. Before the revolution brought about by the Pill, the longing not to have a child may have been far more present in the minds of millions of women. Structured as it is, by formidable, and yet constantly shifting economic, cultural and historical forces, the longing for a child that many women report feeling may be experienced at a level of personal history in a myriad of overlapping ways – as a longing for something to love, or for unconditional love in return, for an anchoring in the world, for something to give meaning to our lives, for that which is simultaneously same and other, for what goes beyond us, for companionship, for something to make up for a founding lack, to name a few. And perhaps we also long for a child purely as a longing for interruption, for something that will break up our egoistic relation with ourselves, open out our thinking, allow us a moment's respite from a consciousness and subjectivity that is experienced as burdensome. In this sense the child, like the Person from Porlock, and following Levinas, is figured as fundamentally outside our consciousness, a figure for a particular kind of alterity, that which comes to interrupt us, to call us into a new relation with ourselves.

MATERNAL LOVE

On mother love and unexpected weeping

I can think of countless instances of my own maternal tears. I admit, I am a crier. I tear easily. The tears that most readily come to mind are those occasioned by physical hurt. Joel, aged 1, unstable yet exacting, dropped a metal wastepaper basket on my face while I was sleeping. It felt like my nose was splintering, bringing hot angry tears of disbelief that I didn't bother to hide. I wanted to show him that I, his mother, hurt just like anyone else. On another occasion, Saul shot me with his brother's submachine gun, the orange-tipped plastic dart grazing my cheek, drawing blood. The ludicrousness of the toy gun drawing real blood should have made us laugh, but it hurt, and in a moment of self-righteousness I sobbed out loud. My body still tenses in response to the memory of being trodden on in bed in the morning, a bicycle crashing into my shin in the park, being kicked in the face while holding a screaming, flailing toddler, being kicked in anger, spite and grievance by a long-past toddler, a particular hollow pain as the solid head of a small child on my lap suddenly collides with my chin, embedding teeth in tongue. When I cry because they've hurt me, I am aghast at the pain. No one does that to me any more! I am thrust back into the rawness of the childhood playground, when things really did hurt, sting, burn, ache and itch, when one's skin was alive with pain. I am infantilized by my children, and I cry from the intense feeling of injustice that this brings on. This is one order of maternal tears, akin to a kind of animalistic howl.

Saul and I pulled a wish-bone. He won. He wished. He then elected to tell me his wish on the grounds that there was no point in keeping the wish secret as he already knew it wouldn't come true. He wished that he didn't have such an angry mum. He wished he had me as his mum, but less angry. He wished that when I said I would try not to get so angry, I would, for once, really mean it. He knew his wish wouldn't come true. I received his wish as if it were a literal blow, and I went to cry alone in the bathroom, hiding my tears, trying to 'get a grip' on myself. When a child's truthfulness is cruel beyond belief, their need to abject me reverberates in me with such force, that despite my internal protests, despite years of schooled resistance to such abjection, it causes me temporarily to embody this state. I cry from a place of profound self-loathing, knowing dimly that perhaps there is no getting away from the abject that clings to motherhood, that being a mother means being prepared to be hated.

And of course there are bleaker moments too. Times when I feel I am very close to hurting them, or when I do hurt them, when I cannot help retaliating. Then there are tears of guilt, horror, pain. I cry because I am sorry, and I wish it were otherwise.

This chapter is concerned with crying, loving and thinking. More precisely, it represents an attempt to articulate maternal love through a particular instance of thinking shown up by an occasion of maternal tears. By maternal love I want to keep my focus on the love that mothers feel for their children, rather than the very real necessities, uses and experiences a child may have of maternal love. I want to try to articulate how maternal love, far from being either a flood of warm, affectionate feeling, or simply a function of speech, is that which remains radically indeterminate, emerging in the most unlikely locations, at times when we least expect it, and occasionally at moments when our children make us cry. Beyond the myriad of reasons a mother may shed tears, I try to home in on an experience of being caught out by one's tears, of crying with no idea why; an occasion that appears at odds with the taxonomy of maternal tears I've charted above. An indeterminate 'tearing' (both in the sense of rip and salty drip) reveals yet another shudder in maternal experience, one that I want to link to the possibility of glimpsing the real of maternal love.

One obvious starting point is Kristeva's notion of *herethics* that emerges from her reading of maternity as a privileged model for the subject-in-process/on-trial, straddling the cleft between semiotic and symbolic. *Herethics* is certainly an important articulation of maternal love:

> For an heretical ethics separated from morality, an *herethics*, is perhaps no more than that which in life makes bonds, thoughts, and therefore the thought of death, bearable: herethics is undeath [*a-mort*], love.
>
> (Kristeva 1977: 263, original emphases)

However, in this chapter I want to read Kristeva against Alain Badiou's work on love as it provides a quite different articulation of the disruption I want to examine, glimpsed in moments of maternal tearing. For Badiou, love is understood as the 'interminable fidelity' to the paradox that there are two positions of experience, but, as he puts it, 'only one humanity' (Badiou 2000: 268). Though Badiou's essay on love is an exposition of sexual difference, I (rather brutally) appropriate his 'two' (man and woman) for my own purposes, substituting 'mother' and 'child', following a small opening in his work that allows an imaginative engagement with different forms of what he describes as the 'disjunction' between two (Badiou 2000: 272). Through paying close attention to Badiou's notion of truth, I think we can tentatively construct a description of maternal love that does not point us back towards the impasses of essentialism, nor force us to adopt a melancholic Lacanian position in which the desiring mother, finally finding in the child that elusive phallus, must ultimately resign herself to coming to terms with her loss for the second time, in order to free her child from her own clutches.

Given the above, my concerns here are also with arithmetic. As I understand it, psychoanalysis counts at least one, two, three.[1] Three is the figure for the Oedipal moment of desire. Two is the figure for the dyad, for love, which appears first through primary narcissism and identification, and one is either the autoerotic infant or the fantasy of wholeness through union or merger with the mother. As we shall see, for Badiou, One can only emerge retroactively after what he terms 'an event', which in a loving situation is the disjunction that is Two. It is by viewing the world from the point of view of there being Two that the One is constituted as singular; it is counted. This view of the world, in which One comes to count through the disjunction that is Two, Badiou calls love, and to be truthful to the event of love, is to be a subject of love. Love can therefore only be thought of in reference to the non-existence of a third. Like the rhythm of syncope, Badiou's sequence misses a beat. He counts 'One, Two, infinity' (Badiou 2000: 272). My aim here is to think about maternal subjectivity as the attainment of a transitory subjectivity achieved through attending to the truth of this disjunction, albeit for discrete and perhaps brief periods of time. In my reworking of Badiou, the disjunction that constitutes love is understood as giving rise to both a mother and child's singularity, and as a consequence, the mother can temporarily attain subjectivity without this being understood purely through the figures of lack or loss.

Mother love

Why love a child? Simone de Beauvoir writes about mother love as a compensation for what a woman cannot get from men:

> The mother finds in her infant – as does the lover in his beloved – a carnal plenitude, and this not in surrender but in domination; she obtains in her child what man seeks in woman; an other, combining nature and mind, who is to be both prey and double.
>
> (de Beauvoir 1949: 527)

Here the child is an object for the mother to act on in frustration, and to pass on what has been done to her in patriarchy. Although de Beauvoir speaks of the mother finding 'an other' with whom she can identify, it is an other to dominate and control as she has been, a receptacle for projections of her own otherness. Mother love for de Beauvoir appears to be access to otherness but only to pass on the abuse. There are other familiar answers to this question too; mother love as biological instinct, as narcissistic cathexis, as the desire for/of the phallus, as an erotic masochistic pleasure, and of course a unique chance for self-abnegation and emotional work. Both essentialism and normativity loom large when the argument veers towards maternal love, and our need to maintain a fantasy of maternal love as a 'given' suffuses a huge variety of psychological discourses that have had a profound influence in the British context in establishing norms in relation to childrearing and ideals of mothering.[2] One of the most dominant discourses that circulates is that mother-as-loving-environment is vital for the healthy development of children. Attachment theory especially has long counselled that not only must 'someone' reliably be there, particularly in the early months and years of a child's life, but also the quality of the interaction between the primary carer and infant is what matters, giving rise to a particular formulation of 'sensitive parenting' that has been much critiqued by feminist researchers (Phoenix et al. 1991: 33). The current marriage between attachment theory and neuroscience is leading to the most recent incarnation of the same normative notion, now propped up by a variety of 'neuroscientific evidence' that sensitivity and a caring response to a baby's needs, now performed through the micro-management of cortisol levels in the baby's brain by the loving sensitivity of the mother, gives rise to healthy, well-adjusted children (Gerhardt 2004). Not only does a carer's love circulate as the essential ingredient for the psychological survival of a child, but also mothers are particularly implicated and continue to implicate themselves through their complex cross-identifications with that 'someone'. Jessica Benjamin writes that due to contemporary changing patterns in mothering, Western culture is in the grip of a sentimental idealization of motherhood, dominated by a fantasy mother who is an 'all-giving, self contained haven' (Benjamin 1990: 211). She argues that this is a dangerously powerful image with whom women are identifying, to the detriment of themselves. More recent articulations of this viewpoint have been put forward by Susan Douglas and Meredith Michaels (2004). The 'new momism' that they identify as emerging in contemporary US culture since the late 1970s imposes an impossible set of ideals that simultaneously appears to celebrate motherhood, while constantly placing this ideal mother further and further out of reach, raising her to unattainable standards of perfection, and in addition, singling out particular forms of deviant motherhood for denigration and derision. And women seem to keep rising to the challenge.

Yet to ask this question, 'Why love a child?' is to realign mother love as both choice and a relation to alterity. For although various formulations within psychoanalytic theory understand the desire for maternity as established in early childhood alongside the often precarious establishment of gendered identity (whether the eventual relations with a child are understood as a drive-motivated emotional, narcissistic investment, a compensatory fleshy involvement with the longed for phallus, or a desire to return to the phallic mother herself by finally becoming her), we do not *just* blindly configure ourselves around our internal ideals, and nor are we purely held in the sway of external representations of idealized motherhood. My focus so far has been to try to notice miniscule examples of the *failure* of the compulsion to repeat – our capacity, through the austerity of certain encounters with otherness, to do and experience something different. I hold with the notion that mothers do draw on their own internal relation to an idealized fantasy of union with a preoedipal mother in their love for their children. But as I have been arguing, the particular alterity that is the child also presents a mother with an enigma that throws her into a certain disarray, that disorganizes her internal world with the potential for new configurations of self and other to emerge. Parveen Adams (1996) writes about the potential for newness within a psychoanalytic frame in *The Emptiness of the Image*:

> I do believe that Freudian psychoanalysis has discovered the human psyche – the necessity of a relation to the phallus and the necessity of unconscious representations which articulate the space between drive and desire. The theoretical issue is this: could these unconscious representations be different? What relation could an unconscious representation have to reality? Does the unconscious simply borrow whatever is most appropriate and ready to hand, in which case the bits of reality which are appropriated in a representation are but possible and predictable materialisations of unconscious life? Or do aspects of reality press forward and make possible a change in the balance of unconscious life, in which case reality produces a possible but unpredictable materialisation of unconscious life?
>
> (Adams 1996: 30–31)

It is a similar question that I want to pose in relation to maternal love. Adams claims that psychoanalysis can theorize new phenomena (or at least unpredictable materializations of unconscious life which arise through contact with 'reality') without transforming itself into either sociology or psychology, in an attempt to work against the tendency for determinism in psychoanalytic theorizing, while holding on to its radical claims. This echoes Laplanche's view about the way that another kind of 'reality' presses forward, changing the balance of unconscious life. The task for contemporary psychoanalysis, as Laplanche sees it, is to understand how 'internal otherness', the alien-ness of the unconscious, is founded on 'external otherness' (Laplanche 1997: 654). Laplanche still presents us with a developmental theory. His account is of the mother's role in the development of the child's unconscious, but I think it has important implications for the mother, and perhaps can be reworked to think about the child's role in the development of maternal subjectivity.

According to Laplanche, the way that internal otherness was founded on external otherness was the 'hidden meaning of the theory of seduction, which has to be rediscovered and re-founded' (Laplanche 1997: 654). If Freud gave us the notion of the unconscious as a kind of internal alien-ness, it is the seduction theory that maintains the alien-ness of the unconscious: *das Andere* (the other-thing or the unconscious) is only guaranteed by the other person (*der Andere*), which for Laplanche can remain other through the workings of seduction. This constant 'going astray' of Freudian theory, in which psychoanalysis' own radical impulse is constantly returned to itself, and reassimilated, is part of an inherent tension within Freudian theory itself. As Laplanche sees it, his own rediscovery of the seduction theory is a classic part of putting psychoanalysis back on its Copernican trajectory, and moving it away from the relentless pull of the Ptolemaic vision that Freud himself succumbed to at a number of key points.

Seduction involves the transmission of a 'message' from the actual mother to the child. This is not exactly the same as a Lacanian view about language guaranteeing the alien-ness of the other. Laplanche holds out for a message that may be non-verbal. He is also interested in maintaining the individuality of the other rather than some transindividual structure such as Lacan's notion of the symbolic. So in Laplanche (1997: 661) we have what he calls an address, a message or an 'index' which makes a sign. The adult uses this 'index' to make a sign to the child, and the sign is both enigmatic, and sexual in its nature. So, for example, the breast transmits to the child a message, and the message is sexual because the breast is an erogenous zone for the mother. What she feels and experiences in breastfeeding (albeit at the level of fantasy) matters and is transmitted to the child. Laplanche's seduction is therefore not the concrete actual seduction that Masson (1988) has argued should be reinstated in order to understand psychopathology. It is the 'universal fact' of the intervention of the adult other, with his or her sexual unconscious that is the underpinning of a general theory of seduction that Laplanche wants to re-establish.

> There is not only the reality of the other 'in itself', for ever unattainable (the parents and their enjoyment) and, on the other hand, the other 'for me', existing only in my imagination; there is also – primordially – the other who addresses me, the other who 'wants' something of me.
>
> (Laplanche 1997: 660)

Furthermore, and crucially, the sexual and enigmatic message is also not transparent to the adult. It issues from the adult's unconscious sexual fantasies, and is set in motion by the adult's relation to the child. So here we have the child triggering the adult's unconscious sexual fantasies, which in turn trigger the child's unconscious sexual fantasies in an interplay between subject and other, both occupying such a position for each other. Here we see that the mother is maintained as an actual other person, a person with sexual fantasies, with thoughts and feelings about her child. She is not just a container, mirror or breast. Neither is she romanticized as part of a loving dyad or nursing couple. A transmission of something enigmatic and sexual takes place between mother and child prompted by the child's presence. In other words, the child calls something forth in the mother (the sucking experience affects the mother at physiological, psychological and unconscious fantasy levels) that in its turn is returned to the child in coded form. Both parties are actively involved, although neither really 'knows' what is going on. I think this usefully moves us closer to a description of maternal love that can include the unexpected, the enigmatic and unknowable, without reducing the mother to an object in the child's world, or romanticizing the union between them.

If this is the case, then the task may be to try to understand maternal love (as distinct from maternal desire) in terms of what emerges in direct response to what the child stirs up in us, rather than the mother's relations with a third term. In making this distinction between love and desire, between dyads and triads, we will again need to re-examine the role of the third. For as soon as the mother is thought about as loving, she appears to lose her precious status as a desirous, speaking subject with access to the symbolic. And yet, as soon as she is configured as desirous, we seem to lose hold of our ability to articulate maternal love as something stemming from the child (the element that Laplanche's theory holds on to), rather than a manifestation of either narcissism or love for our own idealized mothers.

Love/desire

Maternal love is often conflated with maternal desire.[3] However, maternal desire in psychoanalysis is usually understood as the mother's relationship with a third term (be it actual or fantasized) articulated as the mother's desire for the phallus (as in Lacan), for her own mother (as in Kristeva) or other symbolic relations which take the mother away from the baby (as in Benjamin) and effectively break up the dyad. We can see an entanglement of love and desire running through Lacanian theory, despite attempts to keep them separate. In some senses Lacan appears to omit love altogether, in preference for desire. Although Lacan claims that in analytic discourse we only speak of love (Lacan 1972–1973), this is a product of the transference, and as such is proof of the artificial, or at least imaginary nature of love (Evans 1996: 103). We love in order to be loved, in a deeply narcissistic way. Love belongs in the imaginary and is the expression of the fantasy of fullness or union with the loved one. Lacan's 'maternal phallus' is an image of completion that the child desires (Margaroni 2004: 41), whereas the 'paternal phallus' is the signifier of lack or loss of this fantasized fullness, that the child accepts at the dissolution of Oedipus. Love therefore covers over lack that gives rise to desire that marks our entry into the symbolic. However, although areas of Lacan's work indicate the way love and desire are diametrically opposed, there are instances in which the opposition between the two is not so clear (Evans 1996). For instance, it is central to a Lacanian understanding of both love and desire that neither can actually be satisfied. The wish to be loved that is at the core of love is also similar to the structure of desire, in which one desires to become the object of the Other's desire, and both are seen as a feature of the barred subject, a function, that is, of the necessity of speaking. Given that desire is born out of the remainder between need and demand, and demand is always ulti- mately a demand for love, desire is the element of demand that cannot be satisfied, which we may then term love (Evans 1996: 104). So, although Lacan wants to keep the two notions separate, love has a way of suffusing desire when we least want it to.

In thinking particularly then about a mother's desire for a child from a Lacanian perspective, we would have to start from Lacan's premise in his early work that woman is always and only man's other. Her structural position is that she desires to have the phallus, that privileged signifier of the symbolic, which she lacks. Although neither structural position, man or woman, can ultimately have the phallus, she is the subject for whom this is, by definition, an impossibility, and the most she can do is pretend to be the phallus, the object of man's desire and gratification. She cannot have gratification of her own. Hers is a masochistic jouissance, attained through gratifying another. The kind of love a woman then feels for a child is thought about, in Lacanian terms, as the same masochistic jouissance. In other words, there is only maternal desire. In this reading, women desire to have children so they can continue to gain masochistic pleasure from being the object of another's desire. The child is the symbolic substitute for the missing phallus that does not really satisfy her desire, despite having the child (Evans 1996: 118). There is therefore no articulation of the specific loving feelings a mother has towards a child in Lacan; only an articulation of her desire.

Freud did make a distinction between love and desire. He saw all paren- tal love as deeply narcissistic. Parental love becomes a socially sanctioned form of narcissism, without the requirement to move to full object-love. Desire for a child in women, on the other hand, is his well-known formu- lation of the desire for a substitute to make up for the longed-for penis. So we can see that a Freudian/Lacanian trajectory broadly understands love as love for the self, and desire as desire for the phallus.

Drawing on this tradition, Kristeva posits a 'good' loving mother as a desiring mother, as the third term is necessary to rescue the child from a dangerous entanglement with the loving mother who looks only to her child. Kristeva famously warns:

> The loving mother, different from the caring and clinging mother, is someone who has an object of desire; beyond that, she has an Other with relation to whom the child will serve as go-between. She will love her child with respect to that Other, and it is through a discourse aimed at that Third Party that the child will be set up as 'loved' for the other.
>
> (Kristeva 1987b: 34)

The loving mother must 'love' an other in order that the child can feel loved and can go on to love in their own right. The aetiology of love is made possible only through desire. Although she is termed the 'loving' mother, it is her ability to be a 'desiring' mother, desiring of a third party and *not* the child that is the factor that saves the child from being devoured by the clinging and caring mother. To this degree, love is love to the extent that it occurs through desire. However, as I will discuss more fully below, although Kristeva is surely right in insisting that the mother must be understood as desirous in order that she retain access to symbolic functioning, this again leaves love in the realms of either narcissism or idealization. Maternal love therefore gets folded back on itself as either love for the self or love (ultimately) for one's own mother, thereby collapsing the crucial distance between mother and child, negating the child's alterity, and with it the specificity of maternal love for a child. Because desire is always chasing something unrecoverable that the other stands in for, both the child and maternal love in its specificity slips out of sight. My question still remains unanswered. Why love a child? Why stay alongside this ruthless, crying, tantruming, charming, loving, questioning, stammering, enigmatic, unpredictable other, when we could find plenty of other stand-ins for our narcissism and idealization?

I want to suggest that we try to think about maternal love 'otherwise' than a discourse of narcissism and idealization in order to account for the peculiar ethical commitment maternal love entails. My argument is that maternal love can provide a bridge back to the mother's self-experience but via her specific relationship with the child-as-other. Again, I am not looking for a general theory that could account for maternal love, but rather a kind of glimpse in the day-to-day lived experience of mothering that takes us by surprise. And again, I start from the premise that the child's alterity offers the mother something. But contrary to the notion that in love we try to attain 'wholeness' by closing the gap between self and other, which in itself is a hopeless attempt to close what some would describe as an inherent split on which subjectivity is founded, perhaps we can work this idea the other way round and think about how, in moments when a splitting of the self is experienced, something we may call love can emerge. When I cry because I am punctured by my child's otherness, I love you (other) because you (in your radical alterity) provide me with an experience that I can take back as my own; a momentary experience of myself as singular, emerging out of an experience that there are two distinct, and as we shall see, 'disjunct' positions of experience.

Kristeva's *herethics*

Kristeva's enormous contribution to psychoanalytic feminist thought, particularly aspects of her early work on love (Kristeva 1987b), her analysis of the function of the Virgin Mary through the figure of *Mater Dolorosa* and her elaboration of *herethics* (Kristeva 1977), as well as her more recent works on revolt (Kristeva 2000) and feminine genius (Kristeva 2001, 2002, 2004) all appear highly relevant to a discussion of the maternal. However, due to Kristeva's profound and lasting attachment to Freudian thought,[4] despite an extensive engagement with the Kleinian tradition in psychoanalysis, the distance between mother and child which is necessary for maternal love to be understood as something more than narcissism, is proffered at the moment it also folds in on itself. In part, this is Kristeva's point: maternity is one of her examples of a subject-in-process/on-trial who unravels at the point she attains subjectivity by dint of the alterity she contains within; an alterity which acts as a disruptive force, heterogeneous to the symbolic and calling the symbolic itself into question. My difficulty with aspects of Kristeva's work is in part to do with her reliance on the pregnant maternal body to understand alterity at the expense of an account of the alterity of the child 'without', which in my terms bypasses the mother as ethical subject at the very point when she appears to be substantiated. In addition, many feminist writers have articulated their dismay at the way love, as opposed to desire, is understood to emerge through the not-yet-subject's identification with the 'Imaginary Father', Kristeva's term for Freud's 'father in individual prehistory' (Kristeva 1987b: 26), itself understood, as Kelly Oliver has articulated it, as an identification with maternal love. This again situates the emergence of the capacity to love as premised on maternal desire, leaving a void in articulating love in relation to an experience of the child that changes a mother's capacities to love.

Kelly Oliver has persuasively established that Kristeva's overall project is essentially an ethical one (Oliver 1993b). As a psychoanalyst, feminist and mother (as someone, in other words, who exists, or deliberately positions herself at the border, margin or outer limit of the symbolic) Kristeva has a particular view of ethics that moves us away from stable autonomous subjects in relation to stable autonomous objects and their obligations to one another, and towards what she terms a 'subject-in-process/on-trial' (Kristeva 1975: 103), in formation through various practices or discourses that break down identity. Practices that break down identity are in their very nature ethical because they force a reconsideration of the relations between self and other that can allow for difference, rather than being premised on recognition of sameness. Kristeva's privileged practices are poetry, psychoanalysis and maternity, all of which allow the possibility for the multiplicity of the drive to emerge. They bear testimony to the fundamental otherness within, to what Kristeva develops as her notion of 'negativity' (Kristeva 1974: 70), in relation to which a subject-in-process can take shape. Negativity, as distinct from nothingness or negation is both 'the cause and organizing principle of the process' (Kristeva 1974: 70). By *reactivating* process through constantly dissolving it, negativity paradoxically affirms rather than negates. The subject-in-process/on-trial, through a relation to negativity understood as affirmative, creates a new concept of ethics; one that engenders ethics at the point that it engenders the process that gives rise to subjectivity.

The practices Kristeva is concerned with are seen as both the acceptance of the symbolic law and the transgression of this law, a way to shake it up, disturb it and allow the possibility of reconfiguring it. In her famous early essay, *Women's Time* (Kristeva 1981) she argues that feminism as a practice should be engaged in the same process rather than simply repudiating the law altogether, and to some degree her recent return to Oedipus is a reappraisal of the generative aspects of grappling with paternal law (Kristeva 2000). Kristeva's privileged practices (psychoanalysis, poetic language and maternity) deal with the subject's constant battle with symbolic collapse, with the failure of Oedipus' revolt, by releasing the drives into the symbolic, but *without* threatening its collapse. Her argument is that we must have access to heterogeneity, otherwise the symbolic becomes stagnant and there is no possibility for change or in fact for signification, but conversely, overwhelming heterogeneity breaks up the symbolic, and leaves us only with psychosis or borderline states. Kristeva's reading, for example of Freud's paper, *Negation* (Freud 1925), is that complete repression of the erotic drives would stop symbolic function altogether, just as Lacan has asserted that repression is about a 'discordance' between signified and signifier causing the repressed to slip in 'between the lines' (Kristeva 1974: 87). Kristeva's subject-in-process is a way to conceive of the drive transgressing the Law but not destroying it, to conceive of the subject slipping in between the lines. For Kristeva, this is an ethical concern:

> because it assumes that we recognize, on the one hand, the unity of the subject who submits to a law – the law of communication,

among others; yet who, on the other hand, does not entirely submit, cannot entirely submit, does not want to submit entirely.

(Kristeva 1986: 8, quoted in Oliver 1993a: 16)

This subject-in-process, through its relation to the drive (which I understand to be the same as her figure for both negativity and alterity, the part that does not want to submit), then calls for a new concept of ethics that would understand the ethical as the possibility for relations between self and other that can allow for the disruptive involvement of the drive. So, what Kristeva proposes is that the site of the ethical *is* the subject-in-process/on-trial because, by definition, this subject brings with it a disruptive force which calls the symbolic into question, and with it, our relations with others. As I understand it, Kristeva's position is that to be a subject-in-process is to be an ethical subject, but with the understanding that 'ethical' here describes an ethics that emerges out of practice, out of a temporary and provisional relation between subject and other that is constantly being reconfigured. Kristeva writes that the ethical cannot be stated, but only practised to the point of loss (Kristeva 1974).

However, the ethical as a practice to the point of loss is precisely the difficulty in Kristeva's conception of the subject-in-process. Her notion of the ethical rests on reading 'negativity' as 'alterity'. Negativity is what I am not, the process of self-dissolution, which I also carry within me, and that allows 'me' to emerge. But, what I am not is surely not synonymous with the other. The other is not purely a site for what I am not, but for the possibility of what something or someone else is. In other words, negativity and alterity are not the same, and therefore an ethics based on negativity does not necessarily help us rethink our relations with others. I think this is at the core of the difficulties with Kristeva's notion of alterity, and therefore with her ethics. We see this most clearly with her treatment of the maternal.

Motherhood according to Julia Kristeva

Maternity is Kristeva's subject-in-process/on-trial par excellence. For Kristeva, maternity exists at the border between the social and the biological regeneration of the species:

Let us call 'maternal' the ambivalent principle that is bound to the species, on the one hand, and on the other stems from an identity catastrophe that causes the Name to topple over into the unnameable that one imagines as femininity, non-language or body.

(Kristeva 1977: 161–162)

The ambivalent principle that maternity embodies concerns the borders of the social contract, and what we imagine occurs at the edges of the symbolic where we are confronted with the limits of language; where language gives way to the body, biology, non-language and the regeneration of the species. The maternal body, in Kristeva's essay *Motherhood According to Giovanni Bellini* (Kristeva 1975), by its very 'nature' both problematizes the symbolic and through allowing an identification with the fantasy of the phallic mother, maternity is what allows the symbolic to exist: 'She warrants that *everything is*, and that it is representable' (Kristeva 1975: 302, original emphases), given that she too is 'under the sway of the paternal function (as symbolizing, speaking subject and like all others)' (1975: 302). The mother is 'phallic' to the extent that her desire for the phallus is the only way, Kristeva believes, that we can imagine within the symbolic that 'the speaker is capable of reaching the Mother, and thus, of unsettling its own limits' (1975: 305). She is the way in which we represent to ourselves the nature/culture threshold, the limits to language, the point at which biology is instilled into 'the very body of a symbolizing subject' (1975: 305).

Kristeva therefore draws heavily on natality and the maternal body for her formulation of maternity. She describes the maternal body as the place of a splitting that remains a constant factor of social reality. The maternal body is related to as a kind of 'filter', a 'thoroughfare, a threshold where "nature" confronts "culture"' (Kristeva 1975: 302). If no one was in that filter, she writes, then we would be born out of a void. This must be defended against in fantasy, as it presents a permanent threat to the stability of the subject, so the fantasy of the 'phallic' mother, the 'someone' at the threshold is maintained in order to ward off such a threat. It is the maintenance of this fantasy that the maternal body allows.

And yet, for Kristeva, there can therefore be no unified maternal Subject. In maternity, no one is really 'present', as such, to signify what is going on: 'It happens, but I'm not there' (Kristeva 1975: 301). Maternal identity is therefore always under threat, divided, in process. We can neither say she is there, 'master of a process that is prior to the social-symbolic-linguistic contract of the group' (1975: 302), nor that she is not there, for *someone* must exist 'throughout the process of cells, molecules, and atoms accumulating, dividing, and multiplying' (1975: 302). Neither subject nor object, the maternal body is the *materialization* of the split subject, the subject that is both same and other. Given the maternal body problematizes and disturbs the very notions of identities and difference in a similar way to poetry and psychoanalysis, it gives rise, once again, to a new ethics. This Kristeva describes as *herethics*; heretical, feminine and ethical (Kristeva 1977: 185). Again, it is an ethics that challenges the autonomous subject, as it is founded on the indeterminacy of subject and object in pregnancy.

As we have seen, in *herethics*, the divided mother, straddling both culture and biology, sets up her obligations to the other as both obligations to the self, and obligations not just to the child, but also to the *species* (Oliver

1998: 73). In some ways, this is the true alterity of Kristeva's maternal subject. The love for a child is love for the self, but also a willingness to *give oneself up* (Oliver 1998: 73). The mother, in other words, knows that there is something that fundamentally goes beyond herself (something Kristeva terms as 'natural'), but that this alterity is not to be found in the Other of the symbolic, but within herself. The mother sets up these obligations through what Kristeva calls 'love' rather than the Law (Kristeva 1987b). In Kristeva's understanding, the mother's love for her child is a love for herself (a necessary form of narcissism) and a love for the mother's own mother (a resurfacing of primary identification with the Imaginary Father) (Kristeva 1987b: 26). The new kind of love that the mother creates in *herethics* does not require a third term. It is essentially a self-love through identification with the mother's own mother's love. Identification in the sense of *Einfühlung* (the assimilation of other people's feelings) requires no third term (Kristeva 1987b: 24). If there is no third term, the mother's love is outside the law. In Oliver's reading it is 'outlaw love' (Oliver 1998: 73), again underlining the maternal position at the edge of the symbolic.

This point is complex, and we need to look more closely at Kristeva's notion of the 'Imaginary Father' to understand how three becomes two. The sequence seems to go like this. In *Freud and Love: Treatment and its discontents* (Kristeva 1987b), Kristeva rejects the classical Freudian/ Lacanian position where the infant moves into the symbolic at the Oedipal stage, under the threat of castration, experiencing separation from the maternal body as a primordial loss that can only partially be made up for with the consolation of words. Instead, she sees separation beginning prior to Oedipus, prior even to the mirror stage; this separation is not just painful but also delightful, playful, even pleasurable:

> Within sight of that Third Party I elaborate the narcissistic parry that allows me to block up that emptiness, to calm it and turn it into a producer of signs, representations, and meanings, I elaborate it within sight of the Third Party. I seduce this 'father of individual prehistory' . . . . He or I – who is the agent? Or even, is it he or is it she? The immanence of its transcendence, as well as the instability of our borders before the setting of my image as 'my own,' turn the murky source from which narcissism will flow into a dynamics of confusion and delight. Secrets of our loves.
>
> (Kristeva 1987b: 43)

The father of individual prehistory supports a separation from the maternal body, maintaining the initial gap or emptiness that is necessary for signification through love.

In addition, patterns for the separation that is required by language are set up in the infant's body through birth itself, and then through bodily processes that are regulated and overseen by the law of the maternal body. The infant takes in food, for example, which is metabolized and then expelled from the body, setting up a structure of separation that prepares us for language use. So, for example, the expulsion of faeces, both painful and pleasurable, is overseen by maternal law; and through a kind of originary 'reduplication' (Kristeva 1987b: 25), a prototype of identification with this pattern, the scene is set for language.

So Kristeva's argument is that the logic of separation is already operating in the body, and, in part, it is pleasurable. To get to language the infant must abject the maternal body to save itself from identifying with this abject. It must separate, but it can do so without losing the mother completely through identification with what she calls the imaginary father. There is therefore a kind of triangle prior to Oedipus between mother, child and the imaginary father. This originary triangulation stops the subject-to-be from falling into a primary identification with the mother from which it cannot disentangle itself. A third is necessary before Oedipus to save the subject-to-be from being devoured or abjected by the mother.

Kelly Oliver offers a powerful reading of Kristeva's imaginary father *as maternal love itself* (Oliver 1998: 66). Her argument is that it is clear that Kristeva's 'father' is not really a father at all. In fact, Kristeva refers to such a 'father' as a 'father-mother conglomerate' and we have seen that in the quote above she questions her own use of 'he' in reference to such a 'father'. The point Oliver makes is that the 'father' in fact represents a loving couple in the infant's mind, and it is the love that holds the father-mother conglomerate together that the infant identifies with, allowing it to feel loved, even while separating from the mother:

> In my reading, the mother's love enacts the transference from the mother's body to the mother's desire and provides the needed support for the transference to the site of maternal desire.
> (Oliver 1998: 66)

Oliver shows how Kristeva interprets Freud's fantasy of a 'prehistory' as in fact a fantasy of the maternal semiotic. Kristeva's readjustment of Freud is to show that the law of the mother, right from birth, is *already susceptible to meaning*, but still within the realm of the imaginary. The mother is always therefore somewhere between the archaic and the symbolic, a kind of imaginary mother. It is this imaginary mother that Oliver believes Kristeva calls an 'imaginary father', unable quite to sever the link between fathers and symbolization. Because Kristeva believes that archaic 'object' relations are already 'symbolic' then the infant's initial identifications are still with the gap between the mother and her desire, prefiguring the Oedipal moment, but in the imaginary, *this gap is maternal love*. The mother does love the child through the third, but the third turns out to be the mother's love itself, rather than her desire. So we move from three to two. In Kristeva's words, love is

> not a narcissistic merger with the maternal container but the emergence of a metaphorical object – in other words the very splitting that establishes the psyche and, let us call this splitting 'primal repression' bends the drive toward the symbolic of an other.
>
> (Kristeva 1987b: 31)

I find it very difficult to hold on to the mother's experience of maternal love (her love for her child) through this complex discussion of the use of maternal love for the developing child. As we have seen, the child can only separate, abject the mother, through a transference to the imaginary father, protecting a primary 'emptiness' or gap that sets the stage both for representation and for love. This transference is, according to Oliver, a transference to maternal love itself. Rather than primary identification being understood as with the maternal body, it is reinterpreted as an identification with maternal love. The mother's love again has a primary function for the child. It engenders both love and speaking. When Kristeva does talk of the actual mother's love, it is in terms of her love for the child's father, which is really her love for her own mother. When a woman becomes a mother, she identifies with her own mother's love as a form of self-love (she herself is now a mother). But Kristeva's loving mother still remains trapped in the twin elements of narcissism and idealization that make up Kristeva's notion of love. Despite love being organized differently in shifting historical spaces, and despite different amorous forms (mother love presumably being one of them) Kristeva maintains there are some essential points that last in every time and in every space:

> What is universal in the love situation is, on the one hand, for me, the narcissistic investment which is a necessity for the living being to last, to stay alive, to preserve itself. And on the other hand the idealization. The possibility for this living being to project himself through an ideal instance and to identify with it. This can be found in different kinds of friendship, sympathy, love, homosexual, erotic – differently orchestrated. The emphasis may be put in this situation more on violence, or more on narcissism, or more on idealization, or more on the erotic, and so on. But the two components: narcissism and idealization will last, will endure.
>
> (Kristeva 1984: 337)

It is difficult to see how Kristeva can maintain alterity or otherness at all, if all love is either self-love or identification with the ideal other. You are really me. Otherness appears to sustain its alterity only when it is contained within the pregnant mother's body. Once out, the other seems to be no longer other, but an instance of self and one's own mother. Again, the mother seems to have no experience of otherness as there is no 'emptiness' out of which love can evolve.

During an interview in which Kristeva was asked if loving oneself through another, as in *herethics*, was a form of *agape* or of eros, Kristeva replied:

> The difference between the two is that Eros is a sort of ascendant movement, it tries to achieve something that is placed above, it tries to go beyond the possibilities of the person he loves; it aspires to power and it's compared to an erection in an organic sense of the word. Agape is something else, it's a sort of gift, it comes to you from outside, you don't need to merit it, it's a sort of profusion, it's the love of parents for their children, for instance, when it happens which is not very often.
>
> (Kristeva 1984: 342)

So here is the mother's love, understood as a gift; something proffered across a space between mother and child. The child can identify with this gift, feel like a gift, someone chosen and therefore capable of being loved. But how does the mother feel in this loving encounter with her child? If her child is only experienced as an instance of self-love or love for her mother, does the child not disappear, and with it, the mother's access to alterity?

Kristeva (1975) states that the birth of the child constitutes access for the mother to the Other. The mother experiences her being as being for an other, which is woman's only access to the Other, and therefore to love. Kristeva's argument is that the mother 'knows' better than to think of the Other as autonomous. This is what the symbolic needs to believe to maintain a gap between signifier and signified to produce signification. But the mother supposedly already knows that the phallus is a fake, and that the 'true other' is within her. As Oliver puts it, 'she realizes the other is the same' (Oliver 1998: 75), and that this game of keeping them separate is just that, a game to allow the symbolic to exist. But, supposedly, for the sake of her child, she plays the game, she pretends, and out of love she gives the child up. So, not only does she emerge from this account with all her traditional feminine attributes intact (secretive, complicit, duplicitous, while simultaneously guaranteeing everything), but also maternal love and maternal knowledge remain the given or bedrock that Kristeva has so diligently sought to show up as a masculine fantasy. It is not clear how this love for this particular other is maintained, if the mother knows that the other is the same. Neither do we understand its aetiology beyond a kind of knowledge or realization that supposedly comes to a mother during pregnancy and birth.

Maternal tears

Occasionally, very rarely, rather than making me cry, my children move me to tears. Once it happened when I was called out of bed for the umpteenth time, and when I got there, found that my child was already asleep. There he was asleep, and I burst into tears. It would be easy to write this off as a cry of exhaustion, frustration, impotence even. Perhaps I was furious that I wasn't needed after all. Mostly, it has to be admitted, I am so relieved when sleep takes hold of the children that I immediately turn away to get on with something else. But this occasion was more confused. I stumbled on my tears unexpectedly, caught by something left-of-field. It was as if I saw him for the first time, and then my eyes were full of tears. This time no sobs or snivels or hiccups or gulps or gasps. No howling, no crying out in pain. Nothing to show or hide. I can't say this 'being moved' constituted an emotional moment. If emotion has something to do with the perception of feeling, then I can't say I was aware of feeling anything in particular. Neither was I aware of any thoughts; of how beautiful he was, or vulnerable, or of how much I loved him. On the contrary, my mind was blank, conscious thought and emotion suspended. I stood and cried, and then went back to bed.

Tears have their own long and venerable cultural history. Tom Lutz (1999) charts a huge array of cultural meanings of crying, showing, for example how crying can come to signify contrition, grace, sorrow, joy, pleasure or moral worth. Tears have been both interpreted and performed as indicators of conditions as contradictory as truth, empathy, devotion, humiliation, frustration and manipulation. Tears, those pure salty drops, perhaps more than any other bodily secretion, seem to be able to stand in for almost anything.

There are clearly diverse cultural histories of tears that could be written. Lutz (1999) briefly teases out a history of women's tears, stretching from the forbidden tears of Antigone and the public lamentations of women in ancient Greece, through numerous saints, romantic heroines and femmes-fatales, to a present-day fast-changing flux in meaning of 'feminine' and 'masculine' tears. Presumably similar histories could be traced of men's tears and of children's tears, of religious tears, of sporting tears, of comedy tears, of the performance of tears, to name a few. Though Lutz does not chart a particular history of maternal tears, he does pay some attention to the place of the Virgin Mary's tears in the Western cultural imagination. He notes that there are usually two groups of women in Renaissance paintings depicting Mary grieving at the feet of Christ. One group looks up at the dying Christ with a look of extreme anguish, while the other turns away and weeps. Maternal tears appear to allow the weeper to withdraw from the cause of her anguish towards an inner world of bodily sensation. They signal a marking off of the weeper from the group of mourners, as if they can function to create a private, or even sacred space for mourning (Lutz 1999: 23). This image of the intense but private space of maternal tears is in keeping with a number of other images of the unending grief of the mother who has lost her children: Niobe, whom Zeus turns into stone to put her out of her misery after her seven sons and seven daughters are slaughtered, has apparently been weeping ever since; Aurora, the Roman goddess of the dawn, weeps every sunrise over the death of her son, which is supposedly how we get dewdrops (Lutz 1999: 287). The history of maternal tears, in other words, is a history of private, even sacred grief, ineffably linked, once again, to loss and an unending, inconsolable mourning. Perhaps we must sustain the fantasy that someone will weep for us when we have gone. The given of maternal love is culturally represented as the unending grief of the mother in mourning for her dead children. Maternal love and maternal tears are then welded together as one powerful cultural depiction of melancholia.

Despite the complexity of the meanings of tears, Lutz (1999) does make a claim for some common threads. He highlights the function of tears as a signal of desire; a wish or a plea. Given that our emotional life is neither straightforward nor singular, and that we are inevitability caught in a flux of mixed emotions and ambivalent desires, tears often seem to be bound up with moments of intense confusion. Contrary to the idealized figure of the weeping loving mother, tears are rarely simple, and often well up at precisely these moments of disarray. They are also a form of communication; a part of ourselves cries with one eye on an audience even when we are alone; an other who will witness, contain, and make sense of the tears. In addition, there is a long-held cultural elaboration of the way tears make us feel better. Tears are associated with cleansing, particularly cleansing us of the by-products of uncomfortable feelings. This is part of the common assumption that we will feel better after a good cry. There is an almost erotic pleasure in crying, captured beautifully in Henry James' startling description in *The Aspern Papers* that Lutz quotes, of a character who 'clearly had been crying, crying a great deal – simply, satisfyingly, refreshingly, with a primitive retarded sense of solitude and violence' (James 1888, quoted in Lutz 1999: 41). So, although the weeping loving mother is associated with unending loss, Lutz draws attention to the way tears are also bound up with confusion, mixed emotion and competing desires, a need to communicate such confusion, and an almost erotic satisfaction that crying can bring on.

To be with someone while they sleep is to be with them while they have gone elsewhere – while they have gone missing. After birth, when an infant first sleeps they have gone away on their own for the first time. Perhaps then it is not from the mother that they initially separate (she is, after all, often still there), but from the world. If subjectivity is founded on a separation, an 'emptiness' that must be protected and sustained in order

108

that the subject can come to love another, then perhaps this separation is not created by the mother's desire for another, but is first established through this coming and going, from the world, to another place and back again. In sleep the child's capacity for separateness is simply shown up in relief, and for a few moments it makes me weep. These tears are not an outpouring of loss or sorrow. This mother weeps in a confused moment, caught out by her tears, because of a sudden realization that the child already knows how to separate. She is effectively bypassed in this experience, but not in a way that negates her subjectivity. She is neither a lost object herself, nor a lacking subject, and she has not lost her child either. Through this peculiar experience of separation, through a child's example, if you like, something comes back, something that we can reclaim as an aspect of maternal subjectivity. I want to argue that in this instance, through her own distinctiveness returned to her, this mother experiences something we might call maternal love.

A tear is an intellectual thing

Holding in mind the over-determination of the tear at a cultural level, I want to explore further its over-determination at a psychological level. In *The Tear is an Intellectual Thing* (Neu 2000) Jerome Neu takes his title from a poem by William Blake which features tears of love and the power of tears to heal by dint of tears being an 'intellectual thing'. Neu takes up the notion that crying is a form of thinking and tries to unpick the fraught relationship between tears and emotions in psychological theory, since Darwin wrote *The Expression of the Emotions in Man and Animals* in 1872.

Much of the literature on crying starts with Darwin because of his extraordinary uncoupling of crying from psychological and emotional processes. Darwin provides a minute physiological description of crying, particularly in infants. When humans cry, the blood vessels of the eye become engorged and the surrounding muscles contract to protect the eye, something Darwin incorrectly speculated stimulates the lachrymal glands to secrete tears (Frey 1985). This is how Darwin accounted for our tendency to also shed tears when we cough or vomit violently, or become helpless with laughter. Darwin essentially separated out the experience of being relieved of suffering that comes from the total act of weeping, and the shedding of tears themselves. In this sense, tears are an insignificant accompaniment to emotional crying, an unnecessary by-product, caused by the contraction of the surrounding muscles. The production of tears has nothing really to do with emotional expression but with the physiology of the eye. There is something oddly shocking in this assertion. Everything else we secrete or excrete we do for a purpose. Milk, sweat, urine, faeces, menstrual blood and semen have physiological functions to which cultural meaning becomes attached. It is only 'emotional' tears that appear to be produced as meaningless by-products. To some extent this may explain the rich cultural associations that have become attached to emotional tears. However, given that the classic Darwinian stance is that nature hates unnecessary by-products, and tends to select them out, Darwin's account fails to tell us why emotional crying should persist if it is, as he claims, incidental and purposeless.

It is, after all the connection between emotion and crying that appears to be peculiarly human. Animals shed tears, but it remains difficult to assert that they cry because they are sad. It is this coupling and uncoupling of tears and emotions that we can trace through various theories of crying. Theories range from communication as its primary purpose (Treacher-Collins 1932), to the dissipation of aggressive energy (Löfgren 1966), to Frey's more recent work on the biochemistry of emotional tears (Frey 1985). The tears, however, all look alike, whether they are provoked by peeling an onion, or feelings of love, joy, sadness, laughter, loss or despair. To this extent, the tear is not only culturally, but psychologically over-determined. The difference, Neu (2000) suggests, is the thoughts that provoke them. He argues against the assumption that there is a one-to-one correlation of emotions with expressions, even basic emotions and natural expressions. He tries to hold on to the common experience of crying both when we are happy and when we are sad.

William James' (1884) account of the relation between emotion and its expression reverses assumptions between the 'truth' of an inner feeling, and its external manifestation. Rather than understanding crying to be a result of feeling sad, he states that our perception that we are sad is a result of crying, just as our perception that we are angry is a result of our attacking someone (James 1884). We go through the motions to bring on emotions. Emotion, understood as the perception of feeling, is fully grounded in felt sensation. As we saw with Appelbaum (1996), something stirs in the soma before it can be recognized by the psyche. Neu (2000) however argues that James cannot account for the fact that emotions can also exist independently of their bodily expression. We do at times feel sad without crying, happy without laughing, or angry without attacking. In addition, it is clear that crying can be provoked by a number of subtle, complex and nuanced feelings, and for James' account to work, there just aren't enough physiological states to go around.

If the thrust of Neu's argument is that what differentiates tears of sadness and tears of joy is not our bodily state, but the thoughts that provoke them, it stands to reason, he argues, that unconscious thoughts must play a role. When we find ourselves crying and don't know why, we may try to find the answer by thinking back over an event to see if something connects with something else that we may have been less aware of, but which the tears are more likely to be a response to. Sandor Feldman (1956) shows through a series of case studies how crying at a happy event is always a pretext for expressing tears of loss or sorrow. In each case that he details, thoughts of loss or sorrow are brought up by the happy ending, whether they are conscious or unconscious. In Feldman's view, we do not weep from joy. We only ever weep from loss or sorrow. In this sense, the tear is less over-determined than we think. Loss is always searching for something to attach to, a viable and respectable outlet for its energy. Neu notes that as Freud realized when he let go of his cathartic method, it is frustrated desire that we store, not frustrated emotion. And to take it one step further, if desire is a function of language, we cry, like we love, not just because we think, but because we speak.

Neu draws on Freud's (1910) paper, 'The Antithetical Meaning of Primal Words' to try to deal with the implications of Feldman's assertion that there are only tears of sorrow, which would undermine his position that there are tears of all sorts of things, depending on the thought that is provoking them. He notes how pervasive opposites are when it comes to the expression of emotion. For example, we cry from grief and laughter, or we make a similar facial expression for fear and surprise. Freud understood that many words in the oldest languages carry both double and opposed meanings, in the same way one element is represented by its opposite in the dream-work. Neu notes how ambivalence in the language of emotional expression may operate in a similar way to the oldest languages that use comparison as a way of producing meaning. Antithetical meaning is open to two inter-pretations. One is a simple reading of association, in which an experience or object brings up the thought of its opposite – high makes us think of low, etc. However, he believes Freud was getting at something far more radical by referring to a time when contraries themselves are undifferentiated, a point in the history of philology before concepts are sorted out, resulting in *the experience itself* being undifferentiated. To follow this speculation, high/ low is merely a continuum of experience, prior to its differentiation into opposites. In this sense high and low are equivalent:

> On this reading, all tears may be tears of sorrow, but not because there are no tears of joy or because on happy occasions there are associated sad thoughts, but because they come, ultimately, to the same thing. That we cry is a sign that we are moved, but that is an undifferentiated state, which we come (in time) to sort out in terms of associated situations and thoughts.
>
> (Neu 2000: 36)

So, here we are with the psyche and the soma again. Weeping is both one and the other, not purely one or purely the other. An indeterminate, an undifferentiated 'somewhere' between thinking and feeling. 'We come,' Neu writes, 'through multiplying thought and experience to be multiply moved to tears' (Neu 2000: 40).

Eventually he learns to report back, but mostly he decides not to. 'What did you dream Saul?' 'I can't remember'. I wonder if something of the uncanniness of this experience is held over when parents watch their children perform on stage for the first time. The school play works a curious magic. As if in the grip of a mass hysteria, the play begins and the adults begin to weep. It is linked with another feeling I get when I see something at the theatre that makes me urgently want to nudge the person next to me and say, 'Did you see that?' I want to shout out, 'Did you see that thing that just happened? It looked like nothing happened, but something very odd and emotional just happened, did you see that?' knowing that between us, we will have no way of ascertaining that we saw the same thing, or in fact anything at all. In the school play I also want to nudge someone, this time to say, 'Did you see my child? Those are his contours, his edges, his definition. I can only see him now because he is pointed elsewhere. Look, he is in the world. Do you see him too?' Being prohibited from doing this I tear up instead. And there are all the adults, silently crying, longing to nudge their neighbours, to shout out, 'Did you see my child?'

I would like to suggest from the above, that the particular instances of maternal tears that emerge from my anecdote hold precisely this undifferentiated status, somewhere between thinking and feeling, coming from a fusion of these two 'intellectual' states. Like Neu, however, my interest is to try to differentiate maternal tears understood purely as an outpouring of loss or sorrow (the unending grief of the cultural depiction of the weeping mother), from tears that may signal an instance of another maternal state; that of maternal love, which anecdotally seems to be brought on by a sudden realization that the child already knows how to separate, not from the mother, but from the world. The child removed to the place we call sleep, and the child in the school play are examples of their orientation towards the world, whether externally or through the interiority of sleep. It is through this experience of separation that I think we can argue that this mother glimpses maternal love. In the final section of this chapter, I draw on Alain Badiou's notion of love to help articulate this glimpse of the real of maternal love.

Badiou: one, two, infinity

In *Ethics: An essay on the understanding of evil*, Alain Badiou (2001) begins from a position of rescuing Levinas' ethics of otherness from contemporary misuse, diluting it into an account of difference, recognition and ultimately sameness. Badiou berates contemporary thinkers for misusing Levinas' ethics to prop up notions of 'recognition of the other', such as constructing arguments against racism or nationalism on the grounds that these discourses seek to deny this other who deserves recognition. Rather grandly, 'for the honour of philosophy' (Badiou 2001: 20), Badiou sets the record straight on Levinas. The crucial direction of Levinas' thought is that the ethical primacy of the Other over the Same requires that the experience of alterity be ontologically 'guaranteed' (Badiou 2001: 22) as the experience of an infinite distance, or of an essential non-identity. The Other, in Levinas' notion of 'the face' is in the order of the finite (the phenomenon of the other's face), but what the other's face reveals is an infinite distance in relation to the altogether-Other. Ethics is the *traversal* of this infinite spatio-temporal distance. In order to be intelligible, ethics requires that the Other be *'carried by a principle of alterity'* which transcends finite experience (Badiou 2001: 22, emphases added). It cannot then be used in a literal way, for instance, to think about the 'racialized other'. In Badiou's opinion, the dominance of the principle of alterity over the realm of the Same is bound up with a religious axiom, in which the 'Other' signifies the ethical name for God. To try to separate Levinas' thought from this religious axiom is to undo it totally.

> Levinas has no philosophy – not even philosophy as the 'servant' of theology. Rather, this philosophy is . . . *annulled* by theology, itself no longer a theology . . . but, precisely, an ethics.
> (Badiou 2001: 23, original emphasis)

Levinas therefore reminds us that 'every effort to turn ethics into a principle of thought and action is essentially religious' (Badiou 2001: 23).

Badiou works in precisely the opposite direction. He posits his axioms as follows: 'There is no God. Which also means: the One is not' (Badiou 2001: 25). So Badiou's philosophy does not start from singular beings, individuals, or subjects, nor from a relation to an infinitely distant Other. The One is not. Instead, he talks of 'the multiple "without one"' (Badiou 2001: 25). The law of being is that every multiple being is just that: a multiple of multiples. Human beings then are 'ordinary multiplicities'.[5] In terms of the other, Badiou posits infinite alterity as quite simply *'what there is'* (Badiou 2001: 25, original emphases). What he means by this is that there is an infinity of multiplicities. Any experience at all is the infinite deployment of infinite differences, including one's experience of oneself. The difficulties, he maintains, lie not with the Other, but in the realm of the Same, and it is this that we should be concerned with articulating.

The Same is not synonymous with the law of being, this background state of ordinary multiplicities. 'The Same . . . is not what is (i.e. the infinite multiplicities of differences) but what *comes to be'* (Badiou 2001: 27, original emphases). Something emerges out of the ordinary multiplicity of being under certain conditions. And what comes to be is the advent of 'a truth' in the realm of the Same. 'Only truth is indifferent to differences. . . . A truth is *the same for all'* (Badiou 2001: 27, original emphases). So, for

Badiou, there is difference as what is, which becomes punctured by a truth which is that which is not different, but the same for all. What Badiou (2001: 28) calls our 'being immortal' is our capacity for truth – 'our capacity to be that "same" that a truth convokes to its own "sameness"'. And this, in his view, is our capacity for science, love, politics and art, since all truths fall under one or other of these universal names. A genuine ethics is an ethics of the processes of truth, the labour that brings some truth into the world. There is no ethics in general – only an *ethics of*; of politics, love, science and art.

From here Badiou can therefore claim that there is no single Subject, but as many subjects as there are truths, although they resolve into his four fundamental subjective 'types': political, scientific, amorous and artistic.

> There is only a particular kind of animal, convoked by certain circumstances to *become* a subject – or rather, to enter into the composing of a subject. This is to say that at a given moment, everything he is – his body, his abilities – is called upon to enable the passing of a truth along its path.
>
> (Badiou 2001: 40, original emphasis)

The truth, then, which is the same for all, compels us to be true to it, and if we manage it, we temporarily attain subjectivity. However, for this to occur something particular must 'convoke' us. This something extra, something that cannot be accounted for, Badiou calls 'an event'. An event is the supplement that compels us to move from ordinary multiple-being, to a new way of being and on the way to enter into the composing of a subject. This subjectivity can be attested to only for the duration of the truth. *We are not subjects all the time.* We may or may not attain subjectivity for discrete periods of time when we enable this passing of a truth along 'our' paths. When we decide to relate, from now on, to a situation from the perspective of its eventual supplement, then we are being faithful to the event, what Badiou calls fidelity. This requires thinking (although he claims that all thought is a *practice* in terms of a 'putting to the test') the situation 'according to' the event rather than pretending the event has not occurred, and prompting new ways of being and acting in the situation. As examples of situations that turn out to have been events by subjects who come into being through remaining faithful to them, Badiou lists the French Revolution, the meeting of Héloïse and Abélard, Galileo's physics, Haydn's creation of the classical musical style, Lacanian psychoanalysis, a personal instance of falling in love, Grothendiek's creation of Topos theory in maths, and Schoenberg's invention of the twelve-tone scale. To be faithful to the event is to do what Berg and Webern did, by changing the way they approached music after the event that was Schoenberg, and not going on writing neo-romantic music as if nothing had happened. This then changes the post-evental situation although it becomes clear only after the event that this has occurred.

It is important to note that Badiou is not positing 'the truth' as some absolute, external category. The truth is not, for example, Levinas' 'altogether-Other'. It is not external to the situation. It is both within (immanent) and simultaneously 'a break in a situation': a paradoxical 'immanent break' in the situation itself (Badiou 2001: 42). A truth is more like *a process* of truthfulness to an event that changes the situation (an event emerges from within the situation), while still being a break with whatever language and knowledge went before.

Badiou's love

Love is one of Badiou's four domains where truth can function. In 'What is love?' (Badiou 2000), Badiou builds an account of love (as opposed to desire) as a truth-procedure that establishes sexual difference, which for Badiou is the law of difference as such. I want to rather brutally co-opt this account as I think it may provide a model for thinking, not just about the way love establishes sexual difference, but about how other forms of love, particularly maternal love may also establish the One out of a situation in which there are Two.

Badiou's account proceeds by rejecting various traditional or common-place definitions of love, and posting others axiomatically, which are then interrogated against one another. He first rejects the classical notion of love as a fusion in which one is made out of two by merging two ones together. The One can only be supposed beyond Two by suppressing the multiple, and as we saw above, Badiou proceeds from the position that the One is not (there is no God); what there is, is multiplicity. One will somehow have to emerge out of the multiple. Second, he rejects love as a description of a relation with alterity. Love, he maintains, is not even an experience of the Other, but an experience of the *world*, or the situation under the post-evental conditions that there are two. This a startling and brilliant obser-vation. It cuts across any absorption of Levinas into a discourse of love (Levinas is concerned with the realm of responsibility, which is distinct from a notion of love). Badiou, it appears, warns us to keep our eye on the truth (the realm of the Same), which is what creates an immanent break in the world through the event, rather than looking to some exteriority, a relation with which calls us into being. And third, he maintains that love is not an illusion that covers over desire, or the real of sex, as Lacan would have it.[6] Love is an event that 'supplements' a situation, which is something else entirely:

[Love . . .] is only messed up under the fallacious supposition that it is a relation. But it is not. It is the production of truth. The truth of what? That the Two, and not only the One, are at work in the situation.

(Badiou 2000: 266)

So here we begin to see what Badiou's 'love' is. *Love is the production of a particular instance of truth that occurs out of the event that is Two and not One.*

Having established what love is not, Badiou makes a series of axiomatic statements on love. Of all truth processes, love can be 'known' only through axioms because it cannot deliver its identity through experience itself. That, in a way, is what is at the core of love understood as the experience of a radical disjunction. Truth and knowledge are not synonymous. In fact, in love, the opposite is the case: loving subjects depend on the identity of love in order to become loving subjects in the first place – because love is a truth process that attends to a radical disjunction between two positions of experience, love can arrange experience, but cannot deliver 'knowledge' of love from within these experiences. In other words, love, as an experience of thought, does not think itself, despite the fact that to love, according to Badiou, is to think.

Badiou's first axiom in relation to love is that 'there are two positions of experience' which are sexuated, one being named 'woman' and the other 'man'. These are not empirical, biological or social categories. As with Lacan, anyone, male or female, can 'choose' one of these positions. At this point they are only nominal, because it is only after the event that they can be established to have occurred. You can only, in other words, *have been* a 'man' or a 'woman' after the event that is love (which is not to say that love necessarily produces heterosexual encounters between those sexed male or female). Man and woman do not exist prior to love and then come together as loving subjects. They come into existence at the point of love. This is because of Badiou's second axiom: that the two positions are absolutely 'disjunct' (Badiou 2000: 267). There is absolutely nothing in the experience that is the same for the two positions. Between them, they don't divide up a totality of experience, nor are there any zones of coincidence or intersection between the two. 'Man' cannot, by definition, experience what 'woman' can, and vice versa, and neither can you add their experiences together to form a whole. This is what Badiou means by 'disjunction'.

In the event that is love, those positioned within the disjunction can have no knowledge of the disjunction itself, given that there is no point of intersection or overlap that would allow this assessment to be made. Neither of the Two can stand outside of themselves, and there is also no external knowledge of this disjunction because of Badiou's third axiom that states that there is no third position. The idea of a third (an angel) is to appeal to some notion that that there is something outside of the dyad that can assess

116

their experience and verify that it is indeed disjunct. But axiom one tells us that there are only two positions and axiom three that there is no third. So, in order to 'pronounce' the disjunction (as opposed to have knowledge of it) without the help of an angel, Badiou asserts that the situation needs supplementation, which, as we have seen, is performed by the event that is love. The event sets in motion the amorous procedure, which can properly be termed 'an encounter,' and can be understood in terms of Badiou's general philosophical procedure that I described above. So, what we have so far is love understood as the supplement that allows the establishment of two positions of experience that are radically disjunct, and which, in Badiou's schema so far, come to be named 'man' and 'woman'.

Badiou's fourth and final axiom is that there is also only one 'humanity'. This complicates things. Humanity is neither an appeal to idealism or some kind of biologism, but what provides the support for generic or truth-procedures (Badiou 2000: 268). As we already know, truth is transpositional. It is the same for all; that which is subtracted from each position, and is therefore termed 'generic'. The forth axiom establishes that these generic procedures (truth procedures or events that occur in the realm of science, art, politics and love) are supported by a *singular* humanity. In other words, something we can call humanity is attested to if and only if there is '(emancipatory) politics, (conceptual) science, (creative) art or love (not reduced to a mixture of sentimentality and sexuality)' (Badiou 2000: 268). Humanity sustains the *infinite singularity* of truths, or the historical body of truths. If the humanity function is denoted as H (x), as truth procedures traverse the x the humanity function localizes them. As truth (which is transpositional – the same for all) traverses one of these domains (politics, science, art or love), it testifies to the existence of a singular humanity (axiom four – there is only one humanity), which is the localization of a truth in its 'local verification' that is a subject. H is a potential mixture of four types of truth, which it knots together into the particular or historical body. There is only one localization of the generic or transpositional truth. In Badiou's words: 'all truth holds for all its historical body' (Badiou 2000: 268).

So Badiou is describing a paradox that is at the core of 'love': if there is only one humanity, how can there be two positions, man and woman, which are radically disjunct? He does not want to fall into an argument that truths are sexuated: that there is a male and a female truth, as he has already asserted that if they are disjunct and there is no third term, then who could know the difference (and what sex, he asks, would the angel be anyway?). So, love is precisely the place where this paradox is negotiated; the paradox that there is a radical disjunct between the sexes, that there is no third term, and that there is a generic truth supported by one humanity – an element that can be subtracted from every positional disjunction (some indiscernible extra element). Love, he says, *makes truth* of this paradox.

In part the paradox lies back with axiom one, and we see this in all sorts of expositions of otherness, some of which we have strayed upon in earlier chapters. If love is the consciousness of the other as other, then this means the other is identifiable in consciousness as the same, as consciousness always colonizes the other through the very processes of consciousness. Badiou tries to escape this difficulty by presenting the paradox that love is at the same time the disjunction between two radically disjunct positions of experience and that which makes such a disjunction a truth (the same for all). He can do this only by maintaining that love is a process, an ongoing inquiry, rather than a form of consciousness:

> Love is precisely this: the advent of the Two as such, the stage of the Two, which is not to say that it is the being of the Two, which would suppose three, but a work, a process.
>
> (Badiou 2000: 272)

This appears similar to Kristeva's subject-in-progress/on-trial except that the Two appear only as a result of fidelity to the event that is love rather than out of a disruption performed by what is heterogeneous to the symbolic.

> 'I love you' brings together two pronouns 'I' and 'you', that cannot be brought together. The Two who amorously operate is properly the name of the disjunct apprehended in its disjunction.
>
> (Badiou 2000: 272)

So, love is the 'interminable fidelity' to Badiou's first axiom – that there are Two:

> The Two fractures the One and tests the infinity of the situation. One, Two, infinity: such is the numericity of the amorous procedure. It structures the becoming of a generic truth. What truth? The truth of the situation insofar as there exist two disjunct positions.
>
> (Badiou 2000: 272)

Love is a sequence of investigations on disjuncture and the Two, which can only be understood in relation to there being one humanity, the uniqueness of which guarantees the universality of truth (a truth is a truth for all, but in being so, is infinitely singular). Only out of one situation, we can have two absolutely disjunct positions that cannot collapse back into one. One, two, infinity. In Badiou's words:

Love is this place which proceeds when the disjunction does not separate the situation in its being. The disjunction is only a law, not a substantial delimitation. This is the scientific aspect of the amorous procedure. Love fractures the One according to the Two. And it is in virtue of this that it can be thought that, although worked by this disjunction, the situation *is exactly as if there has been a One*, and it is through this One-multiple that all truth is assured. In our world, love is the guardian of the universality of the true. It elucidates virtuality, because it makes truth of the disjunction.

(Badiou 2000: 273, emphases added)

One is what turns out to *have been*, through the paradox of there being Two radically disjunct experiences and only one humanity. Badiou's formulation operates as a reworking of Lacan's notion of the phallus as the signifier that shows up signification but in the opposite direction. Where the phallus works to show up the lack at the core of signification, so love works to show up truth at the core of humanity.

Through Badiou's notion of love, we can now distinguish more adequately between love and desire. Love names the situation that there are Two, whereas desire, chasing its own cause (the *objet petit a* in Lacan's terms), is the fact of the split subject: one divided. One divided is still one. To stop desire being purely masturbatory (given that there is only One in desire) Badiou argues that it is at the point of desire that love 'fractures' the One according to the Two. So, love can suffuse desire, providing the condition of Two that makes the disjunction true without at the same time abolishing the disjunction. Unlike desire, love maintains the disjunction, whereas desire is constantly and hopelessly seeking to plug up the split in itself. Desire itself is homosexual, whereas love, including love between same-sex individuals is in principle heterosexual. Love is '*an inquiry of the world from the point of view of the Two*', not an inquiry of each term of the Two about the other. This latter process would always reveal itself actually as desire, as an inquiry about the One. We cannot occupy two positions at the same time, but we can have a knowledge of the other while that knowledge is still disjunct. The Two then look outwards towards the world.

In keeping with Lacan, Badiou maintains that there is a position 'man' and a position 'woman' which can be occupied by anyone regardless of whether they are sexed male or female, and which have different relations to the Two. In the post-eventary situation that is love, the masculine statement is 'what will have been true is that we were two and not at all one' and the feminine statement is 'what will have been true is that there were two, and otherwise we were not' (Badiou 2000: 279). So the feminine statement is about being, whereas the masculine statement is about the change in number, the painful post-evental rendering of the One through the disjunction of the Two. From here Badiou (2000: 280) argues that the feminine position is the 'bearer of love's relation to humanity' – the function that makes the knot with the other truth-procedures (science, art, politics). The consequences of his final axiom are that 'woman' is the position in which the subtraction of love affects it with inhumanity itself. For 'woman', then, there can be no humanity (One) without love (Two): love is the condition of proof of humanity. Sexual difference is only thinkable by using love as a differentiating criterion:

> The female position sustains itself, in its singular relation to love, so that it can be clear that 'for all x [there is an]H (x)', whatever the effects of the disjunction, or of the disjunctions (for the sexual is perhaps not the only one).
>
> (Badiou 2000: 280)

The return of maternal love

And here, perhaps, we have an opening. If sexual difference is not the only disjunction, then perhaps we can imagine that there are other manifestations of such a disjunction, and perhaps one imagining is that of the Two understood as 'mother' and 'child'. If we work this through, we could think about Badiou's first thesis, 'there are two positions of experience' as those of mother and child in such a way that we do not need to involve ourselves in arguments about empirical, biological or social categories, but can posit them purely as nominal. That there is One would again be established, only retroactively, through what Badiou has described as 'love', due to the disjunction that says that nothing of the two experiences overlaps, that they do not divide up experience, and that there is no third position, no angel to pronounce on the disjunction. The mother cannot 'know' her love for the child, any more than the child can 'know' love for the mother. Love is a process of negotiating the paradox. Likewise, there is no third that can ascertain that there is love. The third can state perhaps that there is a nursing couple, a mother holding a child's hand, a mother watching a school play. This can be seen from the outside, but love cannot be seen from the outside without dissolving the paradox that makes love possible, and it cannot either be seen from within. Only Badiou's 'singular event', the event that initiates the amorous procedure, is visible, and this, which he calls the encounter, is perhaps what I have tried to flesh out in a peculiar moment of maternal tears. The mother realizes that she loves the child, which means that she views the world (not the child) from the point of view of the Two. The world looks different from this perspective, perhaps because, as Badiou states above, 'the situation is exactly *as if* there had been One' (2000: 273, emphases added). Retroactively, and painfully, the One

120

can emerge at the point that it is fractured by the Two that is the event that is love. It is here that a loving subject can be named, and I suggest that the mother could be thought of as attaining, temporarily, a specifically maternal subjectivity (an awareness after the event of her own distinctness or singularity) through her fidelity to the event that Badiou has described as love. When Badiou writes 'love is interminable fidelity to the first nomination. It is a material procedure which reevaluates the totality of experience, traversing the entire situation bit by bit, according to its connection or disconnection to the nominal supposition of the Two', I think he describes maternal anguish, no longer understood as special jouissance in return for the agony of childbirth, but the ongoing, painful and truthful 'traversing of the entire situation bit by bit' (Badiou 2000: 272) according to the realization that now, and for always, there are two. This is perhaps what the child already knows. The child knows there are Two. That perhaps is a way of understanding what is often commented on as the commonplace of children's love for their parents; the way they give it easily and with so much forgiveness. This is how I understand the gift that the child is for the mother, which makes her weep.

6

MATERNAL STUFF

Maternity and the encumbered body

Stuff

I am standing on Brighton Pier on a bleak Saturday in May. A small crowd has gathered to watch a couple of Ukrainians swimming in the freezing grey water below. A few strangers clap as the woman emerges first, followed by her stocky boyfriend. They look sheepish, cold but quietly elated. It becomes clear that they don't have a towel. It seems that they were caught short by a rash desire to swim together off Brighton beach, as if the moment held some kind of romance, some kind of significance. Their audience turns away, distancing themselves from the couple who have enacted their own desire thought better of. Stunned by the water the swimmers try to cover up, pull tight clothes over rubbery limbs. The seagulls eye Saul's chips. We are at the far end of the pier. The wind is blowing hard. Saul sees his cousins dart off, makes to run, doubles back, and clinging to the paper wrapping of the coveted chips, throws me his minna. The chips unravel as the minna flaps for a couple of seconds above my head, wings out over the pier, crumples, and begins to fall, looping slowly, perhaps fifty foot down onto the surface of the sea. We can barely see it, a small bobbing blue rag. Saul moans, 'Minna gone, minna gone'. Pressed against the railings, the children all wait for me to do something. Joel is shouting into the wind, as if the sheer force of his voice may push the minna towards the shore. I try to shout over to the Ukrainians. Maybe they can be persuaded to take another dip. Then we lose sight of it. Saul cries out as the minna resurfaces momentarily and then disappears again. Joel is crying now in place of his brother, the first to catch the full weight of events. If I can let the minna blow off the pier and get swallowed up in the waves, then what chance have I of holding onto them? 'Poor Sauli, poor Sauli'. If I'm to lose one of them, at least in his fantasy it will be his brother. We are all crying now, Saul having finally understood the meaning of his own words, 'Minna gone, minna gone'. There is no substitute for the transitional object. That is precisely its meaning. It has been chosen out from all the other objects, and therefore cannot be swapped or exchanged. The minna is my anchoring in the world. How will I get him to sleep in an hour's time? How else can I comfort him when he's upset? I lamely offer him an ice-cream. Their paternal grandfather, a naval officer, turned a mine-sweeper around during a storm in the middle of the Firth of Forth to look for his son's 'mitt-mat', which had blown overboard. Though there was no hope of finding it, it seemed a desperate attempt to demonstrate that he understood just how difficult the child's realization of parental powerlessness was. Perhaps my children have inherited the gene for losing transitional objects at sea. I am reminded of a film I made on Brighton Pier years earlier in which two men and two children walked to the end of the pier. One of the men, tall and gawky, was holding a big patent-leather red handbag, awkwardly standing in for the missing mother, and then both of the men had inexplicably jumped off the pier, leaving the children looking blankly down at the surface of the sea. Brighton Pier, and mother-loss, forever intertwined.

Maternal embodiment

Imogen Tyler (2000), in a beautiful paper entitled 'Reframing pregnant embodiment', reminds us of the pregnant body's particular capacity for ontological and temporal disturbance, which may account for pregnant subjectivity being largely written out of the philosophical cannon. In a call for animating the maternal object through speech, pregnant embodiment requires a form of 'mattertalk' (Tyler 2000), part autobiographical, part philosophical in that perhaps always already failing task of representing a subjectivity which defies the category 'subject'. Describing a philosophy lecture that she attends while heavily pregnant, she writes:

> My body, my massive pregnant body, wants to stand up, to go to the front of the room, to present *itself* as a question. The dichotomy of subject and object is called into question by this question, as it is already posed by this body, presented, here and now. It dawns on me, that my pregnant embodiment is a topology which remains unmapped, unthought, indeed unthinkable, within a philosophical landscape of stable forms. . . . Am (I) inappropriate? Monstrous? Am (I) obscene? Am I representable as an 'I'? Am I?
>
> (Tyler 2000: 290, original emphasis)

As Braidotti stated, in the mid-1990s:

> The women's body can change shape in pregnancy and child-bearing; it is therefore capable of defeating the notion of fixed bodily form, of visible, clear, and distinct shapes as that which mark the contour of the body. She is morphologically dubious. The fact that the female body can change shape so drastically is troublesome in the eyes of the logocentric economy.
>
> (Braidotti 1994: 80)

And as Irigaray wrote, in the mid-1980s:

> We are luminous. Neither one nor two. I've never known how to count. Up to you. In their calculations, we make two. Really, two? Doesn't that make you laugh? An odd sort of two. And yet not one. Especially not one. Let's leave one to them: Their oneness, with its prerogatives, its domination, its solipsism.
>
> (Irigaray 1985b: 207)

However, the pregnant and lactating body is usually where 'maternal embodiment' in such accounts begins and ends. As Shelley M. Park has argued, pronatalist perspectives on the maternal body, perspectives, that is, that take as their starting point the female body's capacity to biologically reproduce, to change shape in pregnancy and childbearing, render other maternal bodies queer (Park 2006). How do we understand and represent, for instance, adoptive maternal bodies or maternal bodies where a child has been born through surrogacy, where another woman's body has changed shape? Park (2006) argues powerfully that the queering of adoptive maternal bodies creates a useful epistemological standpoint from which to critique dominant views of mothering, particularly the discursive and social regulation of all maternal bodies. She invites us to think about the possibilities of maternal embodiment beyond the trope of the maternal body's morphological ambivalence – its capacity to become two. In many ways I agree with Tyler's statement that 'it's time to make a pregnant self, to reclaim pregnancy as a transient subjectivity by reframing pregnant women as the active subjects of their own gestation' (Tyler 2000: 292). However, her call for more adequate representations of pregnant embodiment, though a vital part of the slow road towards the cultural visibility of maternal subjectivity, emphasizes pregnant embodiment, which may repeat the gesture of returning the maternal to a matter of flesh, whereas the maternal, as Park (2006) points out, encompasses many non-genetic and non-gestational bodily relationships between mothers and children 'that serve to connect parent and child fundamentally in both momentary and long-lasting ways' (Park 2006: 204).

One way to counteract this tendency to couple maternal embodiment and the pregnant and lactating body is to shift our focus towards post-birth, post-lactation embodiment, which also remains curiously unmapped, unthought and perhaps unthinkable, and makes its own challenges to the masculine principles of individuality, non-contradiction and singular temporality that are disturbed by the maternal more generally. After all, once the baby is out, are there 'two' who are so clear for all to see? In addition, is this just a question of how maternal embodiment puts the masculine subject 'on-trial' or is there also something worth charting of the materialist-maternal feminine, something of what it is like to be 'tied' to a child through more than emotional bonds?

Winnicott famously reminded us that there is no such thing as an infant. A mother and baby cannot be thought of in isolation from one another, but are both essential components of a relational dyad (Winnicott 1964: 88). And just as there is no infant thought outside the relationship with a mother, I have tried to trace the transitory attainment of maternal subjectivity that emerges at key destabilizing moments that occur between a mother and child: the first realizations of the child's strangeness, the initial use of a child's first name, the experience of constant interruption, bearing witness to the child in the grip of a tantrum, waiting while a stammering child speaks, love that emerges out of unexpected weeping.

However, what is lacking in this account is the role of objects or 'stuff' through which this relationship is enacted. What would be more accurate to state is that there is no such thing as a mother–infant dyad. Where there is a mother and infant, there is always some stuff. This stuff may be the most minimal cloth covering that a mother wraps a baby in to help retain its precious body heat, or the avalanche of objects that are more likely to furnish the 'nursery' or 'playroom' in a contemporary North American or European home. Much as we may like to bracket off the clutter and characterize the mother–infant relationship as some kind of pure or uncontaminated channel of communication, the 'shadow of the object' is quite literal.[1] Because of its connection with notions of materialism and consumerism, there is a tendency perhaps to characterize stuff as the despised substance, set apart or at least tangential to human-to-human relations. However, contemporary anthropological studies have more recently drawn our attention to the fact that cultures consist not only of social relations, but also of material relations, and that those relations are not just instruments of social relations involved in the creation of symbolic meaning, but essential aspects of culture in their own right (Tonkinwise 2004). Objects, in other words, have a life of their own.

The aim of this chapter is to explore post-birth maternal embodiment through tracing a mother's relation to the 'lives' of various objects that furnish her world, to see what they do to her, and what they offer her. Rather than working from the premise that mother–child relations are mediated, symbolized or constructed by such objects (perhaps such a view would amount to a new incarnation of the third), my aim is to reverse the assumption that objects either mediate or are tangential to the human-to-human, and work towards an idea that objects are themselves both social and ethical. Drawing primarily on the early work of Bruno Latour (1992, 1995, 1997) and Elaine Scarry's monumental work, *The Body in Pain* (Scarry 1985), we can begin to see how such objects both reciprocate and at times fail to do adequate ethical work, and the subsequent consequences for she who mothers.

Through an exploration of the relationship between maternity and stuff, I develop the notion of the maternal subject as a subject both of *heightened sentience* and also of *viscosity*. Through a comparison of the mother as an 'encumbered body' with the figure of the *traceur* or 'freerunner' who navigates the urban landscape with feline ease, the notion of the mother as a new embodied subjectivity beyond that of the pregnant or feeding body is proposed.

Childhood objects and maternal 'tool-beings'

The objects surrounding mothers and their children are often referred to as 'childhood objects': either things we remember from our own childhood, or things that parents procure to provision a child or use in the service of a child. However, many of these objects may be better described as 'maternal objects'. They are, in fact, the things that a mother uses in her child-rearing work. For reasons that I hope will become clearer, these objects may be thought about as either 'actants' (Latour 1997), 'artefacts' (Scarry 1985) or perhaps even 'tool-beings', a term Graham Harman (2001) coins from a reading of Heidegger's famous distinction between the presence-at-hand and readiness-to-hand of *Zeug*, usually translated as 'equipment' (Harman 2001).

It may be possible in a very provisional way to group such tool-beings (to use this evocative term) into recognizable categories. Initially there appears to be an array of objects used by a mother to meet a baby's basic needs for food, warmth and nurturance. Referred to in the Argos catalogue as 'nursery equipment', these include the objects a mother may use to keep a baby warm (clothes, blankets, quilts), to feed a baby (bottles, teats, formula milk powder, sterilizers, breast pumps, feeding spoons and bowls, juice bottles and bibs), to sooth a baby (pacifiers, mobiles, rattles), to change a baby (nappies, wipes, changing mats, creams and powders), to get a baby to sleep (cribs, cots, baskets, baby monitors, mobiles, tapes with nursery rhymes), and to transport a baby (prams, buggies, carry cots, slings, papooses, backpacks, car seats). Though this list is far from exhaustive, it provides us with a preliminary way of grouping maternal objects in terms of the work they do. In keeping with Ruddick's breakdown of maternal work into the three interrelated tasks of preservation, growth and fostering social acceptability, the tool-beings listed above are not initially used directly by the infant as such, but by the mother in her work of sustaining and pre-serving a child's life.[2]

As the baby grows, these initial nursery objects may be replaced with toys and dolls, books, art materials, tapes and videos, games, outdoor equipment such as bikes and skateboards, balls, scooters, skates and trolleys, particular items of clothing, and later still by computers, computer games and mobile phones. Though these are by now largely objects that the child uses, they can still be thought of within the rubric of objects of maternal work, in that they aid the child's independent play and development; they

126

work to foster both the child's growth and their socialization, or work to soothe or amuse the child in order that a mother may find time or space to sustain herself and thereby her capacity to continue her mothering work. In addition, I would argue that these are all objects that furnish the mother's 'workplace', and an investigation of her relation to such objects could be thought of as an inquiry into the ergonomics of motherhood. It appears that little work has been done on such an ergonomics other than the odd research project on the design of a new chair to meet the needs of breast-feeding mothers (Jones 2003) or the different types of back injury related to taking children in and out of car seats (Roca 1997). What may be needed is an understanding of the fact that women find themselves parenting across a vast array of different physical and geographical locations (a wide variety of 'homes', the park, street, playgroup, leisure centre, doctor's surgery, post office, workplace, café, community centre, museum, football pitch, and so on), and takes in an equally vast array of different objects, including her children's toys and multi-various pieces of equipment.

In addition there is an important category of transitional objects used by a child as they move from the nursery world into the world of objects. These are the mitt-mats, minnas and baas that Winnicott (1951) drew our attention to. As the objects shift from being used primarily by the mother in the service of the baby, towards being used directly by the child, the transitional object is understood as the classic 'me/not me' phenomenon, creating an 'unchallenged' area of experience between primary narcissism and true object choice. The mother has her own distinct relation to the child's transitional object, beyond the specific and special relationship the child has developed with the object itself.

The viscous body

The initial set of maternal objects, those classed as 'nursery equipment' appear to precipitate a new set of actions, movements and manipulations on the part of a mother, and in doing so shift a mother's kinetic and sensate experience. Many of these objects require a mother to adjust the scale of her movements towards the extreme points of two poles – the minute and the enormous. Like Alice, she can find herself feeling at once huge and tiny, one moment clumsy as she fiddles with tiny buttons and the next moment tiny as she hauls the huge weight of a growing child up onto her hip. Changing nappies, dressing recalcitrant children, feeding babies pulp with small plastic spoons, carrying children and their equipment, balancing objects in uncertain places, pushing buggies through doors designed to keep the cold out, manipulating prams with buggy-boards attached, getting babies in and out of slings or backpacks, in and out of buses, trains and tubes, loading and unloading cars, packing bags, making up feeds, sterilizing bottles, piecing together breast pumps, manipulating Lego®, threading beads . . . these activities that many an urban-dwelling, late-industrial, consumer-orientated mother may find herself doing often require a new set of skills, actions and movements or the relearning of old ones. In keeping with Merleau-Ponty, our subjectivity resides not in our consciousness alone, but in the lived body (Merleau-Ponty 1962: 121). The lived body orientates itself with respect to its surroundings, adjusting its movements as it goes. If, as Merleau-Ponty claims, the possibilities that are opened up in the world depend on the modes and the limits of the body (1962: 110–112), then as these modes and limits shift, so does our subjectivity. Furthermore, for Merleau-Ponty, the world's spatiality originates in the body. The body is the original subject that constitutes space, without which there would be no space (1962: 102).

Iris Young's early paper, 'Throwing like a girl' (Young 1990), juxtaposed Merleau-Ponty's theory of the lived body with de Beauvoir's theory of the situation of women under patriarchy in order to draw out ways in which women's bodies as lived experience are affected by their objectification; by the experience of their body as, for example, a fragile thing that needs to be protected, or a thing to be looked at and acted upon. Comportment, motility and spatiality are altered by women's awareness of their body as both subject and object, as simultaneously living in space and positioned in space. It seems to me that motherhood represents a major shift in the modes and limits of the body, not just because of patriarchy (a situation that Young (1998) more recently acknowledged as having changed not insignificantly since she wrote her original piece) but because of the specific object-related and spatial tasks that motherhood prompts. If all subjectivity flows from this originary body then the comportment, motility and spatiality of the maternal body surely shifts radically in its newly furnished world.

One of the cleaning staff at the hospital showed me how to put the baby's first nappy on. I caught her watching me across the ward corridor. Her face was expressionless. She neither laughed nor frowned. She simply watched as I haplessly put the nappy on back to front. The notion of 'fit' didn't seem to me to apply. The nappy was practically as long as the baby, his legs sticking out like the drumsticks of a chicken wrapped in a plastic bag. I cooed and fumbled, as I half-heartedly tugged at the plastic, trying to intimate that it was the nappy's fault, it was clearly badly designed, really no good for that all-important job of keeping shit enclosed. She moved silently across the ward, held her broom in one hand, and with the other slowly lifted the drumsticks, flipped out the sticky flaps with her thumb and little finger and rotated the nappy a hundred and eighty degrees. Then without looking at me (I was beneath contempt), she wordlessly moved off.

One of the particularly striking shifts in a mother's kinetic experience is a newfound sense of clumsiness, slowness and delay. Motherhood, I would suggest, has its own kind of *viscosity*. Viscosity is a fluid's internal friction or resistance to flow. And this viscosity becomes evident, or more precisely, is engendered through a mother's interaction with things; small fiddly things, big heavy things, too many things. Being around small children for prolonged periods of time requires working at different economies of scale and different spatio-temporal frameworks. It is not just that mothers often finds themselves 'multi-tasking' (trying to work, have a conversation, or organize a household, while soothing a baby over one shoulder and breaking up a fight between her older children over the other), but through the use of material objects involved in their work, mothers experience their own kinetic being as impeded and resistant in specific ways. Changing a newborn baby can sometimes take hours, despite the fact that a mother previous to mothering may have experienced herself as adept, capable, quick. Getting a number of small children ready in the morning, buckling shoes, brushing teeth, scooping scattered toys into a box can feel like wading through treacle. This new kinetic experience creates and informs the texture of her lived experience.

Simultaneous to this viscosity, a mother may find that she lives in a permanent state of heightened sensation. We forget sometimes that mothers are constantly making decisions in relation to the twin tasks of responding to a child's needs and keeping children literally alive, even the older ones. This receptivity to danger may mean that traffic sounds louder, smells seem more intense, bright light feels more penetrating, people standing close on a bus are experienced as more intrusive. Just as different fluids may move at different speeds due to their different viscosity, so a mother may also experience herself caught in a tension between both heightened sensation and slowed down movement. Think about a mother crossing the road with a newly walking toddler who is proudly pushing a small trolley in imitation of his mother's pram. The mother decides to let the toddler walk, not only facilitating their emerging independence but also avoiding a public and prolonged tantrum that she just can't face today. Painfully slowly they inch into the open terrain between the safety of the two kerbs. She is watching, listening, anticipating, being vigilant, attuned to the signs of danger, hurrying the child along while also trying not to make him trip. In the time it takes to move between the two points of safety she is simultaneously in a heightened sensory state while being physically slowed down. This creates a bodily tension in which both time and space are experienced differently. The mother is impeded, her movement is held back, while at the same time she is opened to a more acute sensory experience than ever before. This kind of tension may be lived with for many years on a day-to-day basis.

My contention here is that mothers are opened up to both their own viscosity and their heightened sentience through multiple encounters with objects. She and the toddler have prams and trolleys, they meet with and negotiate kerbs, cars and street furniture that make up her 'workplace'. She is often weighed down by a number of other objects she brings with her so that her hands are not free, so that her body is not mobile in the same way as it used to be. She is encumbered, not just by the physical presence of a child who needs holding, carrying, who walks at a quarter of her speed, who pulls on her legs, but by the multiplicity of relationships negotiated with child, environment and stuff.

I am aware that my use of 'object' is now getting broader and broader, taking in the built environment and the natural world as well as sound, light, smell and touch. This is not such a crazy idea. There is a long philosophical tradition of teasing out the difference between the reality of an object and its encountered surface, the moment, in other words that objects are revealed through human interaction. If on the one hand Merleau-Ponty wants to assert that space is created by the lived body, there has been a slow accretion of ideas working in the opposite direction, attempting to re-establish the 'objectness' of the world (Harman 2002). I want here to try to trace a strand of such ideas about objects, starting with the difficulty psychoanalysis has with accounting for material objects, and then looking briefly at intentional objects, Heidegger's 'broken' objects, and then moving to the notion of 'ethical objects'. In the final section of the chapter I return to the encumbered body – the mother, her baby, her buggy and her stuff.

Psychoanalytic and philosophical objects

From a psychoanalytic perspective it seems strange and slightly perverse to make a distinction between material objects and embodied subjects. 'Objects' hold a long and specific history within psychoanalysis of blurring the boundary between the material reality of the external world, and what psychoanalysis terms 'internal objects'. In fact 'object' usually denotes the mother herself, or a bit of her, who is deemed the primary object in the child's developing internal world. For Freud objects, both people and material things, are the recipients of the drive, and it is through objects that the drive achieves its satisfaction. Early on, in *Three Essays on the Theory of Sexuality*, Freud makes the distinction between the sexual object and the sexual aim, and shows how deviations can occur with respect to both (Freud 1905). The object is contingent, having no necessary connection with the drive (Laplanche and Pontalis 1973: 273–276; Frosh 2002). Initially this looks like a statement that implies that in its arbitrariness the object's specificity fades. It can be chosen and discarded and replaced by another object in an endless exchange. However, Freud is talking of a mental representation of the object, one that is cathected with aggressive and libidinal energy. As Freud writes right at the end of his life, the mother is 'unique, without parallel, established unalterably for a whole lifetime as the first and strongest love-object and as the prototype of all later love relations' (Freud 1938: 188). Objects are not at all arbitrary for each of us as individuals. They reflect the very particular relations we have established in early childhood, primarily with our mothers.

Alternatively, as with the fetish, the 'thing' itself can be fixated on, but it is still understood as an object that stands in for another missing object. In the case of the fetish, it stands for the missing penis of the mother that is simultaneously accepted and disavowed. Similarly, Fenichel (1938) talks of the drive to amass wealth as an aspect of an instinct to possess; the need, that is, to hold on to the contents of our own bodies, which could in fantasy be taken away. This instinct to possess is itself part of the libidinal drive, originally related to anal eroticism and later to castration. We seek to amass wealth, according to Fenichel (1938), in the same way that we wish to accumulate and possess faeces and fear losing them. Everything essentially returns to the original objects, the internalizations of parental figures and body parts, from which we derive our attitude both towards other people and things in later life. And, of course, this is the basis of the transference (Arlow 1980). The 'person' in the real world gets confused in the transference with the mental representation of the childhood object, which was originally a representation of either a parental figure or a thing.

'Object' in psychoanalysis then comes to denote specifically the original representation of person or thing, usually the parental figure and their body parts. 'Person' appears to remain as a way of denoting real people in the world to whom we relate in our adult lives, and 'possession' comes to signify 'an expanded portion of the ego' (Fenichel 1938), the stuff we want to hold onto partly for anal-erotic reasons, and partly as a defence against castration anxiety, or earlier still, against the potential loss of the breast which is experienced as a diminution of the ego itself. Interestingly, Fenichel (1938) tells us that Ferenczi understood a kind of progression from the child's fascination with faeces to mud, dust, sand and stones and then on to all sorts of made objects that could be collected, and finally to money. In this sense, our relation to material objects and artefacts can be thought about as an extension of our original fixation with breast or faeces, including of course the objects mothers acquire in their adult life to provision their children!

It is, however, the *social function* of such artefacts that allows the 'possessive instinct' to find expression later in the material world. Amassing wealth as opposed to sand is worthwhile only because of its exchange value, making it a culturally significant object to hold on to. Amassing maternal objects, on the other hand, is ostensibly done in the name of provisioning a child or to assist in maternal work. As we shall see later, our relation to such objects may be less to do with needing to hold onto what is precious and more to do with how objects can alleviate our pain.

Although the enormous shift in emphasis brought in by Klein and then the object relations tradition in psychoanalytic theory and practice extends the function of external reality in structuring the internal world of the infant, especially in the work of Fairbairn (1941), who reversed the Freudian notion of 'contingency', making it clear that the internal object is based on very real experiences with, at times, alarmingly real people capable of both abuse and neglect (Buckley 1986), the 'object' remains a person rather than a material object, and that person is usually the mother. Christopher Bollas' notion of the mother as a 'transformational object' is an instructive example. Bollas (1987) argues that one of the things the infant takes in, early in its relationship with the mother, is the mother's capacity to *make things happen*. In other words, there is an aspect of maternal presence and maternal care, Bollas claims, that is experienced by the infant as both transformational and dynamic. Through identification with this aspect, the infant develops its own capacities for experiencing the self as transformational or efficacious. As a result, transformational object-seeking is set up. This describes the ways in which we seek out an object in later life for its 'function as a signifier of transformation'. Thus, in adult life, 'the quest is not to possess the object; rather the object is pursued in order to surrender to it as a medium that alters the self' (Bollas 1987: 14). Bollas is arguing that through the actual alteration of the child's material environment that the mother performs through the daily, routine activities of mothering, the mother is felt to alter the child's *self*, and it is this quality that is pursued in later life. So even though the world penetrates in Bollas' account, it can do so only through a 'maternal object'.

It is only really Winnicott who stops long enough to think about old rabbits with chewed up ears, scraps of cloth, wool, string and songs. It is with his exposition of the function of the transitional object that we come closest to an analysis of the function of material objects without them being totally subsumed by their relation with original objects. In fact it is the very materiality of such objects, their ability to survive our needs to 'love them to bits' as well as more concretely attack and destroy them, rather than their metaphorical function, that allows them to be used as transitional at all.

Lacan also acknowledges the aspect of 'things' that escapes signification. In his reading of Freud's *das Ding* in *The Ethics of Psychoanalysis* (Lacan 1959–1960: 43–70), Lacan suggests that 'reality' is something that is only ever partially 'real'. *Das Ding*, the object of the other place of the Real is what he calls '*Fremde*', or alien, 'strange and even hostile on occasion'. It is just what is there, 'while one waits for something better, or worse, but which one wants' (Lacan 1959–1960: 52). *Das Ding* is then the absolute Other of the subject, the object of the Real, standing in place of the unobtainable object of desire that one is supposed to find but never does. This object, which Lacan also connects with Freud's 'Sovereign Good' (1959–1960: 56), is yet again the mother who does not exist. Here the mother is specifically associated with *das Ding*, the thing in its 'dumb' reality (1959–1960: 55) that is found in the Real, and therefore beyond signification.

How does the subject-mother escape these connotations with 'dumb' reality that cling to her? My suggestion is that, in part, she needs to establish that she has her own understandings and dealings with dumb reality, and in part she is the one who notices that dumb reality is never really dumb. Perhaps it is unfair to call psychoanalysis to question on this issue. Psycho-analysis is largely the study of the effects of unconscious mental processes, of precisely what goes on unbeknown to us. Why should it concern itself with the mundane world of things? However, psychoanalysis also wishes to account for how 'things' get inside us, how the internal is both related to and formed out of its interaction with 'external reality', and must surely, to some extent, deal with an expanded notion of objects or things? What psychoanalysis is less good at acknowledging is that just as there are elements of our internal world that resist self-knowledge, that always remain obscure, so there are elements of the external world that escape our projective impulses, that resist internalization, that remain intact despite our need to relate to them in fantasy as part of our internal world, and that at times take us by surprise or bite back.

Intentional objects

It has been suggested that Freud attended the lectures of the philosopher Franz Brentano (Jones 1953) and drew heavily on Brentano's concept of intentional objects for his own notion of *Besetzung*, translated usually as 'cathexis' or 'psychic investment' (McIntosh 1986). Brentano's notion of intentionality centres on a distinction between intentional contents, inten-tional objects and actual objects (Brentano 1874). In section IX of the Appendix to *Psychology from an Empirical Standpoint*, Brentano discusses how we think about a centaur: 'All mental references refer to things. In many cases, the things to which we refer do not exist'. Although this object, the centaur, may not exist, it is also not purely an idea. Brentano states:

> Every mental phenomenon includes something as object within itself, although they do not all do so in the same way. In presen-tation something is presented, in judgement something is affirmed or denied, in love loved, in hate hated, in desire desired and so on.
> (Brentano 1874: 88–89)

McIntosh (1986) helpfully explicates this distinction by describing the intentional content as a set of blueprints for a building, the intentional object as the building that would be realized if one constructed it exactly as specified in the blueprints and the actual object as the building constructed if building work went ahead. The actual object would always deviate at least in some slight way from the building defined by the blueprints, that is, from the intentional object. The content of the intentional state is then what most closely corresponds to the notion of an 'idea' or 'mental representation', that is, the blueprint. The intentional object is constructed out of such mental contents, but is not itself mental in the way that an idea or feeling is. It appears to be more like the building that the blueprint aims for but is itself impossible to realize. *It retains some of its objectness within the idea.* The actual object then always has some slight deviation from both the set of blueprints and the intentional object that the blueprint aims at, and misses.

In a psychoanalytic grappling with this notion of objectness, one of the meanings of *das Ich*, McIntosh (1986) suggests, is one's self as an intentional object, an object of libidinal or aggressive investment. This corresponds to the person one believes, wishes or hopes oneself to be, and is not the same as the 'actual' object, one's actual person. The 'actuality' of objects, as well as our own status as 'actual objects' for ourselves and for one another, lies in some minor difference, some small overlooked discrepancy between what we take ourselves and objects to be, and what we and they 'actually are'. Although it is clearly impossible to know our 'actuality', perhaps all we can know is that neither ourselves nor the world is exactly what we take it to be. The 'actuality' of the object lies in its minute difference from our intention. 'Actuality' becomes paradoxically the 'discrepancy' or difference; the unnameable bit that leaks out.

The aim of this digression into the nature of intentional objects is to try to pave the way for objects to be thought of as both social and ethical. To do this I have tried to provide a bridge between psychoanalysis and proponents of a social theory of objects such as Bruno Latour, who I will discuss below, by way of the intentional object. But in order to do this, we may need to broaden our terms, and move away from object, thing, and possession all together. Perhaps they are too mired in a psychoanalytical interpretation of objective reality that always renders the mother an object of desire, and fails to articulate the mother's relation to material objects, despite the acknowledged 'failure' to stand up to the test of 'actuality' of the objects involved.

Zeug

There is another set of terms, associated with the work of Martin Heidegger, that includes 'equipment', 'tools', 'gear' or 'stuff'. In a translator's footnote to *Being and Time* (Heidegger 1927), Heidegger's term *das Zeug* is explained in the following way:

> The word 'Zeug' has no precise English equivalent. While it may mean any implement, instrument, or tool, Heidegger uses it for the most part as a collective noun which is analogous to our relatively specific 'gear' (as in 'gear for fishing') or the more elaborate 'paraphernalia', or the still more general 'equipment'. . . . In this

collective sense 'Zeug' can sometimes be used in a way which is comparable to the use of 'stuff' in such sentences as 'there is plenty of stuff lying around'.

(Macquarrie and Robinson 1962: 97)

In the section of *Being and Time* that deals with the 'Worldhood of the World', Heidegger (1927: 97) attempts to describe the 'kind of Being which equipment possesses'. The Being of equipment is always related to the 'in-order-to'; the task that the equipment is geared towards. However, this is not a simple matter of a hammer being designed to beat out metal. Equipment is always experienced *'in terms of [aus]* its belonging to other equipment: ink-stand, pen, ink, paper, blotting pad, table, lamp, furniture, windows, doors, room' (Heidegger 1927: 97, original emphases). In other words, the room is encountered initially as 'equipment for residing' before it is encountered as a set of individual objects, and the 'arrangement' emerges first before any perception of individual objects. Things are then not grasped thematically or initially 'known' about through using them. Rather, Heidegger states, the hammering has 'appropriated' the hammer in the most 'suitable' way. We grab the hammer and use it, and in doing so 'the hammering itself uncovers the specific 'manipulation' of the hammer' (1927: 98), just as we reside in the room, we take up or use the objects, and residing itself is what uncovers the Being of such equipment. Heidegger calls this kind of Being 'readiness-to-hand' (1927: 98).

There are, however, certain situations in which it becomes possible to glimpse the 'worldly character' of what is embedded in the world – the objectness of objects. These situations occur when what is ready-to-hand becomes unusable, or not properly adapted for the use it is needed for, or the tool turns out to be damaged, or the material turns out to be unsuitable. In these situations the object's unusability emerges from our dealings with it, and the equipment itself becomes 'conspicuous'. 'This conspicuousness', Heidegger (1927: 103) writes, 'presents the ready-to-hand equipment as a certain un-readiness-to-hand'. It is at that moment that the thing presents itself as an equipmental Thing. Similarly things show up as things when they are missing: 'which not only are not handy ["handlich"] but are not "to hand" ["zur Hand"]' (1927: 103). When something is missing, the things you do have thrust themselves in your face as not the thing you need, and in Heidegger's terms they 'obtrude'. To miss something amounts to coming across something unready-to-hand. Likewise we can also encounter the unready-to-hand through coming across an obstacle, something that stands in our way and obstructs the ready-to-hand. It is when an assignment is disturbed either by 'conspicuousness, obtrusiveness or obstinacy' (1927: 104), that the assignment becomes explicit.

> Being-in-the-world . . . amounts to a non-thematic circumspective absorption in references or assignments constitutive for the

readiness-to-hand of a totality of equipment. Any concern is already as it is, because of some familiarity with the world. In this familiarity Dasein can lose itself in what it encounters within-the-world and be fascinated with it . . . . The presence-at-hand of entities is thrust to the fore by the possible breaks in that referential totality in which circumspection 'operates'.

(Heidegger 1927: 107)

Joel turns his face away just at the moment the spoon approaches, smearing pumpkin across his cheek, then grabs the spoon and bangs it against the plastic bowl and then throws it across the room.

The spoon, now musical instrument, now extension of his body-flung-away, has met with an Heideggarian 'obstacle', has become 'obtrusive' and momentarily is shown up in its 'tool-being'. 'Feeding' reveals the spoon as a 'feeder' at the point that it fails to feed the baby. *But the spoon is not revealed to the baby, but to the mother.* The-baby-and-spoon is a conglomerate object malfunction, leaving the mother with an experience of a messy and failed attempt to complete her task – to get the spoon plus food inside the baby's mouth. A Heideggerian reading would maintain that the 'presence-at-hand' of things is constantly offered up to the mother, allowing her to glimpse such things in themselves. A mother's experience of 'feeding' reveals to her the presence-at-hand of the spoon, food and child. In so many of her dealings with objects, she meets with obstacles that reveal to her the peculiar being of things. The inherent unpredictability of the baby or child is a result of the child's 'unfamiliarity' with the world. The child is not yet embedded, and therefore provides 'breaks' in the world by revealing to the mother the obtrusiveness, obstinacy and conspicuousness of the objects of her work. Part of the frustration of motherhood appears to be the way that, just as you think you have established a certain set of procedures, got a routine going, found a way to function with the baby, the baby goes and changes, throws the routine out of kilter, goes off a certain food, will not be soothed in the way you thought she liked. But these events take place through a relation with objects, and it is their 'tool-being' that is revealed by the baby's mysterious changes of heart.

Harman (2001: 2) argues that Heidegger's 'tool-analysis' provides the key to the whole Heideggarian project, which he reads as a general 'object-orientated philosophy'. Harman is seeking to invigorate arguments around the philosophy of language by reintroducing the 'brute reality' of objects.

Red billiard ball smacks green billiard ball. Snowflakes glitter in the light that cruelly annihilates them; damaged submarines rust along the ocean floor. As flour emerges from mills and blocks of

136

limestone are compressed by earthquakes, gigantic mushrooms spread in the Michigan forest. While human philosophers bludgeon each other over the very possibility of 'access' to the world, sharks bludgeon tuna fish, and icebergs smash into coastlines.

(Harman 2001: 1)

Harman's argument is that Heidegger is usually read as proposing that ready-to-hand and present-at-hand correspond to the sphere of the subject and object respectively. However, objects do not need human subjectivity to reveal each other to each other. When the billiard balls collide, if one is shiny and hot, these properties will not be 'felt' by the other, but they will be 'felt' by a speck of ice on the surface of one of the balls. Philosophy, Harman writes, must stop lumping 'monkeys, tornadoes, diamonds, and oil under the single heading of that-which-lies-outside', and start building an object-orientated philosophy. This would lead us to start with the object, rather than the mother and child, to think about the objects of motherhood from the point of view of the object. Although this sounds a bizarre approach, it is similar to the main thrust of Bruno Latour's work, and opens us onto the notion of the ethics of objects. In the next section I look at an aspect of Latour's work that thinks about what objects offer human subjects, before turning to Scarry's work on the ethics of objects, in order to try to understand what the objects of motherhood may offer a mother that opens her onto the new.

Ethical objects

The only assignable difference between animal societies and our own resides . . . in the object. Our relationships, social bonds, would be airy as clouds were there only contracts between subjects. In fact, the object . . . stabilizes our relationships . . . . For an unstable bond of baboons, social changes are flaring up every minute. One could characterize their history as unbound, insanely so . . . . The social bond would only be fuzzy and unstable if it were not objectified.

(Serres 1995: 87–88)

It would appear from the quote above that Serres is articulating a view of the social that would need the 'extra-social' element of the object in order to stabilize human sociality (Albertsen and Diken 2003: 20). The object is posited as heterogeneous to the social, the 'stuff' that objectifies the social bond, and makes it possible. Human society, in other words, is held together by the non-human elements.

Heavily indebted to Serres, Bruno Latour and others, in their articulation of actor-network theory (Callon 1986; Latour 1992, 1997), have drawn our attention to the need to examine our relation to the non-human world from a position other than that of the human gazing across the sacred barrier that divides us from a radically different set of objects. This position is one in which the cultural/natural divide is reconceptualized as a continuum, and, in Latour's typically provocative turn of phrase, one in which we are encouraged to embrace our 'brethren' (Latour 1992). Here the object is no longer thought of as 'extra-social'. Rather, the non-human is brought into the realm of the 'social', as one of our fellows, and we are urged to seek to illuminate the 'associations' between humans and non-humans. While Serres' view is that objects are understood to localize social interactions through their ability to frame what is otherwise unstable complexity, Latour refuses a distinction of the human and non-human based on a notion of the social. Instead he sees only 'actors', some human, some non-human, some skilled, some unskilled, some of whom act to make things easier, some to make things harder, in an ongoing exchange of properties (Latour 1992). An actor, for Latour,

> is a semiotic definition – an actant – that is, something that acts or to which activity is granted by others. It implies no special motivation of human individual actors, nor of humans in general. An actant can literally be anything provided it is granted to be the source of an action.
>
> (Latour 1997: unpaginated webpage)

Latour is seeking to show up the ways objects 'act' just as much as their human counterparts. *Things*, in other words, act, including human subjects.

If we are to 'follow' the actors, as he suggests, rather than pour our energies into trying to understand or know them, then we can begin to investigate the mutually constitutive relationships between the human and non-human; the way a door acts to allow human movement across a wall, the action of hinges so that holes do not need to be made and filled and made and filled, the way the door groom acts to store energy from those opening the door within the piston mechanism so that it can release that energy slowly, keeping heat inside the building without the door smashing into the next person's face. Actor-network theory is stubbornly attached to descriptions, not of objects themselves, but of their sociality, of the types of actions that flow from one actor or actant to another, the work actors do for each other, and the changes that their movements produce. In doing so, Latour touches on the ethical relations between the human and non-human by showing us what objects do for us. At once both ironic and thoroughly literal, he writes:

> According to some physicists there is not enough mass in the universe to balance the accounts that cosmologists make of it. They

are looking everywhere for the 'missing mass' that could add up to the nice expected total. It is the same with sociologists. They are constantly looking, somewhat desperately, for social links sturdy enough to tie all of us together or for moral laws that would be inflexible enough to make us behave properly. . . . I expect sociologists to be much more fortunate than cosmologists since they soon will discover their missing mass. To balance our accounts of society we simply have to turn our attention away from humans and look at non-humans. Here they are, the hidden and despised social masses who make up our morality. They knock at the door of sociology requesting a place in the accounts of society as stubbornly as the human masses did in the 19th century.

(Latour 1992: unpaginated webpage)

If we take Latour at face value then we are invited to explore the ethical relations between a mother, a child and the material objects that are used in her maternal work. We would have to write from the point of view of the object itself, to think our way into the position of the object in order to describe in detail its actions. I would take this as an invitation to approach the mother and child as appendages, for example, to the pram, as the pram goes about in the urban cityscape, navigating kerbs, mounting inhospitable buses, buckling under the pressure of too much weight, folding uncomfortably when the rain cover does not fit, upturning when the balance between child and objects hanging from the handle bars is no longer equal, unzipping itself into a bed when the child needs to sleep, pulling a second or third child on a buggy board attached to its back. The pram acts in all sorts of ways to both aid and fail to aid the mother in her work caring for the child. In doing so it changes the relations between mother and child as well as between the mother and her environment, and ultimately the mother and her self.

One of the consequences of 'following the actors' is that things that were previously perceived as background get artificially foregrounded. In doing so, a deliberate disjunction is produced, in some ways a ridiculous one, but one that performs a necessary function in refocusing our attention on what we would usually overlook. In Latour's piece, 'Where are the missing masses? Sociology of a door' (Latour 1992), he describes in detail a number of background elements of experience, artificially anchoring our attention to the door groom in order to make a break with our usual perception of ourselves taking the simple action of walking through a door. This foregrounding of the background performs a deliberate disjunction between the subject and the normally embedded relations within the environment. In doing so, Latour performs a kind of Heideggerian strategy at a textual level, calling into question the relationship between the human and non-human, and reorientating us towards a hybrid network in which facts or artefacts are situated.

139

Furthermore, Tonkinwise (2004) has pointed out that it is through focusing on 'rude things' that Latour shows up the ethical content of objects. The door spring that stores energy to release it later works to allow some humans through, but not others. Children, pregnant women, people with infirmaties, those carrying parcels, Latour points out, struggle to open such a door due to the resistance in the spring. To this extent the object is rude, badly mannered, even immoral. In calling our attention to the rudeness of objects, Latour calls on us to adjust the situation, to design better, to make the object more moral. We might argue then, that by foregrounding not the mother herself, but the mother as an encumbered body, the mother with her pram, her baby, her bags, her stuff, as she encounters doors and buses and stairs and kerbs, the task becomes one of understanding the ethical nature of those objects that are rude to her, what they do and fail to do for the mother, and hence how to aid them to act in a more moral, less badly behaved and less rude manner.

The human endeavour of making objects more ethical brings us to Elaine Scarry's monumental work, *The Body in Pain* (Scarry 1985). The book is subtitled *The making and unmaking of the world*, and despite the apparent grandiosity of such a title, her work is a very concrete engagement with just this. Her concerns are with tracing the structure of 'uncreating', evidenced in the acts of torture and war, which in turn illuminates the structure of 'creating'. Crucial to the link she makes between unmaking and making is her conviction that the problem of suffering must be understood within the wider frame of the problem of creating. *The Body in Pain* is essentially a description of the relation between pain and the imagination, understood as the two interrelated framing poles of all of human activity and endeavour.

My interest in Scarry's work, and its relevance to my exploration of the stuff of motherhood, is to do with her analysis of the production of artefacts. Like Latour, Scarry sees the necessity for examining artefacts in order to understand more fully their relation to human subjects, and in order that they can express and thereby relieve us more fully of our internal sentience. She appears to enact exactly Latour's suggestion that we need an understanding of well-behaved and rude objects in order to understand how we can release the object's ethical capacity. This may provide a way to conceive of a mother's relation to the objects of her work in ethical terms in which the mother is relieved of something by the object, rather than always thinking about the mother's ethical work as entailing the mother's altruistic or self-sacrificial gesture towards the child.

Uncreation and creation

Scarry's intention in the first half of the book is to expose the relation between pain and power, and show how the infliction of pain not only

140

achieves its effects by exploiting the difficulties we have with expressing pain within language, but also mimics this process of the 'deconstruction' of language itself. Not only does the torturer shatter language by inflicting pain, reducing the prisoner to wordless cries, but also torture is almost always accompanied by the verbal act of interrogation. Interrogation involves an insistent, urgent questioning, but very often to people who have no useful answers to give their interrogators, while at the same time, a 'world-destroying' pain is being inflicted. Not only does pain render the prisoner speechless, but also he or she is simultaneously compelled to speak. Through the dual elements of inflicting pain and prolonged interrogation, torture 'graphically objectifies the step-by-step backward movement along the path by which language comes into being and which is here being reversed or uncreated or deconstructed' (Scarry 1985: 20).

Perversely, torture can be successfully presented to the outside world as an activity of 'intelligence-gathering' despite the fact that the true meaning of the word is 'stupidity', in the sense of 'the inability to sense the sentience of other persons' (Scarry 1985: 278). Similarly war, primarily centred on the reciprocal activity of injuring, can be described as though injuring was absent or secondary to its structure. In both instances, what is demonstrated is the ways in which our descriptive powers, our capacities to use language effectively, break down in relation to physical pain. Pain then shows a particular resistance to language inherent in the structure of pain itself. Pain *is* what is unspeakable, an intensely private and incommunicable state that is by definition unshareable. It can be pointed at, we can use metaphors to try to describe our pain, but it cannot be fully grasped by anyone outside the boundaries of the individual body.

In Scarry's view, pain's inherent resistance to language is due to its lack of an intentional object (1985: 164). Unlike other feeling states, such as love, fear, or ambivalence that can be spoken of in reference to their objects (I love ice-cream, I fear the dark, I am ambivalent about my Jewish heritage), pain is not *of* or *for* anything. And it is precisely because it has no intentional object that, more than any other phenomenon, it resists objectification in language. It follows that when states of consciousness are deprived of their object, they begin to approach pain; when the object of love is unobtainable, when fear is no longer fear of the dark, but a nebulous, pervasive fear of the unknown. And conversely, pain is lessened through its transformation into an objectified state.

Having established torture and war as processes of 'uncreation' or 'deconstruction', in which the very ability to communicate or make exterior our interior sentient being is what is being destroyed, Scarry (1985) turns to this principle itself in her descriptions of making or creating. Making and creating are bound up with making exterior or material our internal worlds. Human making entails 'making-up' and then 'making-real', both the imaginative and material phases of creation. What is crucial to her argument is that if we approach creating through an understanding of torture and war we begin to understand that creating may be bound up with morality and justice. Creating is often conflated with 'materialism' and seen as empty of ethical content. However, Scarry argues that creating material objects is part of the original and ongoing project to diminish internal pain, and that in the West this legitimately occurs through material culture or material self-expression.

We have seen that Scarry establishes that pain and the imagination are linked through their position as each other's intentional object. Thinking back to Brentano's work, which Freud took up to develop the notion of psychic investment, the intentional object is the object of our beliefs, desires, wishes, which differs from the intentional content (the blueprint itself) and from the actual object (the material reality of the building that is finally built). The intentional object is the building that the blueprint describes. Scarry establishes that, in effect there is no building that the blueprint of pain describes. And imagination, on the other hand, is the only state that is wholly its objects. You cannot imagine nothing. To imagine is to call forth objects in the mind. This is its meaning. In fact, pain can be thought of as imagination's intentional state, and imagination as pain's intentional object (Scarry 1985: 164). Pushing this notion further, 'pain' and 'imagining' then constitute extreme conditions of intentionality as a state, on the one hand, and intentionality as self-objectification on the other. Between these two boundary conditions all the other, more familiar binary acts-and-objects are located.

Not only are pain and imagination each other's missing intentional counterparts, but also in many different languages there is one word that suggests that pain and the imagination are near synonyms, and this is the word 'work' (Scarry 1985: 170). It is here that the processes of creation and uncreation are linked. The ambivalence of the word 'work', holding connotations of both painful labour and the creation of artefacts, allows us to see how work approaches both ends of the spectrum between pain and the imagination. The more work works to transform itself into objects or artefacts, the closer it is to the imagination and culture, and the more it is unable to bring forth an object or is cut off from its object, the more it approaches the condition of pain.

Thus we can begin to see how Scarry brings back into focus the notion that the act of creating is bound up with ethics. To work to make visible internal sentient experiences (both pain and the imagination) is to counter the processes of both torture and war, which in complex ways act to destroy the capacity to create. In doing so, Scarry claims that the intact form (creating) has a moral claim on us, that we have a responsibility to attempt to eliminate pain in the world through the creating of things and ideas, and that the process of creating is completely bound up with bringing into a shareable space our internal sentient being.

142

Artefacts

Deeply humanist in her orientation, Scarry (1985: 281) claims that made objects are essentially projections of the human body. She gives numerous examples of the ways that specific body parts, needs or capacities can be projected: a gauze bandage over a wound mimics human skin; glasses, microscopes and telescopes are projections of the lens of the human eye; the structure of the human heart has been used to pump water, the institution-alized convention of written history, photographs, libraries, films, different forms of recordings, are all materializations of the embodied capacity for memory. In addition, objects can be projections that specifically deprive the external world of the privilege of being inanimate or unresponsive to sentient beings. To conceive the body as 'aliveness' or 'awareness of alive-ness' is to be aware of the felt-experience of sentience, and this, itself can also get projected out onto the object world.

This last point is an important one. The human imagination

> reconceives the external world, divesting it of its immunity and irresponsibility not by literally putting it in pain or making it animate but by, quite *literally, 'making it' as knowledgeable about human pain as if it were itself animate and in pain.*
>
> (Scarry 1985: 289, original emphases)

It is not that the natural external world knows about the 'hurtability' of human beings, but that the human awareness of its own aliveness is some-thing that gets projected onto the inanimate world as a way to objectify not only internal sentience, but also the awareness of internal sentience.

> A chair, as though it were itself put in pain, as though it knew from the inside the problem of body weight, will only then accommodate and eliminate the problem. A woven blanket or solid wall internalize within their design the recognition of the instability of body temper-ature and the preciousness of nakedness, and only by absorbing the knowledge of these conditions into themselves (by, as it were, being themselves subject to these forms of distress), absorb them out of the human body.
>
> (Scarry 1985: 288)

So, although the chair could be thought of as mimetic of the spine, and even of body weight, it can also most accurately be recognized as mimetic of sentient awareness itself. The chair literally embodies the wish to relieve the other in pain. Scarry claims its shape is the shape of 'perceived-pain-wished-gone' (1985: 290). The chair is the 'materialized structure of a perception; it is sentient awareness materialized into a freestanding design'

(1985: 290). Thus, in her imagining of the chair-maker going through the movements of making the chair, what we would see is a dance entitled 'body weight begone' (1985: 290). The chair-maker sees another in pain and wishes to relieve it, but this perception of the other's pain is replaced by the event of chair-making which becomes translated into a communicable form. The dance, in other words, is recorded on the surface of the wood by the tool. Finally the chair itself *is* a successful object. It will actually relieve someone's pain by giving them something to rest their body on, and it does so in a lasting way. The imagination is therefore not amoral but constantly at work, making the moral distinction between hurting and not hurting, at work on behalf of sentience.

Finally, Scarry closes the loop by taking us from pain and imagination to the artefact and back to the human subject. When human sentience is projected, through the labour of the imagination onto an artefact (a chair, coat, poem, telescope, medicine vaccine and so on), the artefact then refers back to human sentience, 'either directly extending its powers and acuity (poem, telescope) or indirectly extending its powers and acuity by eliminating its aversiveness (chair, vaccine)' (Scarry 1985: 307). The one arc of the loop makes no sense without the other, as the act of projection already assumes that the artefact will reciprocate. 'In the attempt to understand making, attention cannot stop at the object (the coat, the poem), *for the object is only a fulcrum or lever across which the force of creation moves back onto the human site* and remakes the makers' (Scarry 1985: 307, original emphases).

Here we have the object as a lever, always the midpoint in the total action, the movement from human to object and back again. Not only is something returned to the site of the human, but also in returning, the original projection is magnified. What is reciprocated far exceeds what was projected. We always get back more than we put in. Though we are in pain when we work, when we are engaged in the projective act of creating the object, the object, in its use, its durability, its capacity to be exchanged and to recreate itself gives back much more. The human subject then gets caught in a 'cascade of self-revision they have themselves authored' (Scarry 1985: 232), with the object reciprocating in such a way that the imagination is constantly revising the nature of creating.

Motherhood and the ethics of objects

How then does this help us to think about a mother and her objects? Heidegger's hierarchy of authentic objects (for example the bridge, or the Japanese tea cup) is swept away in the tide of objects the mother deals with – a kind of triumph of the proletarian object world. In terms of the thought, creativity and human labour that has gone into the contemporary

144

nappy, the non-spill juice bottle, the three-speed teat, the curved-edged feeding spoon that protects the baby from burning its mouth, let alone the modern pram, each object the mother uses contains something of the hero within it. She is literally overwhelmed by other people's labour. And part of the task some mothers feel they must take on is to sort through the hundreds of objects on offer in order to ascertain the moral quality of the object, trying to separate the 'good' from the 'bad'. Wood versus plastic, organic verses minimally sprayed, hand-made verses mass-produced.

As Daniel Miller (1997) has pointed out in his hilarious and also serious article 'How infants grow mothers in North London', if we rework Klein's interpretation of the infant's development from the mother's perspective, we can trace how mothers move from a paranoid-schizoid position in relation to their infants to a depressive one. In the paranoid-schizoid position the good and bad aspects of the infant have to be kept separate, usually by keeping the infant all good, and keeping the bad for oneself in the form of a crippling sense of guilt or projecting it onto available others such as one's own mother or mother-in-law. The more mature depressive position entails seeing that our infants can be experienced as containing both good and bad elements. Miller (1997) traces how the depressive position can be evidenced in a mother's shopping choices, initially choices about food and later about toys. The middle-class mothers living in a street in North London in Miller's study could initially control their children's food intake, and assessed organic vegetables and breast milk as 'good' and sugar and additives as 'bad'. Eventually the mothers realized they were in a losing battle as their infants gained access to biscuits, sweets and chocolates, and then later to processed foods such as burgers, pizzas, fish fingers and baked beans. In Miller's view, maturity could be achieved if mothers learnt to accept that their children would ingest both good and bad, itself a sign that they could accept that their children contained both good and bad qualities. In a similar way, mothers held out against their son's desires for guns or the daughter's cravings for dresses or Barbie, but again often found themselves bowing in various ways to the pressure, especially of what they perceived to be their child's corruption by materialism, commercialism and capitalism. Some responded by 'buying back' their children through getting them as many Barbies as they wanted. Miller's point is that what lies behind these phenomena is the cultural development of a normative category, 'the mother' within a culture that constantly seeks to define itself both in terms of nature and objects. The particular class fraction he studied used the procurement of objects as ways to construct themselves as mothers within emerging models of both 'nature' and 'materialism'.

If, however, we stay with the ethical content of the object itself, my contention would be that the mother is involved not only in constructing a version of herself through these procurements in relation to powerful norms, but also in assessing what belongs properly to the object. She perhaps understands that the object brings something with it that reciprocates; that a good pram really does alleviate her back pain, a well-thought-out feeding spoon really does protect her children's mouths; that some objects really do help her soothe them, educate them, amuse them. Objects do not just reciprocate in terms of helping her construct her identity. They reciprocate by recognizing in their turn the ethical nature of her work. Perhaps each of us, each mother–child–stuff triad, has their own particular example. I am truly grateful, for example, to the inventors of Lego® in relation to one of my children. But I am equally grateful to the inventors of a small plastic toy phone that played electronic nursery rhymes when you dialled the number. This toy saved me from hurting my child on a number of memorable occasions. The combination of its ability to mimic a coveted but forbidden object (the real phone) while also appealing to the small child's fascination with changes in tone, as well as being built to withstand being turned into a hammer, were acts of creative genius.

The mother in the city: freerunning

In 1990, Iris Young's view was that women in sexist society were physically handicapped (Young 1990). Perhaps we could adjust this somewhat, to a statement that mothers in urban, Western, consumer-orientated society are *encumbered*. I have tried in this chapter to develop a notion of the mother as the subject literally weighed down by stuff. This stuff gives her a certain viscosity that offsets her heightened sentience, but in addition, I have argued, it is stuff that at times reciprocates ethically. I wish to end this chapter by returning to the notion of the mother who is attempting to retain some sense of fluidity in the face of constant physical impediment, to see whether a comparison with the 'freerunner' or *'traceur'* could provide us with a model through which to think about maternal subjectivity that would take into account her encumbered status.

> Draw a straight line on a map of your hometown. Start from point a, and go to the point b. Don't consider the elements which are in your way (barriers, walls, wire fences, trees, houses, buildings) as obstacles. Hug them: climb, get over, jump: let your imagination flow: you're now doing parkour.
> (Urban Freeflow Network 2004: unpaginated webpage)

Parkour, also known as freerun or freerunning, is variously classed as a new urban sport, capoeira on buildings, bungee jumping without elastic rope or, by aficionados, as 'the art of movement', a new art form and in effect, a complete way of life. There is no equipment for freerunning other than the street furniture itself. Freerunners, also known as *traceurs*, move through the urban landscape, leaping from roof to roof, climbing up walls, walking along fences on their hands, vaulting benches, scaling trees, swinging from lampposts, and dropping from great heights. The ultimate childhood fantasy, a traceur is Spiderman without the web. Traceurs use no ropes, pins, crampons, gloves, safety equipment or nets. They walk up walls by training extensively, and developing a balletic level of skill and precision. For some of the hardcore originators, parkour is underpinned by an eclectic mix of new-age philosophical notions drawn from the Samurai's handbook, *L'Hagakure*, the films and personal philosophy of Bruce Lee, a variety of martial art forms, the work of physical educationalist George Herbert, and encompasses notions of freedom through fluidity. Sébastien Foucan, one of the founders, writes:

> Like break dancing and surfing, in their search of perfect fluidity and of the pure gesture, the traceur wants himself to be an imagination, a constant invention of the most limpid gesture.
>
> (Foucan 2004: unpaginated webpage)

There are few rules in parkour. Participants must always go forwards, never backwards, but their path can zig-zag around to take in interesting obstacles. Some moves are dramatic but the overall aim is to execute the move as elegantly as possible. Foucan talks of aiming for movement through the city that is 'feline'. Although the association with cat burglars has been made on a number of occasions, traceurs maintain the aim is to move across the urban landscape in as fluid and graceful way possible, the art being in making continuous movement through a creative encounter with the obstacle. Creativity is released by the obstacle itself.

Related to other slide sports such as skateboarding, parkour remains essentially an urban phenomenon, a way of playing within the urban landscape. However, unlike skateboarding, which has become largely ring-fenced within specifically designated skateboard parks, the essence of free-running means that traceurs can constantly break out of these restrictions, moving across the boundaries of confined spaces. Traceurs sometimes class what they do as the 'art of escaping'. The key objective is to create a 'run' where a series of obstacles are overcome in a creative, athletic, fluid way. Rather than those obstacles being other people, as in rugby or American football, where an individual also breaks free and finds a path through to the goal, the obstacles are the material constraints of the cityscape itself. Parkour requires an imaginative engagement in what goes beyond the confines of the demarcated areas for movement within a city. Instead of taking the evidence of our senses for granted (here is the street, it is a marked-out route through the city and we no longer think about it in terms of whether to take it or not) parkour claims to wonder whether there is another way to move forward, a way that hasn't yet been explored. What is usually seen as impeding movement is something that is then inverted and used to create movement. The encounter with a wall, building, railing, bench, lamppost or kerb throws up the possibility of a creative engagement to navigate such an obstacle through a number of athletic moves.

Foucan (2004) has pointed out that children look at the landscape as a playground. They see concrete bollards as objects to balance on top of, or to leap-frog over, low walls as something to walk along, railings as things to drag their hands along. As we gradually lose this imaginative engagement with the built environment, argues Foucan, the urban landscapes start to contain and channel us along predetermined routes. Walls and street furniture become obstacles rather than opportunities. Parkour becomes a way of reclaiming the city.

The mother-plus-baby-plus-buggy-plus-stuff is out roaming the city. She appears to be the antithesis of the freerunner. Though her body is encumbered she too wishes to 'run', to make a series of feline fluid movements flowing into one another that allow her to navigate the urban landscape.

I think about my journey with my two children from home to visit my mother. I live on the third floor of a block of flats with no lift. I must get my children and stuff and buggy down the stairs, and onto the street, and along the street, and off the kerb across the road, and over another road and another until I get to the tube station where I must find someone to help me carry my buggy-and-baby-and-stuff down the steps at the tube station while holding onto the hand of the older child, and then move through the barrier and down the escalator, balancing the baby-plus-buggy-plus-stuff at a most improbable angle while still holding onto the hand of the older child, and safely (the TERROR of that moment) get them off at the bottom. I am going to move beneath the city, through the tube network and come out in another part of the city, where I will navigate a similar set of stairs and barriers and kerbs and pavements and lights and traffic until I arrive at the door of my mother's house.

Let's slow down and watch this mother more closely.

She manoeuvres the older child out of the front door holding the baby. She must persuade the older child who is only just walking to wait alone while she carries the baby and the buggy downstairs, where she plans to deposit the baby, leaving it unattended while she walks back up to pick up the older child and carry him down. There is no place to leave the buggy downstairs, and the last one, a second-hand battered tatty old thing that she thought no one in their right mind would want to steal, would be safe at the bottom of the stairs, but someone must have thrown it into the communal bins, thinking that no one in their right mind would put a baby in THAT. So now she must carry the new buggy downstairs with the baby lodged on her other hip, and the older child, who has not been convinced to stay behind, crying now and dragging at her trousers. She has her handbag over one shoulder along with the buggy, and over the other, underneath the baby, she carries a second larger bag. It contains a bottle of milk and a change of clothes and nappies and wipes and some spare plastic bags for the baby, and a change of clothes for the older child, who is not completely toilet trained, and a box of snacks and drinks for the journey, and some books to look at. She moves down, one step at a time. She is sweating now. There are 52 steps. She knows as she has counted them with the older child many times.

She has to go on. There is no going back. Otherwise there is no life at all. No visit to the mother who may or may not look after her, and probably has forgotten what it means to have two small children in the city; who looks at her sweating daughter who was meant to have it all and shakes her head at how much hard work it is, keeping it all going. Perhaps, after all, nothing significant was achieved.

She is at the bottom now. The buggy is not one of those that opens on its own. This one needs two hands. Although whoever designed it thought of many things that the mother needs – padded handles, a nice string sack to put the shopping in – they didn't think about the most important thing. They didn't picture her as she is now, laying the small baby on the bottom stair while she unfolds the pram. There is no other solution. Once she handed the baby to a stranger as she got off the bus, smiling openly and saying matter-of-factly, 'Could you just hold the baby while I unfold the pram'. She felt the stranger stiffen. He thought she was crazed. No one in their right MIND would hand their baby to a STRANGER. The immoral object prompts an ethical dilemma, and a rare point of contact between strangers across the precious body of the baby.

The baby is in the pram now, and the bags are hanging from the handle bars, and the older child is standing on the buggy board that sticks out from the back of the pram in such a way that the mother walks tipped forward to avoid tripping, her back hunching over all the stuff. She propels her load out onto the street, avoids dog shit and approaches the first kerb. This is not one of those that the council have redone yet. The older child really has to get off the buggy board otherwise the weight of the buggy as she tips it forward off the kerb makes it almost impossible for her to get it out of the rut without tipping the baby out. The older child doesn't want to get off. The mother bumps the front wheels of the buggy down into the gutter and then shoves hard, twice, to get the back wheels and the buggy board to come with it. The pram looks ready to collapse but rights itself, holding out. They stagger on. The mother dreads getting up the other side so she wheels her load into the road for a while until she can find the next ramped section. The older child reminds her in a singsong voice that it isn't safe to walk in the road.

Perhaps it really is too hard to go on. The mother and the traceur appear so radically disjunct, their experiences so cruelly different, that the latter can only operate as an alter ego for the encumbered, distracted and literally overwhelmed figure that I have traced. However, I want to suggest that there are more similarities between the traceur's run and the mother's than appear at first glance. Parkour allows the traceur to experience the spatial elements of the city anew through engaging directly with its material elements – the surfaces, textures, masses, heights and solidity of the street furniture. The traceur makes momentary and precise judgements about whether to jump, what jump to use, how to land, what to follow with, based on both a sensory experience of the obstacle, and an internal sense of their own capacities and limits. Pushing at the boundaries of their own fear, they are also trying to keep themselves safe.

So too the mother. Though impeded and weighed down by her objects, each obstacle she encounters forces her to renegotiate her relationship with another set of objects: a kerb, stair, entrance, doorway, stranger. She can balk at it, but if she wants to move about the city she must ultimately find a way through. Like the freerunner, she may deliberately make light of the difficulty of her stunts, may not even consciously be aware that she navigates them on a moment-by-moment basis. She too engages with the material elements of the city; sees with fresh eyes both the broken and rude elements, and the occasional objects that reciprocate back.

I want to conclude by suggesting that one overlooked aspect of maternal subjectivity is this encumbered experience that is felt as both burdensome, and in a paradoxical way, oddly generative. I want to suggest that the new kinetic experience that motherhood brings on is one in which the mother re-experiences both her own viscosity (her materiality, if you like), and her own internal sentience (both pain and the imagination) through an encounter with objects, be they the artefacts, the tool-beings of motherhood or the mundane street furniture she stumbles on.

'Oh', she says as she rights herself once more: 'Here I am . . .'

7

INTENTIONS, INCONSISTENCIES, INCONCLUSIONS

I began this book with an anecdote about anecdotes. Not only was Bobby Baker's performance itself a series of anecdotes about mothering, but also I had been told anecdotally about this seminal performance by people who had seen the original show in 1988. At this point Bobby was just emerging from eight long years of motherhood, and beginning to investigate the potentials of her experiences. Literally using food (one of the primary 'materials' of motherhood) as paint, and painting as performance, she thereby rendered motherhood as a kind of artistic practice, and in the process produced a whole new set of artistic materials in the form of food products, which she would then go on to develop as the central materials over her long performance art career.[1] It appears that motherhood offered Bobby a way forwards artistically. *Drawing on a Mother's Experience* evidences new ways of thinking about duration, texture, colour, spontaneity, process-as-production, and performance itself. Perhaps as a result, the anecdotal story I received was that Bobby's original performance held a raw, exciting, enigmatic quality, opening motherhood up as an experience that could not be contained within the dichotomies of pleasure and pain, but that produced its own rich set of possibilities that she had barely begun to trace.

Like all anecdotes, this proved to be something of a tall story, a little embellished, told for effect, rendering an experience more exceptional through the very process of singling out the story for telling. I went to the video of the performance hoping to experience something of that rawness and excitement and of course was disappointed; not just because video always flattens precisely these live qualities that renders performance enigmatic, but because the video was of the performance twenty years on. The 'original experience' was lost. Bobby was herself now recounting anecdotes about anecdotes, reliving her original anecdotes through the lens of twenty years of both mothering and artistic experience.

Realizing that I was longing for the experience to be more than it could be led me to think about anecdotes themselves as a kind of longing for an experience to be more significant, more funny, more interesting than the original. Selecting a particular incident for the purposes of anecdote gave it something extra, elevated it from the mundane to the significant, although its significance could still remain minor in relation to some other more major story. Anecdotal theory seemed like the right kind of vehicle with which to elevate the mundane details of a mother's daily life to the status of 'material' that could then be available for reflection, analysis, even 'research'. It could hold on to the humorous and acknowledge the impulse to make the most of something, without losing sight of theory that would always seek to bring one back down to size. As a quasi-methodology, anecdotal theory seemed to offer a way to investigate something extra issuing from motherhood itself, what I alluded to vaguely as 'new inner resources' that I wanted to conceptualize as somehow beyond a new identity, role or set of tasks. My hope was that an anecdotal approach to maternity would make visible a range of sensations, intensities, experiences, sensibilities, thoughts, emotions, moods and encounters, culminating in a new collection of 'raw materials' with which to think about maternal subjectivity that did not return us directly to notions of containment or holding in tension love and hate. In the introduction I described this kind of longing for something to have been more than or better than it really was as a kind of ethical movement, the difference between what is and what ought to be, holding out, rather grandly for the project itself to have ethical legitimacy as well as wanting to accord the mother an ethics she could call her own.

However, I also sought to undercut my own grandiose aims, trying to steer myself away from the temptation to try my hand at constructing a new account of any kind of subjectivity, let alone a maternal one. In some senses the tensions of this book lie in my attempt to move in two opposite directions at the same time. In one sense I have tried to write an albeit partial phenomenology of motherhood, unhitching maternal experience from any substantive notion of 'maternal subjectivity' where I can, suggesting that the attainment or fragmentation of subjectivity is not perhaps our most pressing current psychological or academic concern. After all, the question of what or who comes after the Subject has prompted a return to much more modest, local interests, inducing a necessary myopia, forcing one to view small sections of a field of inquiry through a limited lens. My attempt to stay close to phenomena by writing off the back of maternal anecdotes has brought a rather limping, distracted, encumbered figure into view; a mother and her child in which the child figures almost as an extra, highly unpredictable limb, attached, yet doing its own thing, and affecting the mother's whole orientation in the world, though not in wholly unpleasant ways.

And yet, I want to question the inherent tension between the mundane and the grandiose; between my attempt at a partial phenomenology of motherhood and questions I have inevitably raised about the nature of maternal subjectivity, as, despite myself, I think that my attempt to unhitch maternal experience from a substantive account of maternal subjectivity has not been completely successful, though perhaps without uninteresting results. For I have found myself unable to fully embrace the kind of dispassionate anti-humanism that is necessary to follow through the phenomenological task in which things and human selves, even oneself, are observed and mined for witty, unusual insights while maintaining a certain aloofness and critical distance, an indifference really, so that maybe nothing really matters, there is nothing to sign up for, no movement to join, nothing to get too excited about. For women of my generation *something is still at stake*, though perhaps no longer identifiable simply in terms of the personal being political, given that both the personal and political are no longer identifiable themselves as stable terms. 'Someone', or perhaps ideally a number of different people, do, after all, *still have to love the children*. In a not completely serious manner, I suggested that an answer to the question what/who comes after the Subject might be informed by taking the maternal subject, glimpsed as a bizarre dis-abled figure, as if she were 'normal'. If, in other words, we are serious about the ethical turn and that we want to account for human subjectivity through some understanding of how we come to be structured by our relation to others, then we could just as well start with the mother, whose structuring through a relation to her child poses all sorts of intractable problems, especially when posed in the feminine, when we begin to examine what it means to 'be for another'. In addition, it is difficult, in the light of the many hundreds of clinical maternal stories I have listened to, to simply abandon the project of trying to write an albeit partial account of maternal subjectivity. Mothers often struggle to make sense of the competing and conflicting emotions, sensations, thoughts, and impulses that they contend with on a daily basis, as well as to juggle identities, social pressures, cultural norms, parental influences and the like. The mothers I have worked with therapeutically over the years have constantly expressed the desire to meet with others to discuss what mothering was like; to share stories, guilts, anxieties, failures and confusions, as well as to try to sort out a way to proceed. The upsurge in confessional books about motherhood, and many thousands of blogs attest to the same need to voice ways in which motherhood changes (and occasionally saves) our lives.

The dis-abled mother

Where did the phenomenological strain in this work take me? The question I began with was 'what is it like to encounter a child?' What is it like to be in the world with this extra unpredictable limb, to be dis-abled by motherhood, made to experience ourselves, our relations, our kinetic being, our spatio-temporal orientations anew, to be constantly 'thrown off the subject' by motherhood? What does it feel like, look like, smell like, what thoughts and feelings can we notice, what dilemmas emerge, what sensations, images, tinglings, moods? In what kinds of moments do we realize our dis-ablement, and what form does this realization take?

What emerged anecdotally were experiences of being impeded, encumbered, slowed down, weighed down, shaken up, disturbed, made strange, dislodged, interrupted, strung-out, punched-drunk, stopped in one's tracks, and pushed close to a simulated death. The mother did nothing exceptional: she crossed a street, burst into tears without knowing why, went to a school play, struggled to get used to using her child's name, lost the vital transitional object, watched her child having a tantrum, did not know how to put a nappy on, found herself thanking the makers of Lego®, waited while her stammering child tried to speak. Many of the overtones of these experiences were of embarrassment, discomfort, exhaustion, shock, surprise, blankness, uncanniness, bewilderment, oddness, terror, frustration and absurdity. And yet, out of these experiences emerged new qualities: those of physical viscosity, heightened sentience, a renewed awareness of objects, of one's own emotional range and emotional robustness, a space to think, an engagement with the built environment and street furniture, a renewed temporal awareness where the present was elongated and the past and future no longer felt to be so tangible, a renewed encounter with oneself as a speaking subject, a realization that love is the condition of remaining truthful to the absolute disjunction between two positions of experience.

Although in many ways the world closed down for this mother – she felt chained to her child, unable to finish a sentence, think or sleep, lost her sense of being agile, capable, quick, self-reflective or as possessing self-understanding – another kind of world opened up. It is not that she saw the world through her child's eyes. She saw it through her own eyes, but the child's relentlessly unpredictable and extreme presence forced her into an appreciation of experiences she had skimmed over before. She noticed herself speaking, moving, thinking, relating, crying . . . 'Oh,' she said as she righted herself once more: 'Here I am . . .'.

At the same time, the philosophical strain of this work attempted to make small forays into unfamiliar terrain to look for alternative ways of articulating maternal subjectivity than those furnished purely by psychoanalytic or discursive accounts. I was concerned to move away from understanding maternal subjectivity in terms of maternal desire which requires the mother to look away from her child, towards her lover, work, hobbies or interests, or unconsciously towards her own father or mother. I also wanted to widen the account by looking beyond the subjective experience of the mother's necessary role as container of the child's emotional extremities. This appeared to negate the specificity of the maternal position, grounded in responsibility for the life of the other whom one elects as one's child, and leave a void in theorizing a specifically maternal subjectivity. I was also unhappy about the way maternity had been co-opted in discussions of female subjectivity to mark sexual difference, and then relegated to the other side of femininity when maternity was seen as the danger of the hardening of desire around the unity of the child, threatening the fluidity of the feminine. It appeared that maternity was being used as a kind of theoretical football, pulled into focus and then shoved away again, in much the same way as the mother has traditionally been used in psychoanalysis to shore up the borders of the subject without achieving subjectivity herself.

Chapter 2 looked at what Levinas could offer in terms of understanding an ethical relation that does not require a self-abnegating subject who disappears for the sake of the other. For Levinas, the subject does not exist prior to the Other, and is called into being only through ethical responsibility. To be *is* to be responsible, grounding ethics as first philosophy. This went some way towards offering an inversion of notions that the mother has a 'self' or a 'life' that she must give up or put to one side when she accommodates the other who is her child, without at the same time negating her ethical relation to the child. Her subjectivity *as a mother* could be then thought to emerge at the point of her ethical responsibility for the other, whatever she was before, and it was the specificity of the other-who-is-one's-child that would then allow an exploration of a subjectivity we could call maternal. This allowed for a certain conceptualization of newness in relation to subjectivity, without newness being folded back into a psychoanalytic notion of repetition or return. We were also immediately situated 'otherwise' than the mired dichotomies around the transition to motherhood that I explored in Chapter 3, whether conceived of as a movement from fluidity to unity or the other way around.

Through Levinas' figure for paternity, we saw the emergence of subjectivity expanded to include the particular relation a parent has with a child. Paternity is the one relation with alterity in which the 'I' transcends itself and is also returned to itself. One sees the possibilities of the other this time *as your own*, allowing an escape from the closure of one's own identity, *while also being returned to yourself.* Unusually in Levinas, paternity is a kind of ontology, but not one that constitutes the 'I am' as a monadic unity. The 'I am' of 'I am my child' is immediately dispersed, as the 'child' is understood as a set of possibilities that one takes to be one's own but is still what is yet to come, itself constitutive of time by engendering a future. The relationship is not reciprocal – I am my child but my child is not me; my child is a stranger, looking already away from the parent towards the next generation. So in this sense, it was not that the mother recognized herself in the child, but that she *discovered* herself there for the first time. Something came back from the relation with the child that was an experience of one's own strangeness, distinctness, particularity and strangeness-to-oneself; an experience, that is, of alterity that does not negate the subject. Through the anecdote about naming and being named by a child, moving from the disturbing experience of taking responsibility for fixing the child in the symbolic prior to their conscious involvement with language, to the experience of being brought out of silence (mum) to speech (Lisa) by the child, this experience of self-discovery through strangeness was glimpsed.

Although my encounter with Levinas allowed some enunciation of maternal subjectivity, it was premised on both upsetting the paternal function in Levinas (paternity being understood as the establishment of relations that are 'beyond the possible' in the figure of the 'son') and upsetting the current historically and culturally specific paternal function of assigning a proper name to my child.[2] Of course, to engage in 'upsetting' the paternal function is a classic characterization of the feminine, being excessive to the symbolic into whose entry the paternal confers the law, as well as being embraced as a feminist strategy. As we saw in Kristeva, the maternal is precisely that which disturbs the symbolic by suggesting that the speaking subject is constantly threatened by the heterogeneity of the drive, seen in maternity as *herethics*; the mother's commitment to both herself and the species. However, unlike Kristeva's *herethics*, in which the child's otherness returns her to her own mother, I think upsetting Levinas' paternal function allowed the mother an experience of her *own* alterity (a relation to herself made strange) without losing either herself or the child. An alterity, if you like, that she can call her own.

As in the early weeks after giving birth, the parent and child in Levinas remained in a kind of 'confinement', theoretically cocooned from other-worldliness, as the Other is conceived of strictly as infinitely distant to the self, and thereby must ultimately be understood as a kind of non-spiritual God. Although Levinas' early work deals with other-worldliness such as the elements (Levinas 1947b), his explorations of paternity, fecundity and maternity emerge out of dyadic relations to the Other, 'social' only in as much as they are relations with alterity conceived of in this way.

Chapter 4 began to move out of the idyllic dyad by focusing initially on the cry, the first puncturing by the not-yet-self (the child) of the not-yet-other (the mother from the child's perspective), but traced through the experience of the not-yet-other (the mother), reconceived, through the lens of Levinas, as also a not-yet-self. The mother's nascent subjectivity, understood as a relation to her child's possibilities that she calls her own, was seen as reliant on the mother withstanding a relentless onslaught of interruption. Psychoanalysis would understand the emergence of the child's capacity for being with, and tolerating proximity to others as occurring through the mother's capacity for constancy, containment, holding or reverie during these early phases, but without fully articulating or addressing how a mother may manage this; what it does to her, and what she does with what it does to her, including how it changes her relation to her child. In Chapter 4, the 'again and again' of the experience was one in which the present tense was constantly re-established as the interruptions accumulated and changed form, moving from the cry to babble, to the tantrum and finally the stammering child who presented the mother with a kind of model for her own experience of interruption, in which the child attempts to establish itself over and over (I I I I I) in the mind of the other. Appelbaum and Clément offered ways of conceptualizing the moment of interruption itself, the blank giving rise to a form of somatic thinking, or as syncope, a faltering or hiccup in time, in which time itself falters, but through which one comes back shaken but changed.

In Chapter 5 the social sphere widened again as maternal love was seen to emerge during uncanny moments of maternal weeping when the child had 'gone away'. Rather than this being understood as a moment of sorrow or loss, it was figured as an indeterminate experience, somewhere between thinking and feeling. The mother wept when she saw her child removed to a place where she couldn't go with him (sleep), nor shout out to name him as hers (the school play). She watched as the child turned away and she found herself in tears. Using Kristeva's notion that love, whether narcissistic or identificatory, is born out of an 'emptiness' prior to the advent of language that needs to be protected by maternal love in the figure of the imaginary father, love was seen as emerging for the mother out of an experience of separation too. However, using Badiou, this was rethought from the perspective of both mother and child. There was no third term in Badiou's account of love. Badiou's sequence was one, two, infinity. Subjectivity was temporarily attained through remaining truthful to the event of love, the disjunction between the two (difference), while managing the paradox that there is only one humanity (sameness).

Finally, maternal subjectivity was spread beyond the confines of the mother–child dyad, to include the concrete world of objects, street furniture and the built environment. Through Scarry's work, the object was seen to reciprocate, recognizing the mother's work, her physical challenges, the complexity of demands made on her, her exhaustion, her need for respite, her need for help. Maternal subjectivity was seen to reside in the mother's interactions, not just with the infant or child, but with all its stuff, and with the environment that she rediscovers through perpetual navigation. If maternity prompts more than a new set of tasks, roles or identities, it is here that this was made most visible, as the mother negotiated a whole new kinetic being, both viscous and porous to sensation, literally changing her orientation in the world.

Inconclusions

If there has been some notional progression through this book, it appears to have been a shift from mother–infant dyad understood as ethical by dint of the mother becoming 'possible' through recognizing her child's possibilities as her own, towards maternity conceived of as 'spread' across the realms of human and non-human interaction, forcing a reappraisal of what we may mean by the mother as an ethical subject. Given my concerns with according the mother a subjectivity where she appeared to have none, I am half-tempted by the latent possibilities of reading this work as a return to an agentive maternal subject, but this time as a kind of tragic-comic heroine, a 'becoming mother' with all her multiplicities and intensities, being dragged along by her child and their stuff, valiantly building Lego®, and becoming conscious of the joys of the contemporary kerb.

I want, however, to return instead to Badiou's notion of truth. For Badiou, a subject *emerges* when an individual decides that something they have encountered which has happened in their situation (however abnormal it may appear), does in fact belong to the situation, and therefore cannot be ignored (Feltham and Clemens 2003). Whether the event belongs to the situation or not is strictly undecidable at the time. This is what makes it 'stick out' or disrupt the situation. It is only through a prolonged investigation of the consequences of the event that a subject can come into being. It is not enough to have named the event once. It requires that the subject is *faithful* to it, for the event to be established as an event retroactively, and for the subject to have been a subject of such an event. The investigation into the event

> is not a passive, scholarly affair; it entails not only the active transformation of the situation in which the event occurs but also the active transformation of the human being. Thus in Badiou there is no such thing as a subject without such a process of subjectivization.
>
> (Feltham and Clemens 2003: 7)

What this means is that one cannot be recruited to the cause of an event while it is happening. If one decides to overlook the event then the event will dissolve back into the situation from which it emerged. Alternatively, it will be retroactively named as an event if one acted *as if it were one*, if one acted with fidelity to it. To become a subject is to declare for the event, acting as if it had happened, placing a 'wager' (Badiou 2003: 62) on the possibility that in doing so, things will in fact be different, after the event.

For Badiou, a truth is manifest only as a retroactive naming of what has been, of an event that erupts out of and so disturbs and alters a situation. An event is not something added from the outside. Its possibility remains immanent in the situation as a universe of untotalizable multiplicities, but it is only ever known to have been, after-the-event. It is retroactively perceived through the process of having attended to its truth, been truthful to it, acted, that is, as if the event were an event. After the event, reflection can then take place that can accord the event a name. The event then is not known through re-cognition, but through naming, an activity that is the task of philosophy (gathering together the names of what has happened in the realms of politics, love, art and science).

Motherhood does not always amount to an event in women's lives. Of course, many women cannot or choose not to have children. But beyond this, we do not always act with fidelity to the event that is a child. The event then dissolves back into the situation from which it emerged. It does not change us. It is returned to the set of untotalizable multiplicities that make up the situation that is motherhood. However, if we do occasionally act with fidelity to the event that is a child, if we notice its anomalous appearance in the situation, if we declare for it, place a wager on the possibility that it may change us, then it may turn out, after the event to have been the case. Then we have, temporarily, through our arduous ongoing commitment to the event that is a child, attained something we could call maternal subjectivity.

This book has been an attempt to name that process. In Badiou's terms, it may amount to doing philosophy – gathering up and attempting to elaborate the name of an event in one of his four domains. We could perhaps consider whether maternity itself would add up to a fifth domain. However, given that love, in Badiou's account, is the binding domain, the one that makes the other three possible, we may conclude that to be a maternal subject, is, after all, to be an occasionally loving subject, when a mother notices the disruption that a child is in her life.

My hair has gone back to being rude, even ruder than before. It is wild, out of control, more Jewish than ever. What did I get from motherhood? More curls? More tsores? Something changed. After the event I can say: 'I put a wager on it, and something changed.'

NOTES

1 MATERNAL ENCOUNTERS

1 Adrienne Rich, in her seminal work *Of Woman Born: Motherhood as experience and institution* (Rich 1976), first made this distinction between two meanings of motherhood: 'the *potential relationship* of any woman to her powers of reproduction and to children; and the *institution*, which aims at ensuring that that potential – and all women – shall remain under male control.' (Rich 1976: 13, original emphasis). Though authors since Rich have made a clear differentiation between 'motherhood' as institution, and 'mothering' as experience (e.g. O'Reilly 2006), I use these terms interchangeably throughout this work, in a bid to trouble the notion that 'experience' may lie outside of the cultural, political and social institutions that both shape and are shaped by it.

2 For discussions of the social regulation of motherhood, particularly the dominance of ideologies such as patriarchy and conservatism, the particular ways motherhood is structured by class, 'race', ethnicity and increasingly sexual orientation, as well as the impact of rapid social changes in the diversification of family forms and the growth of Assisted Reproductive Technologies (ART) on constructions of mothering, the maternal body and parenting more generally, see, for example, Dally 1982; Urwin 1985; Baca Zinn 1990; Rose 1990; Collins 1991; Phoenix et al. 1991; Doane and Hodges 1992; Stack and Burton 1993; Everingham 1994; Glenn et al. 1994; Mann and Roseneil 1994; Thurer 1994; Fineman and Karpin 1995; Ross 1995; Brush 1996; Allen 1997; Bailey 2000; Roseneil and Budgeon 2004; Williams and Roseneil 2004; Pugh 2005; Reynolds 2005; Brakman and Scholz 2006; Franklin and Roberts 2006; Longhurst 2006; Park 2006; Tyler 2008. It is particularly important to note that while motherhood has been understood in much of the early literature in terms of fostering life, growth and socialization, this may be more applicable to white middle-class women who may have had the luxury of staying at home for periods of time with their children, but for women of colour, for example, it may be replaced with the notion that the bedrock of 'motherwork' is redefined in terms of survival, power and identity (Collins 1991, 1994). While research on mothering has begun to take into account the effects of race, poverty and social deprivation on mothering experiences in a rather belated attempt to account for diversity and difference, a substantial parallel literature exists from African American feminists who have continued to describe the lives of mothers, both in theoretical work and in literature (Ross 1995).

3 See in particular Irigaray (1985a), Battersby (1998) and Tyler (2000) for discussions of the difficulties of representing maternal subjectivity and pregnant

subjectivity in the Western philosophical tradition, Betterton (2006) for a discussion of pregnancy and aesthetics, and Stone (2007) for an overview of 'birth' in feminist philosophy.

4 I am referring here to a rich and important strain of work that includes Julia Kristeva (1977, 1987b), Nancy Chodorow (1978, 2000), Luce Irigaray (1985a, 1985b, 1991, 1993a, 1993b), Jessica Benjamin (1995, 1998, 2000, 2004), Susan Kraemer (1996), Rosemary Balsam (2000), Joan Raphael-Leff (2003), Rozsika Parker (2005), Bracha L. Ettinger (2006), Amber Jacobs (2007) and many others working broadly within psychoanalytic feminist perspectives (be they relational, Kleinian or post-Lacanian), who have given much theoretical effort to according the mother a subjectivity of her own. I review and critique many aspects of this work in what follows, but suffice to say that in my view it remains extremely difficult to hold in tension the 'developmental tilt' of psychoanalytic theory in which maternal and paternal figures tend to gravitate towards being viewed as 'functions' through which the child acquires a relation to itself and others, society, culture, language, gender, the body and thought, and an account of the maternal subject through whom many of these capacities are acquired, that does not return her either to these functions or her mothering to being understood purely as a product of her own infantile issues. In addition, although accounts of psychoanalytic work with mothers do now crop up in the literature (e.g. Furman 1996; Balsam 2000; Steinberg 2005), it is still rare to see case studies detailing how mothers consciously and unconsciously view themselves and their own mothering. The emphasis remains on the unconscious fantasies of children and adults in analysis who are reflecting on the mothers of their own childhood. In other words, they are largely still child-centred accounts (Steinberg 2005).

5 I am referring to Gerhardt (2004).

6 Sometimes the flowering of feminist work on the maternal that followed what Ann Snitow called the 'demon texts' of the second wave (e.g. Friedan's *The Feminine Mystique* (1963) and Firestone's *The Dialectic of Sex* (1970)) refers, among others, to the work of Adrienne Rich (1976), Dorothy Dinnerstein (1976) and Jane Lazarre (1976). At other times the term 'maternalist' is used to reference the French feminist tradition that includes the work of Julia Kristeva, Luce Irigaray, Michèle Montrelay and Hélène Cixous.

7 Clément describes syncope as 'time faltering', or a 'little suspension of being' (Clément 1994: 1).

8 There are some similarities between Connor's 'becoming unaccommodated', Clément's 'syncope' and Freud's notion of the uncanny in that they all hold the potential for experiencing the self-made-strange. The uncanny, however, understood as the return of the repressed of castration implies a death-like fear that both syncope and becoming unaccommodated appear to deliberately work against. Connor writes: 'One ought sometimes to be able *not* to be able to describe what one is doing, just as we could do with getting better at not being good at what we do (Connor 2008, unpaginated webpage, original emphasis). In other words, we would do well to seek out and engage with experiences of becoming unaccommodated, rather than finding ways of bolstering against its effects.

9 Adrienne Rich's blend of 'personal testimony mixed with research, and theory which derived from both' (Rich 1976: 2), Kristeva's (1977) autobiographical account of birth that sits alongside her theoretical reflections in *Stabat Mater*, the experimental writing practices Rachel Blau DuPlessis (1990) records in *The Pink Guitar* and the memory-work of Frigga Haug (1987) are early examples of feminist autobiographical strategies used to dislodge the absentee author 'who

lays down speculations, theories, facts, and fantasies without any personal grounding' (Rich 1976: 2). There are many subsequent examples and developments of autobiography, autoethnography and life-writing as research strategies, including the academic journals *Auto/Biography* and *a/b: Auto/Biography Studies*.

10 Weedon (1998) also cites the work of Gallop (1988), Braidotti (1991) and Grosz (1994, 1995) in furthering arguments about an embodied feminine otherness as a site of resistance and transformation.

2 MATERNAL ALTERITY

1 Bion's notion of 'maternal reverie' is an extension of Klein's work in a direction that begins to grapple with maternal agency. In 'A theory of thinking' (Bion 1962), Bion develops the idea that the baby projects into the mother both love and unbearable feelings which the mother then makes bearable by making sense of them in her mind. He writes:

> A well-balanced mother can accept these and respond therapeutically: that is to say in a manner that makes the infant feel it is receiving its frightened personality back again, but in a form that it can tolerate – the fears are manageable by the infant personality. If the mother cannot tolerate these projections, the infant is reduced to continue projective identification carried out with increasing force and frequency.
>
> (Bion 1962a: 114–115).

Projective identification is seen by Bion as the normal mode by which the infant communicates with the mother. The infant cannot yet think like an adult, but through the experience of adult thinking, the baby feels understood and in turn develops a capacity to understand. Thus, thinking in the infant emerges from the mother's ability to think about the infant's unthinkable thoughts and unbearable feeling states. She must allow herself to 'reverie' about her baby, to be receptive to unbearable feelings being put into her, and give them back in a benign form. Although we could argue that Bion's mother has been reduced to a passive, receptive, containing function, this process has been reinterpreted as in fact very active, involving feeling, thinking, organizing and acting (Grotstein 1983; Kraemer 1996; Parker 2005). Bion's notion of reverie is not an ordered kind of thinking, but nonetheless a vital component of reverie is thinking. The important aspect, from my perspective, is that the mother is granted the capacity to think at all. This is a different kind of function than we tend to see in the analytic literature, and one that can be linked to Ruddick's later development of her theory of maternal thinking (Ruddick 1980). It usefully moves us away from associations between the mother and milky preoccupation. Holding on to Bion's insight seems important in the light of the general reduction of the mother, in psychoanalysis, to the status of object or the complementary positions of passivity and malevolence.

2 See, for example, Benjamin 1995, 1998, 2004; Kraemer 1996; Juhasz 2003; de Marneffe 2004; Parker 2005; Hollway 2006.

3 While feminist ethics has largely been concerned with elucidating gender bias in dominant theories of Anglo-American ethics (Walker 1998), a substantial debate arose in the early 1990s about the relation between gender and moral reasoning. This debate largely stemmed from the publication of Carol Gilligan's book *In a Different Voice: Psychological theory and women's development* (Gilligan 1982) and Nel Noddings' *Caring: A feminine approach to ethics and moral education*

(Noddings 1984). Maihofer (1998) notes that the literature this spawned is now so extensive that it is difficult to provide an overview. Examples of contributions, however, include Kittay and Meyers 1987; Held 1993; Larrabee 1993; Jaggar 1995; Shildrick 2001.

4 As far as possible I have used the term 'other' to denote other person or ego, and 'Other' for radical alterity, a transcendent other, although it is not always possible to make such a clear distinction, particularly in Levinas' work.

5 In Levinas, the encounter with the Other occurs in the 'face-to-face', the position also of language. The 'face' is the exteriority of the Other, through which the Other is revealed to the self. However, what is revealed is what goes beyond whatever idea the self has of the Other. The face-to-face is the situation in which the Other's infinite alterity is expressed.

3 MATERNAL TRANSFORMATIONS

1 For similar autobiographical accounts of the transition to motherhood (dubbed 'momoirs' in the USA), see, for example, Figes 1998; Cusk 2001; Buchanan 2003; Enright 2004; Warner 2005.

4 MATERNAL INTERRUPTIONS

1 A stammering song from *That Night in Rio*, with music by Harry Warren and lyrics by Mack Gordon (1941). Ironically, though there are a number of famous stammering songs, stammerers or stutterers tend to become fluent when they sing.

2 Naomi Stadlen devotes five pages to interruption in her book, *What Mothers Do* (Stadlen 2004), but her account is a largely romanticized description of mothers getting over their initial annoyance at being interrupted, leading to an ability to constantly make themselves available for their children.

3 This would be in keeping with Spinoza's conceptualization of being as *conatus*, the effort or tendency for each being to persevere in its being, to exercise the forces immanent in its faculties (Spinoza 1677).

4 Kate Figes' chapter on 'Exhaustion' (in Figes 1998) provides a comprehensive account of the mental, physical and emotional demands on mothers in response to the seemingly unlimited capacity children have to make demands. I have not, however, found anything written about the actual physical damage that children can inflict on mothers. Anecdotally, I know of examples where young children have broken their mother's limbs, bitten them, and kicked and bruised them during tantrums.

5 These quotes are taken from Columbia Market Nursery's verbatim descriptions of Joel's speech, aged 3.

6 According to differential emotions theory, disgust, interest and distress are present at birth, with joy, evidenced by infantile smiling, emerging at between 3 and 6 weeks (Izard and Malateste 1987: 507). However, anecdotal evidence circulates about babies smiling at their mothers from birth. See Janet Balaskas' book, *Active Birth* (Balaskas 1983), for descriptions by mothers of their infants smiling moments after birth.

7 'K-K-K-Katy' was published in 1918 by Geoffrey O'Hara and became an huge hit in wartime America, referred to as 'The Sensational Stammering Song Success Sung by the Soldiers and Sailors' (Wikipedia: The Free Encyclopedia, undated).

5 MATERNAL LOVE

1 See Margaroni (2004) for a brief explication of Lacan's notion of phallus as the invisible, excessive fourth in relation to the Oedipal triangle.
2 See Urwin (1985), Rose (1990) and Phoenix et al. (1991) for discussions of the intensive governmental regulation of families through a particular focus on children during the twentieth century, and Parker (2005) for a discussion of the influence of psychoanalysis and psychology in establishing norms in the British context.
3 For example, Daphne de Marneffe's book is entitled *Maternal Desire: On children, love, and the inner life* (de Marneffe 2004), implying no distinction between maternal love and maternal desire. *Maternal Desire* has been marketed in the United States as a book in defence of motherhood, making the case for mothers enjoying motherhood, feeling a deep compulsion to mother based on a reciprocal experience of love and satisfaction, rather than an exploration of maternal desire (de Marneffe 2004).
4 Kristeva (2000) returned to Oedipus in *The Sense and Non-Sense of Revolt.*
5 There is a stopping point, which Badiou terms 'the void' (Badiou 2001: 68). This is a complex notion, and it is beyond the scope of this brief summary to explore further. Peter Hallward provides an excellent explanation of Badiou's void in *Think Again: Alain Badiou and the future of philosophy* (Hallward 2004).
6 The work of Lacan, however, constitutes an event in and of itself, Badiou claims (Badiou 1999: 81).

6 MATERNAL STUFF

1 *The Shadow of the Object* is the title of a book by Christopher Bollas. Psychoanalytic writing usually refers to internal objects rather than literal ones.
2 During the early childhood period the 'bag' also features heavily in terms of what carries all this stuff about. The bag appears to mutate later into an obsession with 'storage' in the form of a variety of plastic tubs, baskets and boxes on offer to contain this ever-burgeoning nursery equipment. In relation to the bag as a cultural object, Steven Connor's work is particularly instructive (Connor 2000b).

7 INTENTIONS, INCONSISTENCIES, INCONCLUSIONS

1 Bobby Baker's subsequent work has centred around food and cleaning.
2 My children also have my surname.

REFERENCES

Adams, P. (1996) *The Emptiness of the Image: Psychoanalysis and sexual difference*. London: Routledge.

Albertsen, N. and Diken, B. (2003) What is the social? Available at www.comp. lancs.ac.uk/sociology/papers/Albertsen-Diken-What-is-the-Social.pdf. Lancaster: Department of Sociology, Lancaster University (accessed 26 November 2004).

Alford, C. F. (2002) *Levinas, the Frankfurt School and Psychoanalysis*. London: Continuum.

Allen, K. (1997) Lesbian and gay families, in T. Arendell (ed.) *Contemporary Parenting: Challenges and issues*. Newbury Park, CA: Sage.

Andrews, B. S. (2001) Angels, rubbish collectors, and pursuers of erotic joy: The image of the ethical woman, in P. DesAutels and J. Waugh (eds) *Feminists Doing Ethics*. Lanham, MD: Rowman & Littlefield.

Anzieu, D. (1989) *The Skin Ego*, trans. C. Turner. New Haven, CT: Yale University Press.

Appelbaum, D. (1990) *Voice*. Albany, NY: State University of New York Press.

Appelbaum, D. (1995) *The Stop*. Albany, NY: State University of New York Press.

Appelbaum, D. (1996) *Disruption*. Albany, NY: State University of New York Press.

Appelbaum, D. (2001) *Delay of the Heart*. Albany, NY: State University of New York Press.

Arendell, T. (2000) Conceiving and investigating motherhood: The decade's scholarship. *Journal of Marriage and the Family*, 62: 1192–1207.

Arlow, J. A. (1980) Object concept and object choice. *Psychoanalytic Quarterly*, 59: 109–133.

Aron, L. (1991) The patient's experience of the analyst's subjectivity. *Psychoanalytic Dialogues*, 1: 29–51.

Aron, L. (1996) *Meeting of Minds*. Hillsdale, NJ: Analytic Press.

Aulagnier, P. (1975) *La Violence de l'interprétation*. Paris: PUF, 1991.

Baca Zinn, M. (1990) Family, feminism, and race. *Gender and Society*, 4: 68–82.

Badiou, A. (1999) *Manifesto for Philosophy Followed by Two Essays; 'The (Re)Turn of Philosophy Itself' and 'Definition of Philosophy'*, trans. N. Madrasz. Albany, NY: State University of New York Press.

Badiou, A. (2000) What is love? In R. Saleci (ed.) *Sexuation*. Durham, NC: Duke University Press.

Badiou, A. (2001) *Ethics: An essay on the understanding of evil*, trans. P. Hallward. London: Verso.

Badiou, A. (2003) *Infinite Thought: Truth and the return of philosophy*. London: Continuum.

Badiou, A. (2004) *Theoretical Writings* London: Continuum.

Bailey, L. (1999) Refracted selves? A study of changes in self-identity in the transition to motherhood. *Sociology*, 33(2): 335–352.

Bailey, L. (2000) Bridging home and work in the transition to motherhood: A discursive study. *European Journal of Women's Studies*, 7: 53–70.

Bailey, L. (2001) Gender shows: First-time mothers and embodied selves. *Gender and Society*, 15(1): 110–129.

Baker, B. (undated) Bobby Baker's Daily Life Limited. Available at www.bobbybakersdailylife.com/drawing.htm (accessed 1 April 2008).

Balaskas, J. (1983) *Active Birth: The new approach to giving birth naturally*. London: Unwin Paperbacks.

Balsam, R. (2000) The mother within the mother. *Psychoanalytic Quarterly*, 69: 465–492.

Bassin, D., Honey, M. and Mahrer Kaplan, M. (1994) *Representations of Motherhood*. New Haven, CT: Yale University Press.

Battersby, C. (1998) *The Phenomenal Woman: Feminist metaphysics and the patterns of identity*. Cambridge: Polity Press.

Beckett, S. (1958) *The Unnameable*, trans. S. Beckett. London: Pan, 1979.

Benedek, T. (1970) The family as a psychologic field, in E. J. Anthony and T. Benedek (eds) *Parenthood, its Psychology and Psychopathology*. Boston, MA: Little Brown.

Benjamin, J. (1990) *The Bonds of Love: Psychoanalysis, feminism, and the problem of domination*. London: Virago.

Benjamin, J. (1995) *Like Subjects, Love Objects: Essays on recognition and difference*. Cambridge, MA: Harvard University Press.

Benjamin, J. (1998) *Shadow of the Other: Intersubjectivity and gender in psychoanalysis*. New York: Routledge.

Benjamin, J. (2000) Response to commentaries by Mitchell and by Butler: Roundtable on the work of Jessica Benjamin. *Studies in Gender and Sexuality*, 1(3): 291–308.

Benjamin, J. (2004) Beyond doer and done to: An intersubjective view of thirdness. *Psychoanalytic Quarterly*, 73: 5–46.

Betterton, R. (2006) Promising monsters: Pregnant bodies, artistic subjectivity and maternal imagination. *Hypatia*, 21: 80–100.

Bion, W. R. (1962) A theory of thinking, in *Second Thoughts*. London: Maresfield Reprints, 1984.

Blake, W. (1971) *The Poems of William Blake*, edited by W. H. Stevenson. London: Longman.

Blau DuPlessis, R. (1990) For the Etruscans, in *The Pink Guitar: Writing as feminist practice*. New York: Routledge.

Bloom, L. (1993) *The Transition from Infancy to Language: Acquiring the power of expression*. Cambridge: Cambridge University Press.

Bollas, C. (1987) *The Shadow of the Object: Psychoanalysis of the unthought known*. New York: Columbia University Press.

166

Braidotti, R. (1991) *Patterns of Dissonance: A study of women in contemporary philosophy*. Cambridge: Polity Press.

Braidotti, R. (1994) *Nomadic Subjects: Embodiment and sexual difference in contemporary feminist theory*. New York: Columbia University Press.

Brakman, S.-V. and Scholz, S. (2006) Adoption, ART, and a re-conception of the maternal body: Toward embodied maternity. *Hypatia*, 21(1): 54–73.

Brentano, F. (1874) *Psychology from an Empirical Standpoint*. New York: Humanities Press, 1966.

Brody, D. (2001) Levinas' maternal method from Time and the Other through Otherwise than Being: No woman's land?, in T. Chanter (ed.) *Feminist Interpretations of Emmanuel Levinas*. University Park, PA: Pennsylvania State University Press.

Bronner, L. L. (1993) From veil to wig: Jewish women's hair covering. *Judaism*, 42(4): 465–477.

Brush, L. D. (1996) Love, toil and trouble: Motherhood and feminist politics. *Signs*, 21(2): 429–454.

Buchanan, A. J. (2003) *Mother Shock: Loving every (other) minute of it*. Emeryville, CA: Seal Press.

Buckley, P. (1986) Introduction to *Essential Papers on Object Relations*. New York: New York University Press.

Butler, J. (1990) *Gender Trouble*. London: Routledge.

Butler, J. (1994) Bodies that matter, in C. Burke, N. Schor and M. Whitford (eds) *Engaging with Irigaray*. New York: Columbia University Press.

Butler, J. (2000) Longing for recognition: Commentary on the work of Jessica Benjamin. Roundtable on the work of Jessica Benjamin. *Studies in Gender and Sexuality*, 1(3): 271–290.

Byatt, A. S. (1985) *Still Life*. London: Vintage.

Callon, M. (1986) The sociology of an actor-network: The case of the electric vehicle, in M. Callon, J. Law and J. Rip (eds) *Mapping the Dynamics of Science and Technology*. London: Macmillan.

Carle, E. (1969) *The Very Hungry Caterpillar*. New York: World Publishing.

Chanter, T. (2001) Introduction, in T. Chanter (ed.) *Feminist Interpretations of Emmanuel Levinas*. University Park, PA: Pennsylvania State University Press.

Chernin, K. (1999) *The Woman Who Gave Birth to her Mother: Tales of change in women's lives*. London: Penguin.

Chodorow, N. J. (1978) *The Reproduction of Mothering: Psychoanalysis and the sociology of gender*. Berkeley, CA: University of California Press.

Chodorow, N. J. (2000) Reflections on *The Reproduction of Mothering*: Twenty years later. *Studies in Gender and Sexuality*, 1(4): 337–348.

Clément, C. (1994) *Syncope: The philosophy of rapture*, trans. S. O'Driscoll and D. M. Mahoney. Minneapolis, MN: University of Minnesota Press.

Cohen, R. A. (1998) Foreword to E. Levinas, *Otherwise than Being, or, Beyond Essence*, trans. A. Lingis. Pittsburgh, PA: Duquesne University Press.

Coleridge, S. T. (1816) A note to Kubla Khan, available from *The Electronic Text Centre*. Available at http://etext.lib.virginia.edu/stc/Coleridge/poems/notes.html (accessed 18 September 2005).

Collins, P. H. (1991) The meaning of motherhood in black culture and black mother-daughter relationships, in P. Bell-Scott et al. (eds) *Double Stitch: Black women write about mothers and daughters*. New York: HarperCollins.

Collins, P. H. (1994) Shifting the centre: Race, class, and feminist theorizing about motherhood, in D. Basin, M. Honey and M. M. Kaplan (eds) *Representations of Motherhood*. New Haven, CT: Yale University Press.

Connor, S. (2000a) *Dumbstruck: A cultural history of ventriloquism*. Oxford: Oxford University Press.

Connor, S. (2000b) Bags. Available at www.bbk.ac.uk/english/skc/magic/bags.htm (accessed 18 September 2005).

Connor, S. (2008) A few don'ts (and dos) by a cultural phenomenologist. Available at www.stevenconnor.com/cultphen.htm (accessed 1 April 2008).

Cornell, D. (1992) *The Philosophy of the Limit*. New York: Routledge.

Craig, K. D., Gilbert-MacLeod, C. A. and Lilley, C. M. (2000) Crying as an indicator of pain in infant, in R. G. Barr, B. Hopkins and J. A. Green (eds) *Crying as a Sign, a Symptom and a Signal: Clinical, emotional and developmental aspects of infant and toddler crying*. London: MacKeith Press.

Cusk, R. (2001) *A Life's Work: On becoming a mother*. London: Fourth Estate.

Dally, A. (1982) *Inventing Motherhood: The consequences of an ideal*. London: Burnett.

Darwin C. (1872) *The Expression of the Emotions in Man and Animals*. Chicago, IL: University of Chicago Press, 1965.

Davies, K. (1990) *Women, Time and the Weaving of the Strands of Everyday Life*. Aldershot, UK: Avebury.

De Beauvoir, S. (1949) *The Second Sex*, trans. H. M. Parshley. New York: Vintage, 1989.

Deleuze, G. (1977) I have nothing to admit, trans. J. Forman. *Semiotext(e)*, 2(3): 111–116.

De Marneffe, D. (2004) *Maternal Desire: On children, love, and the inner life*. New York: Little, Brown.

Derrida, J. (1976) *Of Grammatology*, trans. G. Spivak. Baltimore, MD: Johns Hopkins University Press.

Derrida, J. (1999) *Adieu to Emmanuel Levinas*, trans. P. A. Brault and M. Naas. Stanford, CA: Stanford University Press.

Dinnerstein, D. (1976) *The Mermaid and the Minotaur*. New York: Harper and Row.

Doane, J. and Hodges, D. (1992) *From Klein to Kristeva: Psychoanalytic feminism and the search for the 'good enough' mother*. Ann Arbor, MI: University of Michigan Press.

Douglas, S. and Michaels, M. (2004) *The Mommy Myth: The idealization of motherhood and how it has undermined all women*. New York: Free Press.

Enright, A. (2004) *Making Babies: Stumbling into motherhood*. London: Jonathan Cape.

Ettinger, B. L. (2006) From proto-ethical compassion to responsibility: Besideness and the three primal mother-phantasies of not-enoughness, devouring and abandonment. *Athena: Philosophical Studies*, 2: 100–135.

Evans, D. (1996) *An Introductory Dictionary of Lacanian Psychoanalysis*. London: Routledge.

Everingham, C. (1994) *Motherhood and Modernity: An investigation into the relational dimension of mothering*. Buckingham: Open University Press.

Fairbairn, W. R. (1941) A revised psychopathology of the psychoses and psychoneuroses. *International Journal of Psychoanalysis*, 22: 250–279.

Featherstone, B. (1997) Crisis in the Western family, in W. Hollway and B. Featherstone (eds) *Mothering and Ambivalence*. London: Routledge.

Feldman S. (1956) Crying at the happy ending. *Journal of the American Psychoanalytic Association*, 4: 477–485.

Feltham, O. and Clemens, J. (2003) An introduction to Alain Badiou's philosophy, in A. Badiou, *Infinite Thought*. London: Continuum.

Fenichel, O. (1931) *Outline of Clinical Psychoanalysis*, trans. B. D. Lewin and G. Zilboorg. New York: Psychoanalytic Quarterly Press, 1934.

Fenichel, O. (1938) The drive to amass wealth. *Psychoanalytic Quarterly*, 7: 69–95.

Figes, K. (1998) *Life after Birth*. London: Viking.

Fineman, M. A. and Karpin, I. (eds) (1995) *Mothers in Law: Feminist theory and the legal regulation of motherhood*. New York: Columbia Univeristy Press.

Fink, B. (1997) *A Clinical Introduction to Lacanian Psychoanalysis: Theory and technique*. Cambridge, MA: Harvard University Press.

Firestone, S. (1970) *The Dialectic of Sex: The case for feminist revolution*. New York: Morrow.

Foucan, S. (2004) Birth of an art: Art in motion, trans. 'Jeremy'. Available at www.urbanfreeflow.com (accessed 1 July 2004).

Franklin, S. and Roberts, C. (2006) *Born and Made: An ethnography of preimplantation genetic diagnosis*. Princeton, NJ: Princeton University Press.

Freud, S. (1905) Three essays on the theory of sexuality. *Standard Edition*, 7: 125–245, in J. Strachey (ed.) *The Standard Edition of the Complete Psychological Works of Sigmund Freud*. 24 vols, trans. J. Strachey et al. London: Hogarth Press, 1974.

Freud, S. (1910) The antithetical meaning of primal words. *Standard Edition*, 11: 155–161.

Freud, S. (1915) Letter to Ferenczi dated 21.11.1915, in E. Falzeder and E. Brabant (eds) *The Correspondence of Sigmund Freud and Sandor Ferenczi*, Volume 2: *1914–1919*. Cambridge, MA: Belknap Press of Harvard University Press, 1996.

Freud, S. (1925) Negation. *Standard Edition*, 19: 235–239.

Freud, S. (1938) An outline of psycho-analysis. *Standard Edition*, 23: 141–207.

Frey, W. H. (1985) *Crying: The mystery of tears*. New York: Harper & Row.

Friedan, B. (1963) *The Feminine Mystique*. New York: Norton.

Frosh, S. (1997) Father's ambivalence (too), in W. Hollway and B. Featherstone (eds) *Mothering and Ambivalence*. London: Routledge.

Frosh, S. (2002) *Key Concepts in Psychoanalysis*. London: British Library.

Furman, E. (1982) Mothers have to be there to be left. *Psychoanalytic Study of the Child*, 37: 15–28.

Furman, E. (1996) On motherhood. *Journal of the American Psychoanalytic Association*, 44S: 429–447.

Gallop, J. (1988) *Thinking through the Body*. New York: Columbia University Press.

Gallop, J. (2002) *Anecdotal Theory*. Durham, NC: Duke University Press.

Gerhardt, S. (2004) *Why Love Matters: How affection shapes a baby's brain*. London: Routledge.

Gilligan, C. (1982) *In a Different Voice: Psychological theory and women's development*. Cambridge, MA: Harvard University Press.

Glauber, I. P. (1968) Dysautomatization. A disorder of preconscious ego-functioning. *International Journal of Psychoanalysis*, 49: 89–99.

Glenn, E. N., Chang, G. and Forcey, L. R. (eds) (1994) *Mothering: Ideology, experience and agency*. London: Routledge.

Gordon, M. (1941) I, Yi, Yi, Yi, Yi (I like you very much), Si, Si, Si, Si, Si (I think you're grand), *That Night in Rio*, music: H. Warren. Available at http://libretto. musicals.ru/text (accessed 13 September 2005).

Grosz, E. (1994) *Volatile Bodies: Towards a corporeal feminism*. Bloomington, IN: Indiana University Press.

Grosz, E. (1995) *Space, Time, and Perversion: Essays on the politics of bodies*. New York: Routledge.

Grotstein, J. S. (ed.) (1983) *Do I Dare Disturb the Universe? A memorial to Wilfred R. Bion*. London: Maresfield.

Hallward, P. (ed.) (2004) *Think Again: Alain Badiou and the future of philosophy*. London: Continuum.

Harman, G. (2001) Object-oriented philosophy. Available at www.webcom.com/paf/OOP.html (accessed 18 September 2005).

Harman, G. (2002) *Tool-Being: Heidegger and the metaphysics of objects*. Peru, IL: Open Court.

Haug, F. (1987) *Female Sexualization: A collective work of memory*, trans. E. Carter. London: Verso.

Hegel, G. W. F. (1807) *The Phenomenology of Spirit*, trans. A. V. Miller. Oxford: Oxford University Press, 1977.

Heidegger, M. (1927) *Being and Time*, trans. J. Macquarrie and E. Robinson. Oxford: Blackwell, 1962.

Held, V. (1993) *Feminist Morality: Transforming culture, society and politics*. Chicago, IL: University of Chicago Press.

Hirsch, I. (1987) Varying modes of analytic participation. *Journal of the American Academy of Psychoanalysis*, 15(2): 205–222.

Hollway, W. (2001) From motherhood to maternal subjectivity. *International Journal of Critical Psychology*, 2: 13–38.

Hollway, W. (2006) *The Capacity to Care: Gender and ethical subjectivity*. Hove, UK: Routledge.

Irigaray, L. (1985a) *Speculum of the Other Woman*, trans. G. C. Gill. Ithaca, NY: Cornell University Press.

Irigaray, L. (1985b) *This Sex Which Is Not One*, trans. C. Porter and C. Burke. Ithaca, NY: Cornell University Press.

Irigaray, L. (1991) The bodily encounter with the mother, trans. D. Macey, in M. Whitford (ed.) *The Irigaray Reader*. Oxford: Basil Blackwell.

Irigaray, L. (1993a) *An Ethics of Sexual Difference*, trans. C. Burke and G. C. Gill. Ithaca, NY: Cornell University Press.

Irigaray, L. (1993b) *Sexes and Genealogies*, trans. G. C. Gill. New York: Columbia University Press.

Izard, C. E. and Malateste, C. Z. (1987) Perspectives on emotional development I: Differential emotions theory of early emotional development, in J. D. Osofsky (ed.) *Handbook of Infant Development*, 2nd edition. New York: Wiley.

Jacobs, A. (2007) *On Matricide*. New York: Columbia University Press.

Jaggar, A. M. (1995) Caring as a feminist practice of moral reason, in V. Held (ed.) *Justice and Care: Essential readings in feminist ethics*. Boulder, CO: Westview Press.

James, H. (1888) *The Aspern Papers: Louisa Pallant – The modern warning*. London: Macmillan.

James, W. (1884) What is an emotion?, in M. B. Arnold (ed.) *The Nature of Emotion*. Harmondsworth: Penguin, 1968.

Jones, E. (1953) *The Life and Work of Sigmund Freud, Volume 1*. New York: Basic Books.

Jones, L. S. (2003) The research, design and concept development of a new chair to meet the needs of breast-feeding women and their infants. Thesis (PhD), Brunel University.

Juhasz, S. (2003) Mother-writing and the narrative of maternal subjectivity. *Studies in Gender and Sexuality*, 4(4): 395–425.

Jump London (2003) (DVD) Video Collection Int. Ltd.

Kittay, E. F. and Meyers, D. T. (eds) (1987) *Women and Moral Theory*. Totowa, NJ: Rowman and Littlefield.

Klein, M. (1935) Contribution to the psychogenesis of manic-depressive states, in M. Klein, *Love, Guilt and Reparation and Other Works 1921–1945*. London: Vintage, 1998.

Koppelman, C. (1996) The politics of hair. *Frontiers*, 17(2): 87–88.

Kraemer, S. B. (1996) Betwixt the dark and the daylight of maternal subjectivity: Meditations on the threshold. *Psychoanalytic Dialogues*, 6: 765–791.

Kristeva, J. (1974) *Revolution in Poetic Language*, trans. M. Waller, reprinted in K. Oliver (ed.) *The Portable Kristeva*. New York: Columbia University Press, 1997.

Kristeva, J. (1975) *Desire in Language*, trans. T. Gora, A. Jardine and L. S. Roudiez, reprinted in K. Oliver (ed.) *The Portable Kristeva*. New York: Columbia University Press, 1997.

Kristeva, J. (1977) Stabat Mater, in T. Moi (ed.) *The Kristeva Reader*. Oxford: Blackwell, 1986.

Kristeva, J. (1981) Women's time. *Signs*, 7(1): 13–35.

Kristeva, J. (1984) Julia Kristeva in conversation with Rosalind Coward, in K. Oliver (ed.) *The Portable Kristeva*. New York: Columbia University Press, 1997.

Kristeva, J. (1986) An interview with Julia Kristeva, I. Lipkowiz and A. Loselle. *Critical Texts*, 3(3): 8.

Kristeva, J. (1987a) *Black Sun: Depression and melancholia*, trans. L. S. Roudiez. New York: Columbia University Press, 1989.

Kristeva, J. (1987b) Freud and love: Treatment and its discontents, in *Tales of Love*, trans. L. S. Roudiez. New York: Columbia University Press.

Kristeva, J. (2000) *The Sense and Non-Sense of Revolt: The powers and limits of psychoanalysis, Volume 1*, trans. J. Herman. New York: Columbia University Press.

Kristeva, J. (2001) *Hannah Arendt, Volume 1. Female Genius: Life, madness, words – Hannah Arendt, Melanie Klein, Colette*. New York: Columbia University Press.

Kristeva, J. (2002) *Melanie Klein, Volume 2*, trans. R. Guberman. New York: Columbia University Press.

Kristeva, J. (2004) *Colette, Volume 3*, trans. J. M. Todd. New York: Columbia University Press.

Lacan, J. (1953–1954) *The Seminar of Jacques Lacan, Book I: Freud's Papers on Technique, 1953–1954*, trans. J. Forrester, edited by J.-A. Miller. Cambridge: Cambridge University Press.

Lacan, J. (1956) *The Seminar of Jacques Lacan, Book III: The Psychoses*, trans. R. Grigg. London: Routledge, 1993.

Lacan, J. (1959–1960) *The Seminar of Jacques Lacan, Book VII: The Ethics of Psychoanalysis*, trans. D. Porter, edited by J.-A. Miller. New York: Norton, 1992.

Lacan, J. (1972–1973) *Encore,* trans. B. Fink. New York: Norton, 1998.

Laplanche, J. (1997) The theory of seduction and the problem of the other. *International Journal of Psychoanalysis*, 78: 653–666.

Laplanche, J. (1999) *Essays on Otherness*, edited by J. Fletcher. London: Routledge.

Laplanche, J. and Pontalis, J.-B. (1967) *The Language of Psychoanalysis*. London: Hogarth Press, 1973.

Larrabee, M. J. (1993) *An Ethic of Care: Feminist and interdisciplinary perspectives*. New York: Routledge.

Latour, B. (1988) Mixing human and nonhuman together: The sociology of a door-closer. *Social Problems*, 35(3): 298–310.

Latour, B. (1992) Where are the missing masses? Sociology of a few mundane artefacts, in W. Bijker and J. Law (eds) *Shaping Technology/Building Society*. Cambridge, MA: MIT Press. Also available at www.ensmp.fr/~latour/articles/article/050.html (accessed 25 November 2004).

Latour, B. (1995) A door must be either open or shut: A little philosophy of techniques, in A. Feenberg and A. Hannay (eds) *Technology and the Politics of Knowledge*. Bloomington, IN: Indiana University Press.

Latour, B. (1997) On actor-network theory: A few clarifications. Available at www.keele.ac.uk/depts/stt/stt/ant/latour.htm (accessed 26 November 2004).

Lazarre, J. (1976) *The Mother Knot*. New York: McGraw-Hill.

Law, J. (2004) *After Method: Mess in social science research*. London: Routledge.

Levinas, E. (1947a) *Time and the Other and Additional Essays*, trans. R. A. Cohen. Pittsburgh, PA: Duquesne University Press, 1987.

Levinas, E. (1947b) *Existence and Existents*, trans. A. Lingis. Pittsburgh, PA: Duquesne University Press, 1978.

Levinas, E. (1961) *Totality and Infinity: An essay on exteriority*, trans. A. Lingis. Pittsburgh, PA: Duquesne University Press, 1969.

Levinas, E. (1974) *Otherwise than Being, or, Beyond Essence*, trans. A. Lingis. Pittsburgh, PA: Duquesne University Press, 1998.

Levinas, E. (1985) *Ethics and Infinity: Conversations with Philippe Nemo*, trans. R. A. Cohen. Pittsburgh, PA: Duquesne University Press.

Levinas, E. and Lichtenberg-Ettinger, B. (2006). What would Eurydice say? Emmanuel Levinas in conversation with Bracha Lichtenberg-Ettinger. *Athena: Philosophical Studies*, 1: 137–145.

Lichtenberg-Ettinger, B. (1995) *The Matrixial Gaze*. Leeds: Feminist Arts and Histories Network.

Lichtenberg-Ettinger, B. (1997) The feminine/prenatal weaving in matrixial subjectivity-as-encounter. *Psychoanalytic Dialogues*, 7(3): 367–405.

Lingis, A. (1978) Translator's introduction to E. Levinas, *Otherwise than Being, or,*

Beyond Essence, trans. A. Lingis. Pittsburgh, PA: Duquesne University Press, 1998.

Löfgren, B. L. (1966) On weeping. *International Journal of Psychoanalysis*, 47: 375–381.

Longhurst, R. (2006) A pornography of birth: Crossing moral boundaries. *ACME: An International E-Journal for Critical Geographies*, 5(2): 209–229.

Lutz, T. (1999) *A Cultural History of Tears*. New York: Norton.

McIntosh, D. (1986) The ego and the self in the thought of Sigmund Freud. *International Journal of Psychoanalysis*, 67: 429–448.

Macquarrie, J. and Robinson, E. (1962) Translators' notes to M. Heidegger, *Being and Time*. Oxford: Blackwell.

Maihofer, A. (1998) Care, in A. J. Jaggar and I. M. Young (eds) *A Companion to Feminist Philosophy*. Malden, MA: Blackwell.

Mann, K. and Roseneil, S. (1994) 'Some mothers do 'ave 'em': Backlash and the gender politics of the underclass debate. *Journal of Gender Studies*, 3(3): 317–331.

Margaroni, M. (2004) The trial of the third: Kristeva's Oedipus and the crisis of identification. In J. Lechte and M. Margaroni (eds) *Julia Kristeva: Live theory*. London: Continuum.

Masson, J. M. (1988) *Against Therapy: Emotional tyranny and the myth of psychological healing*. New York: Atheneum.

Merleau-Ponty, M. (1962) *The Phenomenology of Perception*, trans. C. Smith. New York: Humanities Press.

Miller, D. (1997) How infants grow mothers in North London. *Theory, Culture and Society*, 14(4): 67–88.

Miller, T. (2005) *Making Sense of Motherhood: A narrative approach*. Cambridge: Cambridge University Press.

Mitchell, S. A. (1988) *Relational Concepts in Psychoanalysis: An integration*. Cambridge, MA: Harvard University Press.

Mitchell, S. A. (2000) Juggling paradoxes: Commentary on the work of Jessica Benjamin. *Studies in Gender and Sexuality*, 1: 251–269.

Moyers, B. and Tucher, A. (1990) *A World of Ideas: Public opinions from private citizens*. New York: Public Affairs Television.

Neu, J. (2000) *A Tear is an Intellectual Thing: The meanings of emotions*. New York: Oxford University Press.

Noddings, N. (1984) *Caring: A feminine approach to ethics and moral education*. Berkeley, CA: University of California Press.

O'Driscoll, S. and Mahoney, D. M. (1994) Translator's preface to C. Clément, *Syncope: The philosophy of rapture*. Minneapolis, MN: University of Minnesota Press.

Oliver, K. (1993a) Julia Kristeva's outlaw ethics, in K. Oliver (ed.) *Ethics, Politics, and Difference in Julia Kristeva's Writing*. New York: Routledge.

Oliver, K. (ed.) (1993b) *Ethics, Politics and Difference in Julia Kristeva's Writings*. New York: Routledge.

Oliver, K. (ed.) (1997) *The Portable Kristeva*. New York: Columbia University Press.

Oliver, K. (1998) *Subjects without Subjectivity: From abject fathers to desiring mothers*. Lanham, MD: Rowan & Littlefield.

Oliver, K. (2001) Paternal election and the absent father, in T. Chanter (ed.)

Feminist Interpretations of Emmanuel Levinas. University Park, PA: Pennsylvania State University Press.

Olsen, T. (1978) *Silences.* New York: Delacorte Press.

O'Reilly, A. (2006) *Rocking the Cradle: Thoughts on motherhood, feminism and the possibility of empowered mothering.* Toronto: Demeter Press.

Orenstein, P. (2000) *Flux: Women on sex, work, love, kids, and life in a half-changed world.* New York: Doubleday.

Oxford English Dictionary (1989) 2nd edition. Oxford: Clarendon Press.

Paes de Barros, D. (2004) *Fast Cars and Bad Girls: Nomadic subjects and women's road stories.* New York: P. Lang.

Park, S. M. (2006) Adoptive maternal bodies: A queer paradigm for rethinking mothering? *Hypatia*, 21(1): 201–226.

Parker, R. (1997) The production and purposes of maternal ambivalence, in W. Hollway and B. Featherstone (eds) *Mothering and Ambivalence.* London: Routledge.

Parker, R. (2005) *Torn in Two: The experience of maternal ambivalence.* London: Virago.

Phoenix, A., Woollett, A. and Lloyd, E. (1991) *Motherhood: Meanings, practices, and ideologies.* Newbury Park, CA: Sage.

Plänkers, T. (1999) Speaking in the claustrum: The psychodynamics of stuttering. *International Journal of Psychoanalysis*, 80: 239–256.

Plato (1977) *Timaeus and Critias*, trans. D. Lee. Harmondsworth: Penguin.

Pollock, D. (1999) *Telling Bodies Performing Birth: Everyday narratives of childbirth.* New York: Columbia University Press.

Pollock, G. (1990) Review of 'Drawing on a mother's experience' by Bobby Baker. *Performance Magazine*, November. Available at www.bobbybakersdailylife.com/drawing.htm (accessed 14 June 2005).

Potegal, M., Kosorok, M. and Davidson, R. (2003) Temper tantrums in young children. II. Tantrum duration and temporal organization. *Developmental and Behavioural Pediatrics*, 24(3): 148–154.

Pugh, A. (2005) Selling compromise: Toys, motherhood and the cultural deal. *Gender and Society*, 19: 729–749.

Raphael-Leff, R. (ed.) (2003) *Parent-Infant Psychodynamics: Wild things, mirrors and ghosts.* London: Whurr.

Reynolds, T. (2005) *Caribbean Mothers: Identity and experience in the U.K.* London: Tufnell Press.

Rich, A. (1976) *Of Woman Born: Motherhood as experience and institution.* New York: Norton.

Roca, L. L. (1997) This infant carrier is too heavy: An ergonomic redesign of infant carriers. *Proceedings of the Silicon Valley Ergonomic Conference, 1997*: 142–148.

Rose, J. (1996) Of knowledge and mothers: On the work of Christopher Bollas. *Gender and Psychoanalysis*, 1(4): 411–428.

Rose, N. (1990) *Governing the Soul: The shaping of the private self.* London: Routledge.

Roseneil, S. (2004) Why we should care about friends: An argument for queering the care imaginary in social policy. *Social Policy and Society*, 3(4): 409–419.

Roseneil, S. and Budgeon, S. (2004) Cultures of intimacy and care beyond 'the family': Personal life and social change in the early 21st century. *Current Sociology*, 52(2): 135–159.

Rosolato, G. (1974) The voice: Between body and language. *Revue Française de Psychanalyse*, 38: 75–94.

Ross, E. (1995) New thoughts on 'the oldest vocation': Mothers and motherhood in recent feminist scholarship. *Signs*, 20(2): 397–413.

Rouche, H. (1987) Le placenta comme tiers. *Langages*, 85: 71–79.

Ruddick, S. (1980) Maternal thinking. *Feminist Studies*, 6: 342–367.

Ruddick, S. (1989) *Maternal Thinking: Towards a politics of peace*. London: Women's Press.

Ruddick, S. (1997) The idea of fatherhood. In H. L. Nelson (ed.) *Feminism and Families*. NewYork: Routledge.

Scarry, E. (1985) *The Body in Pain: The making and unmaking of the world*. New York: Oxford University Press.

Schwab, G. M. (1994) Mother's body, father's tongue: Mediation and the symbolic order, in C. Burke, N. Schor and M. Whitford (eds) *Engaging with Irigaray*. New York: Columbia University Press.

Serres, M. (1995) *Genesis*. Ann Arbor, MI: The University of Michigan Press.

Sevenhuijsen, S. (1998) *Citizenship and the Ethics of Care*. London: Routledge.

Sevenhuijsen, S. (2003) The place of care: The relevance of the feminist ethic of care for social policy. *Feminist Theory*, 4(2): 179–197.

Shildrick, M. (2001) Reappraising feminist ethics: developments and debates. *Feminist Theory*, 2(2): 233–244.

Sikka, S. (2001) The delightful other: Portraits of the feminine in Kierkegaard, Nietzsche, and Levinas, in T. Chanter (ed.) *Feminist Interpretations of Emmanuel Levinas*. University Park, PA: Pennsylvania State University Press.

Smith, S. (1975) *The Collected Poems of Stevie Smith*. London: Allen Lane.

Snitow, A. (1992) Feminism and motherhood: An American reading. *Feminist Review*, 40: 33–51.

Soltis, J. (2003) The signal functions of early infant crying. Available at http://www.bbsonline.org/Preprints/Soltis-11072002/Soltis.pdf (accessed 10 November 2003).

Spinoza, B. (1677) *Ethics and Treatise on the Correction of the Intellect*, trans. A. Boyle. London: J. M. Dent Orion, 1993.

Spitz, R. A. (1955) The primal cavity: A contribution to the genesis of perception and its role for psychoanalytic theory. *Psychoanalytic Study of the Child*, 10: 215–240.

Stack, C. and Burton, L. (1993) Kinscripts. *Journal of Comparative Family Studies*, 24: 157–170.

Stadlen, N. (2004) *What Mothers Do: Especially when it looks like nothing*. London: Judy Piatkus.

Steinberg, Z. (2005) Donning the mask of motherhood: A defensive strategy, a developmental search. *Studies in Gender and Sexuality*, 6(2): 173–198.

Stern, D. (1985) *The Interpersonal World of the Infant*. New York: Basic Books.

Stern, D. (1998) *The Motherhood Constellation: A unified view of parent-infant psychotherapy*. London: Karnac.

Stern, D. and Bruschweiler-Stern, N. (1998) *The Birth of a Mother: How motherhood changes you forever*. London: Bloomsbury.

Stone, A. (2007) *An Introduction to Feminist Philosophy*. Cambridge: Polity Press.

Thurer, S. (1994) *Myths of Motherhood: How culture reinvents the good mother*. Boston, MA: Houghton Mifflin.

Tonkinwise, C. (2004) Ethics by design or the ethos of things. Available at www.desphilosophy.com/dpp/dpp_journal/paper4/body.html (accessed 10 December 2004).

Tronto, J. (1993) *Moral Boundaries: A political argument for an ethic of care*. New York: Routledge.

Treacher-Collins, E. (1932) The physiology of weeping. *British Journal of Ophthalmology*, 1: 1–20.

Tyler, I. (2000) Reframing pregnant embodiment, in S. Ahmed, J. Kilby, C. Lury, M. McNeil and B. Skeggs (eds) *Transformations: Thinking through feminism*. London: Routledge.

Tyler, I. (2008) 'Chav mum, chav scum': Class disgust in comtemporary Britain. *Feminist Media Studies*, 8: 17–34.

Urban Freeflow Network (2004) Art in motion. Available at www.urbanfreeflow.com/urbanfreeflow/artinmotion.htm (accessed 06 December 2004).

Urwin, C. (1985) Constructing motherhood: The persuasion of normal development, in C. Steedman, C. Urwin and V. Walkerdine (eds) *Language, Gender and Childhood*. London: Routledge & Kegan Paul.

Verhaeghe, P. (2000) The collapse of the function of the father and its effects on gender roles, in R. Salecl (ed.) *Sexuation: Sic 3*. Durham, NC: Duke University Press.

Walker, M. U. (1998) Moral epistemology, in A. J. Jaggar and I. M. Young (eds) *A Companion to Feminist Philosophy*. Malden, MA: Blackwell.

Walsh, L. (2001) Between maternity and paternity: Figuring ethical subjectivity. *Journal of Feminist Cultural Studies*, 12(1): 79–111.

Warner, J. (2005) *Perfect Madness: Motherhood in the age of anxiety*. New York: Riverhead.

Weedon, C. (1998) Postmodernism, in *A Companion to Feminist Philosophy*. Malden, MA: Blackwell.

Whitford, M. (ed.) (1991) Introduction to Part I, *The Irigaray Reader*. Oxford: Basil Blackwell.

Wikipedia (undated) Stuttering. Available at http://en.wikipedia.org/wiki/Stuttering#Stuttering_in_Music (accessed 13 September 2005).

Williams, F. (2001) In and beyond New Labour: Towards a new political ethic of care. *Critical Social Policy*, 21(4): 467–493.

Williams, F. and Roseneil, S. (2004) Public values of parenting and partnering: Voluntary organizations and welfare politics in New Labour's Britain. *Social Politics*, 11(2): 181–216.

Winnicott, D. W. (1951) Transitional objects and transitional phenomena, in *Collected Papers: Through pediatrics to psycho-analysis*. London: Tavistock, 1958.

Winnicott, D. W. (1963) From dependence towards independence in the development of the individual, in *The Maturational Processes and the Facilitating Environment*. London: Karnac, 1990.

Winnicott, D. W. (1964) *The Child, the Family, and the Outside World*. Reading, MA: Addison-Wesley, 1987.

Winnicott, D. W. (1968) The use of an object and relating through identifications, in

C. Winnicott, R. Shepherd and M. Davis (eds) *Psycho-Analytic Explorations.* Cambridge, MA: Harvard University Press, 1989.

Wolf, N. (2001) *Misconceptions: Truth, lies and the unexpected on the journey to motherhood.* London: Chatto & Windus.

Woolf, V. (1942) Professions for women, in *The Death of the Moth and Other Essays.* New York: Harcourt Brace Jovanovich, 1970.

Young, I. (1990) Throwing like a girl, in *Throwing Like a Girl.* Bloomington, IN: Indiana University Press.

Young, I. (1998) *Throwing Like a Girl* revisited, in D. Welton (ed.) *Body and Flesh: A philosophical reader.* Malden, MA: Blackwell.

INDEX

Locators for headings which have subheadings refer to general aspects of that topic.

abjection 4, 6–8
actor-network theory 137–9
Adams, Parveen 94
adoptive mothers 20, 124; *see also*
    biological kinship
Agape 106
aggression, maternal 20, 35; *see also*
    ambivalence; destructive impulses;
    hate
alien 17, 25, 95; *see also* alterity; Other/
    otherness
alterity 17, 24–9; anecdotes 24, 36, 46,
    47; and difference 28; and ethics 113;
    femininity/maternity/paternity 40–5;
    intersubjective turn 29–33; Levinas
    on 35–9; and maternal love 98–9,
    105–6; and maternal subjectivity 39,
    103; meanings of term 26; and
    naming 45–7; and negation 33–5,
    101; notes 162–3; and self 155–6; *see
    also* Other/otherness
ambivalence 21, 31–2, 54–5; emotional
    expression 111; *see also* aggression;
    destructive impulses; hate
analytic interpretations 83–4
anecdotal theory 12–13, 17, 152
anecdotes 12–15, 151–2, 159; alterity
    24, 36, 46, 47; interruptions 66, 68,
    73, 80, 85–7; maternal love 90–1,
    107, 112; maternal stuff 122–3, 128,
    136, 148–50; maternal
    transformations 48–9, 61–4; naming
    156
anger, maternal 20, 35; *see also*
    ambivalence; destructive impulses;
    hate

Anzieu, Didier 70, 71–2, 87
Appelbaum, David 17, 76–9, 84, 110,
    111
art, performance 1–4, 7, 151
artefacts 143–4; *see also* maternal stuff;
    objects
attachment theory 93
autobiographical writing 13–15, 17; *see
    also* anecdotes
autonomy, maintaining 31
awareness, sentient 143–4, 146; *see also*
    heightened sentience
axioms of love 115–17, 120, 159

babbling 84–5, 157
Badiou, Alain 9, 17, 157–9; axioms of
    love 116–17, 120; disjunction 116,
    119, 120; event 92, 114–15; maternal
    love 91–2, 115–19; one, two, infinity
    112–15, 116, 118–21
Baker, Bobby 1–4, 7, 13, 151
Battersby, Christine 10
becoming unaccommodated 11–17
being-in-the-world 135–6
being there to be left 5; *see also* loss
Benjamin, Jessica 9, 20, 26, 28–33, 55
Benjamin, Walter 18
binary: melancholia/murder 6, 7, 8; and
    third *see* one/two/three
biological kinship 42, 44, 45; *see also*
    adoptive mothers
Bion, Wilfred 25, 79
Blau DuPlessis, Rachel 13, 14
blueprints 133–4
Bollas, Christopher 5, 18, 51, 132
boundaries, setting 31, 33

179

breaches in experience 68; *see also* interruptions
Brentano, Franz 133
Bruschweiler-Stern, N. 54
Butler, Judith 17, 28, 33–5, 46, 59–60
Byatt, A. S. 25

care: ethics of 26–7; temporal nature of 75
caring and clinging mother 56
cathartic method 111
celebration of motherhood 7
chairs 143–4; *see also* maternal stuff; objects
child: destructive impulses/attacks 30, 31, 32; as event 158–9; fantasy 61; I 43; naming 24, 25; as open structure 11, 25, 26; as stranger/other 8–9, 46; as unknowable 26
childbirth, and loss/mourning 48, 49, 51
childhood: emotions 71; objects 126–7; *see also* maternal stuff; objects
Chodorow, Nancy 20, 51
chora 59
Clément, Catherine 9, 11, 15, 17, 81–2, 88–89
Coleridge, Samuel Taylor 88
compassionate waiting 87–8
complementarity 30
confinement 156
Connor, Steven 11, 15, 69, 70
conscience, development of 76, 78–9
consciousness: development of 76–9; and maternal love 118
containment 5, 19–21, 74, 152, 154
contingency 132
Cornell, Drucilla 18
creation/uncreation 140–2
crisis, psychic *see* psychological threat of motherhood
crying 17, 69–74, 156–7; adult responses to 72–3; maternal *see* weeping; *see also* tantrums
cultural phenomenology 15, 17; *see also* phenomenological perspective
culture and nature 101–2
Cusk, Rachel 50

Darwin, Charles 109–10
das Andere 95; *see also* alien; alterity; Other/otherness

daughters 44
Davies, Karen 74–5
de Beauvoir, Simone 40, 92–3
Deleuze, Gilles 9, 18, 47
denigration of the mother 4, 5, 27
dependence 10, 21
depressive position 32, 145
Derrida, Jacques 16, 40
desire: for lost mother 56; and love 96–9, 119
destructive impulses 30–2, 34, 35, 39; *see also* aggression; hate
development: maternal 28, 31; parental 53–4
diaries 13–15, 17; *see also* anecdotes
difference, and alterity 28
dis-abled mother 153–7; *see also* encumbrance; maternal stuff
disjunction 17, 116, 119–20, 139, 154
disruption 13, 17, 18, 75–80; *see also* interruptions
divided mother *see herethics*
domains of love 115–17, 120, 159
doors 138–40; *see also* maternal stuff; objects
Dostoyevsky, F. M. 37
dumb reality 132–3
dyad, mother–infant 125, 156, 157; *see also* one/two/three

embodiment, maternal 123–6
emotions: expression 109–11; intensity of childhood 71
emptiness 103, 105–6, 157
encounters, maternal 117, 120, 160–2
encumbrance 146, 150, 152; *see also* maternal stuff
equipment 126–7; *see also* maternal stuff; objects
Eros 42, 44, 106
ethical: objects 137–40; turn 28
ethics 17, 23; and alterity 113; of care 26–7; Kristeva on 100–1; Levinas on 36–7, 39, 41, 155; maternal 4–7, 26–8; of objects 144–6; outlaw 16; and psychoanalysis 19
Ettinger, Bracha 41, 44–5
events 92, 114–15, 158–9
experience: lived 12; woman/man positions of 116–17, 119–20; of world 115–19

exteriority/interiority 38, 39
external/internal otherness 95

face 38, 42
Fairbairn, W. R. 132
fantasy: child 61; perfect child 33, 34;
  perfect mother 52; see also
  idealization of the mother; imaginary
  father
fatherhood/fathers: role in separation
  104, 105; turn to 4; see also
  imaginary father; paternity/paternal
fecundity 42, 43–4, 45, 156
female/feminine: and alterity 40–5;
  characterization 40, 41; and maternal
  10–11, 60; and otherness 28, 44;
  qualities 27; subjectivity 7, 8, 10; see
  also maternal subjectivity
feminist perspective 2, 27, 156; post-
  modern 15
fetish 131
fidelity 114, 158–9; see also truth
Fink, Bruce 83
fleshy continuity 10
fluidity/unity dialectic 49–52, 58–60,
  63, 146, 155
Foucan, Sébastien 147
freerunning 146–50
Freud, Sigmund 9, 17, 30, 46, 54;
  'The Antithetical Meaning of
  Primal Words' 111; cathartic
  method 111; love and desire 97–8;
  Negation 100; prehistory 104;
  psychic investment 142; sovereign
  good 132; stammering 87; Three
  Essays on the Theory of Sexuality
  130; unconscious 95
Frosh, Stephen 33, 87–8
Furman, Erna 5

Gallop, Jane 12, 13, 16
gaps 69; see also emptiness
gear see maternal stuff; objects
gendering of maternal 19–23, 78
giving oneself up 103
good-enough mother 32, 33, 51

hate, maternal 20, 21, 51–2, 90–1; see
  also aggression; ambivalence;
  destructive impulses
Hegel, G. W. F. 28, 29–34
Heidegger, Martin 135–6

heightened sentience 125–6, 129,
  154
herethics 16, 91, 99–103, 106, 156
heterogeneity 17
Hollway, Wendy 20
hope 52
humanity 117, 120

I/non-I 41, 43, 44, 155
idealization of the mother 4, 5, 27,
  93–94, 105; see also perfect mother
  fantasy
identity 10, 154; and motherhood 22,
  102
imaginary father 99, 103, 104, 105; see
  also fatherhood/fathers; paternity/
  paternal
imaginary mother 104; see also
  idealization of the mother; perfect
  mother fantasy
imagination, human 143–4
immediacy 48
immune system 62
index/sign 95
infant–mother dyad 125, 156, 157
infinite 38, 44; responsibility 37
injury to children see aggression;
  ambivalence; destructive impulses;
  hate
institution of motherhood 22
intentional objects 133–4, 142
interiority/exteriority 38, 39
internal/external otherness 95
internal objects 130
interpretations, analytic 83–4
interrogation 141
interruptions 11, 15, 17, 156–7;
  anecdotes 66, 68, 73, 80, 85–7;
  breaches in experience 68; crying
  69–74; disruption 13, 17, 18, 75–80;
  gaps 69; and maternal subjectivity
  67, 74; maternal time 74–5, 79–80,
  81; nature of 68–9; as normality
  73–4; notes 163–4; and
  psychoanalysis 83; punctuation 69,
  72, 73, 83; and reverie 73;
  stammering 84–8; tantrums 80–4;
  and thinking/thought 73–4, 79
intersubjectivity 28–34; unconscious
  19, 21
Irigaray, Luce 7, 15, 17, 56–63, 123
introjection 67, 71

James, William 110
Jewish women 63–4

Kant, Immanuel 78
Klein, Melanie 32, 131
knowing the other 37
knowledge 116
Kraemer, Susan 16, 20–1, 51–2, 67, 70–1
Kristeva, Julia 5–7, 14–17, 156–7; ambivalent principle 101–2; caring and clinging mother 56; Eros 106; ethics 100–1; *Freud and Love* 103; *herethics* 91, 99–101; maternal love 86, 89, 98, 101–6; 'Motherhood according to Giovanni Bellini' 102; mother's mother 54; negativity 100, 101; subject-in-process 100–1, 118; vocation of motherhood 27; *Women's Time* 100

Lacan, Jacques 9, 17, 46, 58, 69; love and desire 96–7; objects/things 132; symbolic 95
Laplanche, Jean 17, 18; index/sign 95; internal/external otherness 95; unconscious development 94–5
Latour, Bruno 9, 17, 125, 135–6, 138; 'Where are the missing masses? Sociology of a door' 138, 139, 140
Law, John 12
Levinas, Emmanuel 17, 29, 35–9, 156; alterity 36–9; ethics 36–7, 39, 41, 155; femininity/maternity/paternity 40–5; other 38–9, 113; *Otherwise than Being, or Beyond Essence* 38, 39, 41; Same 113; *Time and the Other* 40; *Totality and Infinity* 38, 39, 40, 42
Lichtenberg-Ettinger, Bracha 52
lived: body 128, 130; experience 12
loss/mourning 5–6, 9, 32, 62–3; after childbirth 48, 49, 51; *see also* separation
lost: mother 56; years 9
love, maternal 89, 157, 159; and alterity 98–9, 105–6, 106; anecdotes 90–1, 107, 112; attachment theory 93; axioms of 115–17, 120, 159; Badiou on 91–2, 115–19; and consciousness 118; and desire 96–9, 119; as experience of world 115–19;

Freud on 97–8; giving oneself up 103; and hate 90–1; *herethics* 91, 99–101, 106; intellectual meanings of tears 109–12; Kristeva on 86, 89, 98, 101–6; Lacan on 96–7; and narcissism 105; nature of 92–6, 154; notes 164; one, two, infinity 112–15, 116, 118–21; paradox of 117–18, 157; return of 120–1; and separation 103–4, 106; and splitting 99; tears, maternal 107–9; and truth 113–16, 117, 118

male: subjectivity 10, 45; time 74–5; *see also* imaginary father; paternity
man/woman positions of experience 116–17, 119–20
masculinity 44; *see also* imaginary father; paternity
master-slave model 30, 34
material relations 125, 145; *see also* maternal stuff; objects
maternal/maternity: desire for 94, 97; development 28, 31; encounters 117, 120, 160–2; and ethics 26–8; and feminine 56–62, 63; gendering of 19–23, 78; meanings of term 19, 22; and paternal 20; praxis 14; relations 22, 23; time 74–5, 79–80, 81; *see also* love; maternal stuff; maternal subjectivity; motherhood/mothers
maternal stuff: anecdotes 122–3, 128, 136, 148–50; artefacts 143–4; encumbrance 146, 150, 152; equipment 126–7; and ethics 137–40, 144–6; freerunning/*Parkour* 146–50; intentional objects 133–4, 142; maternal embodiment 123–6; and maternal subjectivity 157; objects 126–7, 130; psychoanalytic/ philosophical objects 130–3; tool-beings 126–7; uncreation/creation 140–2; viscosity 126, 127–30; *Zeug/* tool analysis 134–7; *see also* objects
maternal subjectivity 2–11; and alterity 39, 40–5, 103; biological/adoptive mothers 20; construction 152–3, 154, 158, 159; development 31; emergence 14, 16, 17, 28; and ethics 26–8; and femininity/maternity/paternity 40; heightened sentience 125–6, 129, 154; and interruptions 67, 74;

meanings of term 19–21, 22; and naming 47; and otherness 28; in relation to child 31; as remainder 35–6; self realization needs 55–6; and stuff 157; as transformed state 52
matricide 6, 60, 61
matrixial 45
matter 59
melancholia/murder binary 6, 7, 8
Merleau-Ponty, Maurice 128, 130
mess 49, 61, 63; see also performance art
metaphors: containment 20–1; for imagining 12; mother 3, 6–7, 59–60; receptacle/chora 59; veil/wig 57, 62–5
mimesis 64–5
monstrosity 10
Morrison, Toni 8
motherhood/mothers: caring and clinging 56; celebration of 7; and the ethics of objects 144–6; good-enough 32, 33, 51; idealization of 4, 5, 27, 93–94, 105; and identity 22, 102; imaginary 104; as love object 130–1; metaphorical 3, 6–7, 59–60; mother's mother 54, 105; psychological threats to 2–3, 5, 23, 35, 51–2; and sexuality 95–6, 155; symbolic 6, 17; vocation of 27; see also herethics; maternal/maternity; perfect mother fantasy
mother–infant dyad 125, 156, 157
mothering: meanings of term 19; qualities 25, 26
mother-writing 14–15
mourning see loss
mouth 70, 71, 87
mummers 47
murderous impulses 34; see also matricide
mutuality 30

naming child 24, 25, 159; and alterity 45–7; anecdotes 156; and maternal subjectivity 47
narcissism 30, 97–8; and love 105; of parenting 53–4
natality 10
nature and culture 101–2
needs, self/other conflict 55

negation 33–5, 100
negativity 100, 101
Neu, Jerome 17, 109–12
Nom-du-Père 46
normality/norms: interruptions 73–4; male subjectivity 10; of motherhood 11
nurse/mother 59–60

object-position of motherhood see maternal subjectivity
object relations theory 131
objects 17, 126–7, 130; brute reality 136–7; intentional 133–4, 142; part 52; rude 140; transformational 132; transitional 64, 122–3, 127, 132; use of (Winnicott) 30; see also maternal stuff
Oedipal complex 46, 100, 104
Oliver, Kelly 16, 99, 103
omnipotence 29, 30, 32, 33, 35
one, two, infinity (Badiou) 112–15, 116, 118–21, 157
one/two/three 56, 59, 92, 96, 103–5; see also dyad; third position
open structure, child as 11, 25, 26
Other/otherness 6, 8–9, 18, 28–9, 45; alien 17, 25; femininity as 44; as God 38; internal/external 95; and intersubjectivity 30; knowing 37; Levinas on 38–9, 113; and maternal subjectivity 29; and paternity 44 ; and Same 41; and self 31, 34–9, 42, 49–50, 55; transcendent 38, 40; turn to 26; see also alterity

pain 125, 140–4
paradox: of love 117–18, 157; of maternal transformations 57
paranoid-schizoid position 145
parental: body 19; development 53–4
parenting 4, 19–20; and narcissism 53–4; sensitive 93
Park, Shelley 20, 124
Parker, Rozsika 54
Parkour 146–50
part objects, mother/child 52
paternity/paternal 42–4, 155; and alterity 40–5; daughters 44; differences from maternal 20; function 156; sons 43–4; see also fatherhood/fathers; imaginary father

perfect child fantasy 33, 34
perfect mother fantasy 52; *see also*
  idealization of the mother
performance art 1–4, 7, 151
phallus 96–8, 102, 106, 119
phenomenological perspective 15, 23,
  152–3
philosophical: objects 130–3;
  perspectives 8–9, 18–19, 28, 159
placenta 61, 62, 63; *see also* veil/wig
  metaphors
post-modernism 15
prams 139, 146; *see also* maternal
  stuff
praxis, maternal 14
pregnant embodiment 123–4
primal repression 105
projection/projective identification 67,
  71
psychic investment 142
psychoanalysis 19, 67–8; crying 72–3;
  ethics 19; one/two/three 56, 59, 92,
  96, 103–5; and philosophy 28;
  projection/projective identification
  67, 71; and punctuations 83;
  regression/repetition 53–4, 56;
  stammering 87
psychoanalytic objects 130–3
psychological threat of motherhood
  2–3, 5, 23, 35, 51–2
punctuations 69, 72, 73, 83; *see also*
  interruptions

Raphael-Leff, Joan 53, 54
rapture 17
readiness-to-hand 135–7
Real 6
receptacle 59
recognition 37–8, 39
regression/repetition 53–4, 56
repression, primal 105
research methodology 11–12
responsibility, parental 22–3, 28, 31,
  38–40, 155–6; infinite 37
reverie 19, 25, 73, 79
Rose, Jacqueline 5, 51
Rosolato, Guy 70
Rouch, Hélène 62
Ruddick, Sara 11, 20, 25, 43–4
rude objects 140
ruthlessness, infant 30–2, 34, 35, 39;
  see also aggression, maternal

Same 9, 28, 37, 44, 69; Levinas on 113;
  and Other 41
Scarry, Elaine 17, 157; *The Body in
  Pain* 125, 140–4
seduction theory 17, 95–6
self: autonomy 31; discovery 155;
  identity 10, 154; and other 31, 34–9,
  42, 49–50, 55; realization, maternal
  55–6
sensation 78, 80
sensitive parenting 93
sentient awareness 143–4, 146; *see also*
  heightened sentience
separation 103–4, 106, 157; role of
  fathers 104, 105; and sleep 108–9,
  112
sexual difference 59; *see also* gendering
  of maternal
sexuality, maternal 95–6, 155
shadow-figure, mother as 4–5
sign 95
signification 103, 119, 132
sleep 108–9, 112, 157
Smith, Stevie 88–9
Snitow, Ann 22
soma/somatic 77–80, 110, 111,
  157
sonorous envelope 70
sons 43–4, 156
sovereign good 132
Spinoza, Baruch 9
Spitz, René 70, 71, 87
splitting 30, 53, 71, 99, 105
stammering 84–8
Stern, Daniel 54
strangers/strangeness *see* alterity; Other/
  otherness
stuff *see* maternal stuff; objects
stuttering *see* stammering
subject/object reciprocity 40–1
subject-in-process 100–1, 118
subjectivity: female 7, 8, 10; male 10,
  44; maternal *see* maternal
  subjectivity
substitution 41–2, 43
symbolic: function 100–2, 104, 106,
  156; Lacan on 95; mother 6, 17
syncope 11, 17, 81–2, 92, 157

tantrums 80–4, 157; *see also* crying
tears in experience 68; *see also*
  interruptions

tears: children's *see* crying; maternal *see* weeping
terminology 19–23
theatre 57; *see also* performance art
thinking: about mothers 5; interruptions 73–4, 79; maternal 44
third position, absence of 104–5, 116–17; *see also* one/two/three
time, maternal 74–5, 79–80, 81
tool: analysis 134–7; -beings 126–7; *see also* maternal stuff; objects
torture 141–2; *see also* pain
transcendent: I 43; other 38, 40
transference 105, 131
transformational objects 132
transformations, maternal 17, 19, 159; anecdotes 48–9, 61, 62, 63–4; loss/mourning 49, 51; maternal feminine 56–62, 63; and maternal subjectivity 52; meanings of term 57; notes 163; paradox of 57; psychic crisis 52; unity/fluidity dialectic 49–52, 58–9, 60, 63; veil/wig metaphors 57, 62–5
transitional: objects 64, 122–3, 127, 132; space 25
trans-substantiation 43
truth 9, 154, 158–9; and knowledge 116; and love 113–16, 117, 118
triads *see* one/two/three; *see also* third position, absence of
turn, to other 26
Tyler, Imogen 123

umbilical cord 61, 62
unconscious 17–19, 21, 55; development 94–5; meanings, maternal tears 110–11
uncreation/creation 140–2

unity/fluidity dialectic 49–52, 58–60, 63, 146, 155
unknowable, child as 5–6, 9, 26
unknowing 18
unspeakability of motherhood 5–6
unthought 18

veil metaphor 57, 62–5; *see also* placenta
Virgin Mary 107–8
viscous body/viscosity 126, 127–30, 146, 154
vocation of motherhood 27

wager 158, 159
war 141–2; *see also* pain
weeping, maternal 107–12, 120–1, 157; *see also* crying
wig metaphor 57, 62–5; *see also* placenta
Winnicott, D. 25, 34, 51, 64; babbling 84–5; mother–infant dyad 125; transitional objects 132; use of an object 30; *see also* containment
Wolf, Naomi 49, 70
woman 40, 41, 42; *see also* female/feminine
woman/man positions of experience 116–17, 119–20
Woolf, Virginia 27
work, meanings of term 142
world, experience of 115–19
writing 13–15; *see also* anecdotes

Young, Iris 128

Zeug 134–7